CRITICAL ACCLAIM FOR
MASCULINITY RECONSTRUCTED

"Most books do not change lives; this one will."
—E. Anthony Rotundo, author of
American Manhood

"A long overdue *action plan* for m⸻ ⸻ ⸻e
emotional intelligence to b⸻
masculinity."
—Dr. Marlin S. ⸻
psychotherap⸻ ⸻ *⸻uas:*
What's Really C⸻ *⸻uonships*

"A smart, compassionate, readable, interesting book about
men that pulls not a single punch."
—Kathy Weingarten, author of *The Mother's Voice:
Strengthening Intimacy in Families*

"An excellent guide . . . I wish every man and woman would
read it." —Susan Jeffers, author of
Feel the Fear and Do It Anyway

"Significant new insights . . . Levant's clear-headed approach
could prove helpful for men ready to reconstruct."
—*Publishers Weekly*

"An important addition to men's studies." —*Booklist*

RONALD F. LEVANT earned his doctorate in clinical psychology and public practice from Harvard, has taught at Boston
University and Rutgers, and is currently on the faculty at
Cambridge Hospital/Harvard Medical School. He is the co-
author of *Between Father and Child* (Viking/Penguin) and has
frequently appeared on such major national television shows
as *Oprah*, *20/20*, and *ABC News*. He lives in Belmont,
Massachusetts. GINI KOPECKY has written about psychology,
relationships, and gender issues for a number of national
magazines. This is her first book.

DR. RONALD F. LEVANT
WITH GINI KOPECKY

MASCULINITY RECONSTRUCTED

CHANGING THE RULES OF MANHOOD— AT WORK, IN RELATIONSHIPS, AND IN FAMILY LIFE

A PLUME BOOK

PLUME
Published by the Penguin Group
Penguin Books USA Inc., 375 Hudson Street, New York, New York 10014, U.S.A.
Penguin Books Ltd, 27 Wrights Lane, London W8 5TZ, England
Penguin Books Australia Ltd, Ringwood, Victoria, Australia
Penguin Books Canada Ltd, 10 Alcorn Avenue, Toronto, Ontario, Canada M4V 3B2
Penguin Books (N.Z.) Ltd, 182–190 Wairau Road, Auckland 10, New Zealand

Penguin Books Ltd, Registered Offices: Harmondsworth, Middlesex, England

Published by Plume, an imprint of Dutton Signet,
a division of Penguin Books USA Inc.
Previously published in a Dutton edition.

First Plume Printing, March, 1996
10 9 8 7 6 5 4 3 2 1

 REGISTERED TRADEMARK—MARCA REGISTRADA

The Library of Congress has catalogued the Dutton edition as follows:

Levant, Ronald F.
Masculinity reconstructed : changing the rules of manhood : at
work, in relationships and in family life / Ronald F. Levant with
Gini Kopecky.
p.   cm.
Includes bibliographical references and index.
ISBN 0-525-93846-X (hc.)
ISBN 0-452-27541-5 (pbk.)
1. Men—United States.   2. Men—United States—Psychology.
3. Masculinity (Psychology)—United States.   4. Sex role—United
States.   I. Kopecky, Gini.   II. Title.
HQ1090.3.L48   1995
155.3'32—dc20   94-31382
                                                            CIP

Printed in the United States of America
Original hardcover design by Julian Hamer

To Harry and Wilma Levant,
Carol Slatter, Caren Levant and
Adam, Adrian, and Jeremy Shanker;
and to Anton and Helen Kopecky,
Bob Lascaro, and Marc Wallace.

ACKNOWLEDGMENTS

We would like to thank our agents, Barbara Lowenstein and Joy Harris, and writers John Kelly and Sheila Weller who helped launch this book. We would also like to acknowledge Arnold Dolin, our editor at NAL/Dutton, whose capacity for patience is truly admirable, and John Paine, the manuscript editor, for his skillful editorial suggestions.

Dr. Levant would also like to thank his colleagues from whom he has learned much about the psychology of men. Joseph Pleck, Ph.D., the "Dean" of the psychology of men, has long been a source of wisdom, and has always given generously of his time. "Fellow-traveler" Gary Brooks, Ph.D., has long been a colleague to whom he could turn in moments of doubt and confusion, and also to share the excitement of discovery. The past and present members of the "Men's Studies Seminar and Play Group," a group which meets once a month to discuss men's studies, and also to goof off, have been a source of inspiration and an aid in testing new ideas: William Pollack, Ph.D., Joel Eichler, Ph.D., Steven Krugman, Ph.D., Robert Weiss, Ph.D., Gene Bocknek, Ph.D., Jon Reusser, Ph.D., and Alan Gurwitt, Ph.D. Finally, he has learned from many other colleagues in Gender Studies in general and the Society for the Psychological Study of Men and Masculinity in particular: James O'Neil, Ph.D., Louise Silverstein, Ph.D., Richard Lazur, Ph.D., Richard Eisler, Ph.D., Jeffrey Fischer, M.A., Ellen

McGrath, Ph.D., Barbara Wainrib, Ed.D., Marlin Potash, Ed.D., Glenn Good, Ph.D., Murray Scher, Ph.D., Sam Osherson, Ph.D., James A. Levine, Ed.D., Lenore Walker, Ph.D., Marion Gindes, Ph.D., Penelope Russianoff, Ph.D., Richard Majors, Ph.D., Judith Jordan, Ph.D., Dwight Moore, Ph.D., Richard Osborne, Ed.D., Kathy Weingarten, Ph.D., Stephen Bergman, M.D., Ph.D., Robert Pasick, Ph.D., E. Anthony Rotundo, Ph.D., Jerry Shapiro, Ph.D., Charles Hoffman, Ph.D., Michael Diamond, Ph.D., and Robert Brannon, Ph.D.

Dr. Levant would also like to express his gratitude to the men who participated in his Fatherhood Courses and Reconstructing Masculinity Workshops, and his clients, from whom he has learned an incalculable amount about the new psychology of men.

Last but not least we would like to thank Bob and Rita Lascaro, Kalia Doner, Mary Brown, and Linda Lee for providing moral and technical support, and Carol Slatter and Marc Wallace for putting up with us during the very long haul that writing this book became.

Contents

Authors' Note

The men's stories told in this book include both case histories and composite portraits. These stories are drawn from the experiences shared by the many men who have participated in Dr. Levant's Fatherhood Courses and Reconstructing Masculinity Workshops, or who have consulted Dr. Levant.

Names, backgrounds, physical descriptions, and other identifying details have all been changed to protect the privacy of the men whose stories provide the basis for these case histories and composites.

CHAPTER ONE

Masculinity at the Turning Point

MEN IN CRISIS

We're grown-ups. We're strong. We can handle the truth, and it's time we faced it: American manhood is in crisis—has been for a generation.

You don't like hearing that. Most men don't. Men bristle in lectures and workshops when I use the word *crisis* to describe the current state of American manhood—just the way you're probably bristling right now: "Crisis! What's he talking about? I don't know what kind of men he's been talking to, but he sure isn't talking about me."

Yes I am. I'm talking about the crisis facing all American men now that the social changes wrought by the feminist movement and the influx of women into the work force have left our traditional code of masculinity in a state of collapse. And, no, *crisis* isn't too strong a word. You may not like its emotional (read: "feminine") connotations or what seems to be the implied insult to your masculine sense of mastery and control. But a crisis needn't trigger an emotional reaction to qualify as a crisis. To be in crisis simply means to be at a turning point, to have reached a decisive or crucial time or stage. I use the word crisis to describe the current state of American manhood because we are at such a stage.

But you probably know that, or you wouldn't be reading this book. Perhaps you've reached a point in life where you're willing to at least consider rethinking your beliefs about manhood—simply because some of those beliefs don't seem to work anymore. Maybe, like other men, you're feeling the strain of living in a world in which many of the masculine ideals men learned early on have lost their cachet and we're now being told we're supposed to be something else. Raised to believe that "real men" don't feel fear, sadness, or much of any other emotion, we're now told we should not only feel these emotions but also express them. Trained to be cool-headed, action-oriented protectors and problem-solvers, we're now told that these masculine ways of demonstrating love don't quite cut it anymore and that our success as lovers, husbands, and fathers now hinges on our ability to develop the more traditionally feminine skill of being sensitive and responsive to other people's feelings. Taught early on that a man's primary role is that of breadwinner and that his primary dedication must be to his work, we now find ourselves having to share that role with our female partners and take on, in exchange, some of the household and child care duties that have traditionally been considered women's work.

It's been a real shock.

Some men recovered and adapted fairly swiftly, sensing that there might be something to be gained from becoming more flexible in their ideas about "what's manly." Others experienced a sense of liberation—a sense not of having to refashion themselves to suit a changing Zeitgeist but of the Zeitgeist finally changing to suit them. The majority of men, however, weren't having any of these changes. Their initial response was to resist—angrily at times, to cover their fear and confusion and try to beat back the forces of change.

But of course there is no beating back change, and after a while men began to realize—some sooner, some later—that their resistance was not only futile but foolhardy. Like mule-headed sailors who'd dared to pit themselves against what they'd been warned was the approaching storm of the century, they were now being bashed around by a raging sea, and their boat was going down. Their intimate relationships were becoming increasingly strained and contentious. The harder they tried to connect with their children, the more they seemed to push them away. The things they'd once found most pleasurable in life—such as sex, professional accomplishments, material comforts—no longer seemed as fulfilling. They were feeling more anxious and stressed, more fatigued and irritable, more confused and unsure than they'd ever thought possible about their purpose and value as men.

Which isn't to say men started falling apart. Nothing as drastic or obvious as that has occurred. For the most part men continue to function quite well—especially in those areas in which traditional masculine values still prevail, such as work. To all outward appearances, most men seem to be managing just fine. Their lives seem busy, productive, successful. But the inside story is different. They put up a good front—as they've been trained to do—but inside they're not feeling so hot. There's a kind of emptiness; a hollowness; a vague feeling that something is missing. The sense of masculine purpose and pride has gone out of their lives, and they want it back.

That's where men are now. For twenty years, both in my work as a practicing psychologist specializing in counseling men and in my research and writings on men and masculinity, I've been tracking how men have been responding to the collapse of our traditional masculine code. And the evidence overwhelmingly suggests that men have indeed reached a turning point. The more I listen to men talk in individual therapy sessions and in men's groups and workshops, and the more I exchange findings and thoughts with other researchers, the more convinced I become that men are now *ready to change*. They're ready to rethink their ideas about a man's proper role, rights, and responsibilities—to take a close look at the various components of the traditional masculine belief system in order to determine which have outlived their usefulness and which should be preserved. They're ready to get to work developing and mastering the skills not imparted during their early-life training that are being required of men now. And, very important, they're ready to set aside the belief that there is or should be any one "right way" to be a man because they now see how confining and crippling that belief is.

That's one good thing to come out of the collapse of our traditional masculine code. As painful and confusing as it has been, it has introduced us to a freedom we've never known—the freedom to define manhood for ourselves. It took a while to adjust to this new freedom. Like "lifers" suddenly released from prison with no preparation for life outside, many men's first impulse was to embrace a substitute set of masculine dictates—the sensitive man ideal. But it didn't take long for men to realize that in trying to turn into some combination of Alan Alda and Mr. Mom they were only trading one form of incarceration for another. The only course left was to forge a new middle path between traditional masculinity and the sensitive man ideal—one that allows every man to decide for himself what combination of old and new traits he wants to incorporate into his reconstructed masculine code.

Beating Drums in the Woods Isn't the Answer

Perhaps you've read or heard about the book *Iron John* by poet and storyteller Robert Bly. In it, Bly retells an ancient fairy tale about a young prince who runs off into the woods with a Wild Man—Iron John—and argues that the reason men feel so lost and ineffectual is because, unlike the prince, we were never properly initiated into manhood by our male elders and, partially as a result, have lost touch with the wild man in ourselves. You've probably also heard about the weekend-long men's gatherings that Bly and his associates conduct and the various

Wild Man retreats and New Warrior training programs that have spun off from them in which men are encouraged to reconnect with the wild man or warrior within by engaging in ritualistic practices such as beating drums and sitting in sweat lodges. The popularity of these programs and the commercial success of *Iron John* and other books for men attest to the fact that huge numbers of men are searching for a way out of the current male crisis.

But are they searching in the right place?

Bly and his associates deserve much credit for popularizing the concept of men coming together in groups to re-examine their ideas about masculinity. As women discovered during the early days of feminism, coming together to share thoughts and experiences can be an extremely effective method of raising consciousness—one to which few men had been exposed before Bly and his colleagues began conducting these gatherings. Bly also deserves credit for using the example of his own struggle to resolve his feelings toward his alcoholic father to encourage other men to work through the grief and pain that are part of their own complicated feelings toward their fathers. In almost every other respect, however, the guidance being offered by Bly is pointing men in the wrong direction: not into the future, but back into the past.

To propose, first of all, that men can restore their lost sense of masculine purpose and pride by engaging in modern-day versions of rites and rituals practiced in early Native-American and other premodern societies is a romantic pipe dream at best. These rites and rituals serve an important function in the cultures from which they derive, but ours is not one of these cultures. Nor would we want it to be. Much as we bemoan the ills of our postmodern society and enjoy escaping in fantasy to what we imagine to have been the nobler way of life of these premodern cultures, the truth is that, given a choice between living in their world or living in ours, most of us would choose the comforts and conveniences of modern life—even with all its problems. The current male crisis is one of these problems—a contemporary problem requiring contemporary solutions that aren't going to be found by taking on animal names and dancing naked in the woods.

Nor are they going to be found by following Bly's interpretation of the metaphorical instructions for attaining manhood contained in the Iron John fairy tale—that is, by separating from women in order to throw off their feminizing influence and finding male mothers to guide us, as our own fathers failed to do, in our journey to become "initiated men." Bly would argue that he's not urging men to literally separate from women—that his message, like the fairy tale's, is metaphorical. But the problem with metaphorical messages is that people can interpret them however they wish—including literally. And what an unfortunate number of men want to hear is that they're right to blame women—i.e., the feminist movement—for creating the mess they're in and are justified in maintaining or increasing their emotional distance from their female partners. This thinking couldn't be more wrong-headed. In fact, just as men need to resolve their feelings toward their fathers, they also need to work through the deeply conflicting feelings about intimacy instilled in infancy by their mothers that prevent them from drawing closer to their partners. What men need to do, in other words, is take down the walls they've erected between themselves and their partners—not build them up. The same goes for the importance Bly places on making contact with the elemental fierceness of the Wild Man within. Again, Bly would argue that his message is metaphorical—that he's talking not about giving freer rein to anger, aggression, rage, and violence, but about reclaiming masculine strength, courage, vigor, and resolve. During a men's gathering that I attended, however, that distinction wasn't made very clear. The talk was simply about developing fierceness. And I was disturbed by how hungrily many of the men drank it in.

What Men's Gatherings Can and Can't Do for Us

Another problem with these gatherings and retreats is that men often come away from them fired up with the belief that they've found quick-fix solutions to long-standing difficulties—only to discover days or weeks later that they haven't. But male-only gatherings can serve a valid purpose—and at their best, they serve two purposes. First, they offer a man an opportunity to learn from other men that he's not the only one feeling demoralized and confused—and this discovery alone can do much to alleviate the secret shame men attach to these feelings. Second, these gatherings offer men a safe place in which to begin re-examining their beliefs about manhood. They can't guide a man all the way through the process of identifying and executing the changes he wants to make in his traditional belief system, but they can inspire him to continue that process when he returns to his daily life.

I know one man, Ted, who returned from a three-day men's conference precisely so inspired. Shortly after his return he entered therapy for the first time—at age forty-seven—for the primary purpose of figuring out why he tended to get involved with women who treated him unkindly and then stay involved with them, despite his unhappiness, until they called it quits. Ted remained in therapy for two years, during which time he met and began dating the woman to whom he is now married—his first marriage, her second. He couldn't be happier—with his marriage, with his new stepson, with the warm, supportive family life to which he now returns at the end of each workday seldom later than six-thirty, instead of working late as he always did before. Ted takes credit for having worked hard in therapy to turn his life around. But he also credits the unexpectedly powerful experience of attending the men's conference with inspiring him to do it.

The conference Ted attended wasn't one of Bly's men's gatherings or any of its spin-offs, however, but just the opposite. It was a large, mainstream conference offering a wide range of lectures and workshops, most of which simply offered men a chance to come together to discuss and explore the positives and negatives of their adherence to various facets of the traditional masculine code. No way, he says, would you ever get him to go off into the woods with a bunch of other grown men to beat drums around a fire.

In a way, in other words, the whole question of what these retreats and training programs do or don't offer is moot because, like Ted, the vast majority of men won't go anywhere near them. Sure, they have issues and problems they realize they need to work on. But they just can't see themselves doing it in such a setting. Many men refuse, in fact, to attend any conference, seminar, or workshop that takes the current male crisis as its subject matter, fearing that all men's gatherings operate along these same lines.

And that's unfortunate. Because, as Ted's story illustrates, these meetings can motivate men to make constructive changes in their lives. But, then, so can the simple awareness that their lives aren't working and that something has to change. And that's good. Because, as I've learned over the course of my career, once men decide that they need to change some deeply entrenched attitude or behavior, they're extremely good at actually making that change. That's one of the many still valuable components of the traditional masculine code. Men are nowhere near as skilled as women are at identifying, analyzing, and discussing feelings, but they're much better at translating talk into action. Having been trained to take a pragmatic, problem-solving, action-oriented approach to life, men are very skilled at meeting problems head on and getting down to the business of solving them.

MEN IN TRANSITION

Indeed, the more I listen to men talk, the more convinced I become that they aren't just ready to change—they've already begun changing. A few years ago, I decided to investigate whether the shift in values I was noticing was happening within the male population at large. To find out, my colleagues and I devised a test comprised of fifty-eight statements that either reflect or contradict seven traditionally masculine norms: (1) avoidance of femininity; (2) restricted emotions; (3) sex disconnected from intimacy; (4) pursuit of achievement and status; (5) self-reliance; (6) strength and aggression; and (7) homophobia.* We then administered the test to a sample group of men by asking them to read each statement and indicate how much they agreed or disagreed with it. As we reported in the July 1992 issue of the *Journal of Mental Health Counseling*, our sample included 117 predominantly white, predominantly middle- and upper-middle-class men. Because this obviously was not a representative sample of the American male population our findings must be regarded as somewhat preliminary. But the responses were so strikingly different from the conventional wisdom about the beliefs men hold that we felt it was important to report them. Here's what we found:

1. Avoidance of Femininity. It used to be that men drew a hard line between masculine and feminine behavior. Indeed, according to various studies, avoidance of femininity was one of *the* most unviolable tenets of the traditional masculine code. In the last ten years this stance has softened considerably. The men in our study still felt it was important to encourage certain traditionally masculine traits in their sons. They agreed, for example, that "boys should prefer to play with trucks rather than dolls" and that "boys should not throw baseballs like

* See Appendix for the complete test.

girls." But they were nowhere near as rigid about adult behavior. These men slightly disagreed, for example, with the idea that "a man should prefer football to needlecraft" and basically scoffed at the notion that "a man should avoid holding his wife's purse at all times." As far as they were concerned, it was also perfectly acceptable for men "to wear bracelets." More important, they rejected the idea—at least in theory— that "housework is women's work" and also rejected the notion that "jobs like fire fighter and electrician should be reserved for men."

2. Restricted Emotions. Another traditional norm states that men should never show emotion: not fear, sadness, vulnerability, tenderness—not anything, except maybe anger. The men in our study believed there are times when it's important and appropriate for men to control emotions. But they also believed there are times when men should be allowed to express them. They disagreed, for example, with the ideas that "fathers should teach their sons to mask fear" and that others "should not be able to tell how a man is feeling by looking at his face." And they strongly rejected the notion that "a man should never reveal worries to others"—strongly agreeing, instead, that "if a man is in pain, it's better for him to let people know than to keep it to himself." They disagreed slightly with the notions that a man should never cry in public and that being "a little down in the dumps is not a good reason for a man to act depressed." But they strongly disagreed with the idea that men "should not be too quick to tell others that they care about them" and strongly endorsed the idea that "men should be allowed to kiss their fathers."

3. Sex Disconnected from Intimacy. Traditionally, men have separated sex from emotional intimacy. Lately, however, they've begun rethinking their beliefs about sex. The men in our study were still concerned about their capacity to perform sexually. They disagreed, for example, that "a man doesn't need to have an erection in order to enjoy sex" and agreed that it's important for a man "to be good in bed." But they rejected the stereotypical "male as stud, female as sex-object" ethic in favor of a more intimate, egalitarian, less goal-oriented approach to sex. They disagreed moderately to strongly, for example, with the traditional notions that "a man should always be ready for sex"; that "touching is simply the first step toward sex"; that "hugging and kissing should always lead to intercourse"; and that a man "shouldn't bother with sex unless he can achieve an orgasm." And they thoroughly rejected the notions that men should always do the sexual initiating and that men "shouldn't have to worry about birth control." They also repudiated the notion that men don't care who their sex partner is so long as she's willing by agreeing, instead, that "a man should love his sex partner."

4. Pursuit of Achievement and Status. Men have been trained to measure their masculine worth by their ability to compete and excel, and, to a large extent, they still do. The men in our study agreed, for example, that a man should try to win at any sport in which he participates, agreed strongly that "men should have goals and be determined to achieve them," and disagreed with the notion that "it's not important for men to strive to reach the top." But men are beginning to realize that achievement isn't the only thing that matters and are also becoming more willing and able to share power and status with women. The men in our study disagreed with the notions, for example, that a man should do "whatever it takes to be admired and respected" and that "if necessary, a man should sacrifice personal relationships for career advancement." They expressed only slight disagreement with the notion that a man should always be the major financial provider, but they were much clearer in rejecting the notion that men should always have the final word in financial decisions and also disagreed with the idea that "in a group, it's up to the men to get things organized and moving ahead."

5. Self-Reliance. Very early on, a man learns that his status as a man rests on the ability to stand and act alone. This isn't entirely a bad trait. There's much to be said for self-reliance.

And our findings indicate that men count it as one of their strengths. The men in our study expressed moderate to strong agreement, for example, with the traditional beliefs that a man should always be realistic and level-headed; that he should "think things out logically and have good reasons for what he does"; that he should "never count on someone else to get the job done"; and that he "must be able to make his own way in the world." But men are beginning to realize that self-reliance can also be carried too far. The men in our study agreed, for example, that "it's okay for a man to ask for help changing a tire." And while they expressed only slight disagreement with the notion that a man who takes a long time making decisions will not be respected, they expressed clearer disagreement with the traditional belief that "a man should never doubt his own judgment."

6. Strength and Aggression. Men have always considered strength, courage, and aggression to be among the most valuable of the many manly virtues. Our findings indicate that men still value these traits and consider them important to pass on to their sons, but our test results also show that men are beginning to discriminate between healthy and unhealthy uses of strength and aggression. The men in our study disagreed, for example, with the notion that "a boy should be allowed to quit a game if he is losing," and yet they agreed only slightly with the idea that "boys should be encouraged to find a means of demonstrating physical prowess." They agreed that "when the going gets tough, men should get tough" and agreed even more strongly that when there's a strange noise in the house at night, men should be the ones to "get up to investigate." They also agreed that it's "important for a man to take risks, even if he might get hurt" and, more moderately, that a man with no taste for adventure "is not very appealing." But they were disinclined to support the traditional masculine ethic of meeting every act of aggression with an even greater display of aggression. Instead of strongly disagreeing, for example, with the idea that a man "should not force the issue if another man takes his parking place"—as this traditional ethic dictates they should—the men in our study remained neutral. And they edged just past neutrality toward slight endorsement of the notion that "when physically provoked, men should not resort to violence."

7. Homophobia. As is reflected in the highly charged, ongoing debate concerning whether gay men and women should be allowed to serve in the military, homophobia is still very much alive in this country. The men in our study rejected homophobia only ever so slightly. Given the depth and power of this particular norm, however, the fact that they rejected it at all should be taken as an encouraging sign that men are becoming less uncomfortable with homosexuality than they once were. The men in our study agreed, for example, that "being called 'faggot' is one of the worst insults to a man or boy" and that "it is disappointing to learn that a famous athlete is gay." But their agreement with both these statements was rather mild. More important, they had worked free enough of homophobia to agree, at least mildly, that "a man should be able to show affection to another man" and to disagree fairly strongly with the notion that a man should end a friendship with another man "if he finds out the other man is homosexual." And that represents progress.

Yes, We Know We Have to Change —In Some Ways, Not All Ways

The answer to the question "Are men changing?" seems clearly, then, to be yes—but it's a fascinatingly textured and qualified one that reflects men's commitment to forging a new middle path between opposing "traditional man" and "sensitive man" ideals by carefully selecting what's useful from both. Men know that the traditional masculine code needs to be reconstructed, but they also know it doesn't need to be completely replaced. They're ready to rework certain parts of it, but they have no intention of relinquishing the still-valuable masculine traits.

Unfortunately, these still-valuable traits haven't been receiving much recognition lately. It's as if when the traditional masculine code collapsed all these good traits got buried at the bottom of the pile. The first step in reconstructing masculinity, therefore, is to give these traits the recognition they deserve. Over the course of my career I've compiled a fairly extensive list of the traits men consider worth preserving and celebrating. Here are a few of them:

- **The willingness to sacrifice personal needs and desires for the sake of providing for dependents.** One of my clients spoke often and fondly, for example, of how hard his father had worked to be able to send his seven children to Catholic school—the only way, in his time and community, that he could be sure they received a good education. "He was a superintendent for an apartment building," said my client. "The job didn't pay much. But he managed by never missing a day of work, never getting sick, never taking a vacation, and never spending one penny on himself."

- **The willingness to withstand hardship and pain to protect loved ones.** Another client told me of the time, as boys, when he and a cousin got lost in the woods during a family camping trip. Darkness fell. A vicious rainstorm hit. They holed up in a cave—dry and safe, but scared to death. Hours later, between claps of thunder and flashes of lightning, they heard his father calling them. They'd been found! On their way back to camp, my client realized that his father was limping badly—wincing with each step he took. When he asked what was wrong, his dad insisted it was nothing. The next morning his mother drove the family to a hospital emergency room, where his father's foot was put in a cast. It turned out that, while searching for them in the darkness and rain, his dad had tripped on a fallen tree branch and broken his ankle—and had kept right on searching until he'd found his boys.

- **The willingness to take on and try to solve other people's problems.** Literally and figuratively, men have strong shoulders. Another former client took over all responsibility for his ailing mother-in-law's medical care when it became clear that his wife, who'd never gotten along with her mother—a selfish, arrogant, unpleasant woman—couldn't handle that responsibility herself. The duties he took on included chauffeuring his mother-in-law to and from doctors' appointments and hospital visits, consulting with her physicians, arranging to have her prescriptions filled and making sure she took her medication, and handling all medical bills and insurance claims. The demands on his time were endless and exhausting. But I never once heard him complain. "Someone has to do it," he said, shrugging. No one else seemed willing to do it, so he did.

- **Expressing love by doing things for others.** Many men feel that this trait is vastly underappreciated now that the pressure is on them to express their feelings in words. An example of the ways in which men show affection through deeds comes from a couple I counseled a few years ago. For a few weeks the wife had been making noises about "how nice it would be" if they had more shelf space in their study. "What kind?" the husband casually asked one evening. Together, they sketched out a design for an entire wall of built-in shelving. A month later the wife left town for a week to visit her mother. When she returned and walked into the study she discovered that her husband—a teacher by vocation and skilled carpenter by avocation—had installed the shelves. He hadn't told her he was going to do it. He'd just done it—as he said, "because I knew she wanted them." She was overwhelmed with emotion. He insisted it was "no big deal." That's what you do, was his philosophy. When you love someone, you do things to make her happy.

• **Integrity, steadfastness, and loyalty to commitments.** A man keeps his promises. He doesn't go back on his word—even when he's sorely tempted. A former client of mine had to work very hard to resist the temptation to violate his marriage vows when his wife confessed that she'd had an affair. His first angry impulse was to divorce her; his second, to get her back by having his own affair. But he resisted. As he said, "That's not going to get us anywhere. It'll only make things worse, and I don't want that. I married her. I love her. I made a commitment to her, and I'm going to see it through." Which he did. It took a lot of hard work—which included examining his own contributions to the marital unhappiness that had caused his wife to stray and learning to feel and express the pain her affair had caused him. But such was his dedication that he was eventually able to put his wife's infidelity behind him and concentrate on repairing and strengthening their bonds.

• **The will to hang in until a difficult problem is resolved.** Men can be stubborn, all right—wonderfully stubborn when it comes to plugging away at a problem until it's resolved. I know another man who became seriously concerned that his unemployed bachelor brother, who lived out of state, was sliding into alcoholism. He tried to share his concerns with his widower father, but his father didn't want to hear about them. He called a long-distance business contact and lined up a job interview for his brother, but his brother never showed. He tried talking to his brother by phone, telling him he was concerned about his drinking and encouraging him to attend an Alcoholics Anonymous meeting. His brother said he'd think about it. He never went. Frustrated and frightened that his brother was slowly drinking himself to death, he finally took it upon himself to fly out to confront him, stay with him until he admitted he had a problem, and persuade him to enter a rehabilitation clinic. That was three years ago. His brother hasn't had a drink since. The last time they talked by phone, his brother thanked him, for the first time, for caring enough to keep kicking his ass when everyone else had given up on him—and helping him save his own life.

- **The ability to think logically, solve problems, take risks, and stay calm in the face of danger.** Getting up in the middle of the night to investigate a strange noise in the house is just one example of the ways in which men manifest these traits—and it's a small example at that. Think of something you're particularly proud of having accomplished. Think of a friend, colleague, mentor, or role model whose achievements you admire. Ask yourself what traits made possible your own accomplishment—what traits enable the other person to do his work. It's hard to imagine how men would ever achieve anything were it not for our well-honed abilities to (1) envision a goal, devise a strategy for accomplishing it, and work steadily toward it; (2) hold true to our vision despite the scoffing of naysayers; (3) think on our feet, outwit opponents, and identify and overcome obstacles; (4) bull through in the face of fear, frustration, and exhaustion; and (5) roll with the punches, overcome setbacks, and pick ourselves up after being knocked down by defeat and get back into the game. And that's just for starters. Keep thinking. You'll come up with more.

Are these traits worth preserving and celebrating? Absolutely. And the sooner men realize that, the sooner they'll be on the road toward recovering their sense of masculine purpose and pride.

But reclaiming and celebrating these valuable traits is only the first step in the work I call reconstructing masculinity. An important step, but only the first—and a relatively easy one at that. Once these valuable traits have been separated out, the next task is to identify those aspects of the traditional code that have now become obsolete and/or dysfunctional and set to work changing them.

During my years of research and practice I've developed what I think is a pretty clear sense of what these main problem areas are. More important, I've found that when men are provided with a program for change that plays to their pragmatic, action-taking, goal-oriented strengths, they're extraordinarily successful at resolving these problem areas. In each of the nine chapters that follow, I'll be focusing on one of these problem areas and sharing some of the techniques I've found most effective in helping men resolve them. Listed in the order in which I'll be discussing them, these main problem areas are:

- **Difficulty sensing and responding to other people's emotions.** Men are extremely good at figuring out what another person is likely to do and then encouraging or blocking that action to achieve a desired goal—a skill I call action empathy. What they're not good at is intuiting and responding to another person's feelings—a skill I call emotional empathy. Unlike females, in whom this skill is encouraged in infancy and who then perfect it in childhood while engaged in intimate, cooperative play with a small circle of female friends, males are neither encouraged nor allowed to master it. The major thrust of our training is in how to compete, how to be aggressive, how to strategize, how to take action—not how to be sensitive to our own or other people's emotions. Unfortunately, this skill deficit often gets men into trouble —especially in their relationships with women, to whom emotional empathy comes so easily that they often mistakenly assume men are good at it, too. The usual scenario: A woman tells her husband about some problem she's having. He immediately plunges in and tries to fix it. She becomes angry and hurt. He becomes confused. What'd he do wrong? What he did wrong was to immediately swing into action mode without first pausing to empathize with her feelings—a response she sees not as the loving and helpful response he thinks it is but as unbelievably insensitive and cold. The good news is that although emotional empathy often seems like some kind of ESP women are born with and men aren't, it's actually a fairly easy skill to master—not so different from action empathy. In Chapter Two, we'll discuss how men can develop this skill simply by building on the action-empathy skills they already possess.

- **Inability to feel, identify, and express feelings.** Pretty much from the moment a male is born, he begins absorbing the message imparted by his parents, peers, and society that he isn't supposed to feel or express sadness, fear, tenderness, vulnerability, or much of any other emotion. Throughout infancy and childhood, while females learn to feel, name, and express their feelings, males learn to suppress theirs. The result is that by the time men reach adulthood, most are so emotionally numb that they don't know they're having an emotional reaction even when they're having it! In Chapter Three, we'll look closely at the causes and unfortunate consequences of this emotional numbness—a condition called alexithymia—and run through the various steps in a kind of detective game I've devised to help men identify these emotional reactions, figure out what's causing them, and learn to express feelings more directly.

- **Overindulgence in anger.** The one emotion males are allowed and encouraged to express is anger. Unfortunately, this means that many of the emotions they're not allowed to express get compressed and transmuted into anger—which too easily turns into rage and too often spills out as violence. Some of that violence gets directed at other men, but most of it gets directed at women, to whom men unconsciously look to minister to their needs and who they are quick to punish when things don't go their way. In Chapter Four, we'll explore how men learn to transmute emotions into anger, the obvious and subtle ways in which they vent anger on women, and how they can short-circuit anger by learning to feel, identify, and express the emotions that trigger it.

- **Propensity to simultaneously depend on, distance from, and take advantage of female partners.** Males have a rough time in early life—beginning in infancy, when mothers unconsciously limit the nurturing they give sons, and continuing through childhood, when boys are denied closeness with their fathers. As a result, males come into adulthood with a whole host of unmet dependency needs that are unconsciously transferred onto their partners. Without realizing they're doing it, they look to their wives not only for the nurturing they still crave but also to feel, express, and manage their emotions. And yet, having learned first from their mothers and then from their fathers that to be masculine means to be separate, men also find intimacy threatening. When their partners come close, an unconscious need for self-sufficiency kicks in and they distance—which women find hurtful and confusing. To complicate matters further many men also come to adulthood with an unconscious belief that they're entitled to take more than they give to compensate for the early-life traumas they suffered. In Chapter Five, we'll discuss how men can break these patterns by doing the difficult but ultimately liberating work of bringing these deep hurts up to consciousness and mourning them. Only then can a man finally put them behind him and free himself of the destructive behaviors to which they give rise.

- **Chronic fear and secret shame of failing to measure up as a man.** If there's one thing all men know—without even knowing they know it—it's that manhood is an unattainable goal. Men feel called upon to prove their manhood over and over by passing a never-ending series of tests. And no matter how many tests they pass, they live in fear of failing the next one. In Chapter Six, we'll examine how fear of the punishment attached to failing these tests keeps a man striving to fulfill traditional manhood requirements that (a) no longer serve his best interests and/or (b) have now become difficult or impossible to fulfill. We'll also look closely at how the excruciating shame attached to failing these tests keeps a man silent about his failures and, thus, mistakenly convinced he's the only one keeping shameful secrets when the fact is all men have them. Finally, we'll examine how trying to fulfill unfulfillable manhood ideals can lead to a vicious cycle of self-sacrificing and self-indulging and discuss how men can break out of this cycle.

- **Over-investment in work.** That's what men know how to do best—work. In fact, a lot of men don't know how to do anything but work. In Chapter Seven, we'll examine how a man's early-life training sets him up to seek validation and fulfillment almost exclusively from work—and how this leads, in turn, to such unhealthy outcomes as workaholism and work-related stress disorders and exacerbates the negative repercussions of being trapped in work he finds unfulfilling or being temporarily or chronically unemployed. We'll also examine the quandary in which men find themselves now that the amount of validation they *can* derive from work has diminished and they find themselves being encouraged and/or pressured to find compensatory fulfillment in fuller participation in family life. This isn't an easy adjustment for men, but the rewards make the effort worthwhile.

- **Lack of awareness of—or disregard for—the health risks associated with conforming to the traditional masculine code.** Men are taught to be unemotional, self-sufficient, impervious to pain—supermen, in other words. But we're not supermen. We're human beings who don't hold up well under the strain of trying to be what we're not. In Chapter Eight, we'll examine the serious health risks involved in trying to live up to these unrealistic masculine ideals. Statistics make troublingly clear that far more men than women fall victim to heart disease, lung cancer, stress-related disorders, alcoholism, drug addiction, suicide, and accidental or violent death—in large part because males are trained according to a code that (a) encourages them to indulge in unhealthy habits and risky behaviors; (b) discourages them from heeding signs of injury or illness; and (c) discourages them from seeking medical care when they need it. Men also pay a price in physical well-being for not being allowed to express emotion, admit imperfections, and experience closeness with loved ones—all of which promote health.

- **Discomfort with sexual intimacy.** Men are now beginning to re-examine their long-standing tradition of separating sex from intimacy and seeing women primarily as a means of satiating lust. In Chapter Nine, we'll examine how early-life experiences and training conspire to instill these nonrelational sexual attitudes in men by teaching them, among other things, to fear closeness, to suppress and deny tender emotions, to see sex not as a form of intimate communication but as a means of proving their manhood, and to see females not as human beings but as objects of sexual arousal and gratification. We know women suffer as a result of our holding these nonrelational sexual attitudes. What we often don't realize, however, is that we suffer, too. Satiating lust is gratifying, certainly. But satiating emotionally disconnected lust doesn't hold a candle to the more enduring delights of sexual intimacy, which men can't experience until they overcome nonrelational attitudes toward sex.

- **The overall lack of relationship skills that makes closeness to others unattainable.** The problem isn't that men don't want to establish closer ties with other people. The problem is they don't know how. In the final chapter, we'll look at how men who develop the emotional skills needed to rectify the trouble areas we've examined can use these skills to become more sensitive, involved fathers; resolve unresolved feelings toward parents; draw closer to male friends; and create and sustain satisfying relationships with their partners. As our nation's abysmal divorce statistics attest, sustaining a long-term relationship is no easy task in these days of shifting values. The more emotionally skilled, or emotionally intelligent, a man is, the better his chances are of beating these grim statistics.

RECONSTRUCTING MASCULINITY: A PROGRAM THAT WORKS

The bottom line is that men possess a host of admirable skills and traits—but emotional intelligence isn't one of them. And that's what we need. Back in our fathers' and grandfathers' and great-grandfathers' day, men and their dependents were better off if they weren't too emotionally inclined. Too much emotional self-awareness and sensitivity would only have compromised their ability to do the things a man had to do: withstand long hours of back-breaking, sometimes dangerous work in fields, mines, and factories to provide food and shelter for their dependents; be prepared at all times to lay their lives on the line to rescue their families from danger and protect them from harm; leave their loved ones behind to seek work in distant locales when there was none to be found near home; go off to war—never knowing when or if they'd return—to maim and kill, or be maimed and killed by, other human beings.

And so on. Hard business that required men to harden themselves. Until as recently as the 1950s, when it was still a man's job to function as sole financial provider and chief family disciplinarian and decision-maker, being cut off from emotion still served some useful purpose. *But it doesn't anymore.* The world is changing. Professional and community life is changing. The nature and structure of family life and intimate relationships are changing. More and more, men are being urged to relinquish their traditional role and join in partnership with women in providing for their families, nurturing children, creating and sustaining satisfying relationships, and resolving the many ills that plague our communities, society, and world. Men possess a number of valuable skills that they can apply toward resolving these problems. But unless their efforts are guided by sensitivity to and respect for their own and other people's feelings, the outcome will be mixed at best. Before men can effectively tackle these problems, they first have to do the work of becoming more emotionally intelligent human beings.

I've had the privilege of helping many men do this work—and the pleasure of seeing them succeed in making profound, lasting, constructive changes in themselves, their relationships, and their lives. Not flashy changes. The vast majority of my clients have no desire to change their lives radically. What they want to do and what I help them to do is to pinpoint and remove the obstacles preventing them from deriving more satisfaction from the lives they're living right now. Together, we figure out the ways in which their adherence to traditional values prevents them from doing that, then decide how best to reconstruct these aspects of their masculine code. The approach I use is very down-to-earth and grounded in men's reality—designed to take advantage of men's traditional training and strengths by allowing them to do what they do best: identify a problem; devise a strategy for solving it; and implement that strategy via a series of concrete steps until the desired goal is reached.

In the chapters that follow, you'll meet a number of men who committed to doing this work and who, by dint of their motivation, determination, and courage, succeeded in making positive changes in their lives. In Chapters Two through Five, you'll sit in as I work with men in individual counseling sessions to identify and resolve the deep-rooted, often unrecognized problems that stem from having been trained to distance themselves from emotion, fear closeness, and deny the pain they suffered when their early nurturing needs went unfulfilled. In the second half of the book, when we examine how men's lives are shaped by larger societal and cross-cultural manhood ideals, you'll listen in as men speak in workshops about the ways in which they're still caught up in trying to meet these impossible standards, and you'll learn through abbreviated case histories how I've helped other men put these standards in a healthier perspective.

When relating incidents from men's lives and discussing case histories, I've taken the precaution of changing names and other identifying details to protect privacy. But the men are real. Their stories are real. And, most important, the positive changes they made in their lives are real. I share their stories with you in the hope that you'll see yourself in these men and be inspired by their example to begin the serious work of re-examining and reconstructing your own beliefs about manhood—so that you, too, can derive more meaning and satisfaction from the life you're living and begin, once again, to feel proud of being a man.

CHAPTER TWO

From Action Empathy to Emotional Empathy

THE EMOTION SOCIALIZATION OF MALES

"Women," said Dave, dropping his long, lanky frame onto my office sofa at the start of one of our weekly counseling sessions. He removed his glasses and massaged the bridge of his nose. "I swear, Ron, I do not understand them."

Hardly an original complaint. I'd have smiled if it weren't obvious Dave was angry and frustrated. What man hasn't said that? It used to be that this was about as close as men got to expressing concern over their inability to fathom the female psyche—and they usually had to be feeling pretty lost down a dark tunnel of misunderstanding to say even that much. Whatever serious worries men might have had over relationship problems they pretty much kept to themselves. And they certainly never voluntarily sought help in solving these problems. Worrying too much about relationships just wasn't manly. And working at relationships—that was women's terrain. Men worked at making money. Women worked at their relationships with men.

But times have changed. No longer so dependent on their mates for economic survival, women today are also no longer so willing to do all the relationship work. Now they're saying, "Look, if you care about this relationship, you're going to have to work at it, too." Men do care, of course—always have. But, never before having had to do this kind of relationship work, they find themselves clumsy at it—at best. That doesn't mean they can't develop the necessary skills. They can. And, as the results of my study indicate, they want to. Men have begun rejecting the traditional male norm of restricted emotions in favor of a reconstructed masculine code that allows them to open lines of emotional communication with their loved ones. They just need coaching in how to do that.

That's why Dave had come to me.

Action Empathy Versus Emotional Empathy—The Great Male–Female Divide

Dave was a forty-eight-year-old cross-cultural media consultant for a commercial pharmaceuticals company and the divorced father of two girls. He had entered counseling with me when the woman with whom he'd become involved after his divorce had suddenly ended their relationship—for reasons he hadn't understood. He'd been seeing Joyce, a divorced, forty-four-year-old attorney, for two months. "We were talking on the phone last night," he said, smoothing back a shock of unruly blond hair and replacing his glasses. "She found out yesterday that the bid she and another female colleague had put in to work on this big case their firm is handling had been turned down—that it had been assigned to two of their junior male colleagues instead. She was really upset about it. But it seemed she had a pretty good fix on the situation—which is what I told her. She was talking about glass ceilings and under-the-table discrimination, and I said, 'Sounds right to me. Sounds like you've got a good handle on things.' So, there I am, agreeing with her, and what does she do? She gets angry! 'I don't know why I even bother talking to you,' she says. And I'm like, 'Huh? Wait a minute. I thought I was being supportive.' And she snorts and says, 'If you call *that* being supportive.' I was stunned. So I just shut up. There was this dead silence. And then she said, 'Well, it's late. I should get to sleep. I'll call you tomorrow.' And then we hung up."

Of course Dave was shocked—all the more so because Joyce's seemingly unwarranted attack flew in the face of his own image of himself as a rather astute and sensitive guy. Which he is—in his way. An anthropologist for ten years before he acquired an MBA and switched to a more lucrative business career in order to put his girls through private school, Dave was hired by his Fortune 500 employer precisely because of his keen ability to gather information about people, view a problem or situation from their vantage point and, on the basis of that, predict what they will do. It's this skill in perspective-taking, applied on an international level, that makes him so good at his job—enabling him to pick out which lines in an advertisement for insect repellent will confuse sub-Equatorial Africans, pinpoint the reason upwardly mobile Peruvians and Bolivians shun chewing-gum laxatives, and chart the different connotations the word *deodorant* carries in Eastern versus Western Europe.

It is this skill, which I call action empathy, that Dave had called upon in his genuine attempt to be supportive of Joyce. "It's all there in your language," I said. " 'Clear fix,' 'good handle'—these are action-empathy terms." Basically, he had complimented Joyce on what he saw as her ability to do what he and most other men do so well: watch people move, figure out what they'll do next, and devise strategies to counter or encourage that predicted response to achieve a desired goal. It's very much a male skill—a legacy, in part, of the thousands of boy-hours we spent playing competitive team sports. Women, for the most part, don't have this skill, because they were never socialized in it. They passed their childhoods in intimate play, smiling, giggling, and sharing secrets with friends in small groups of two or three—which puts them at a disadvantage when they enter the competitive professional arena.

"So I *was* being supportive of Joyce," said Dave, sounding annoyed. "So, why did she bite my head off?"

"Because you weren't giving her what she wanted," I said. "She didn't want action empathy. She wanted a different kind of empathy—what I call emotional empathy."

If action empathy is a male skill, emotional empathy is its female counterpart. "What women learn in their childhoods," I said, "is how to put themselves in another person's place in a different way—not to figure out what the other person will do, but to read and respond to what the other person is feeling. That's what Joyce wanted from you. You had no way of knowing this, of course, but when she talked about glass ceilings and discrimination, she wasn't asking you to confirm her view of the game board. She wanted you to empathize with her feelings of hurt, anger, and frustration."

Dave was really irked now. "Well, then, why didn't she just say so, for God's sake?"

"You're right. She wasn't being direct." But it probably hadn't occurred to Joyce that Dave wouldn't understand what she was asking for. Operating on the assumption that they thought the same way—a mistake men and women often make with each other—she'd probably been as flummoxed as he'd been by their miscommunication. Like many women, Joyce also may have no trouble expressing mildly negative emotions but may find it difficult to express strong negative emotions directly, and so had fallen back on indirectness, counting on Dave to use the emotional-empathy skills she'd assumed he possessed to intuit her needs and meet her halfway.

"In other words, I'm supposed to read her mind."

"No, not her mind. Her heart. You're already pretty good at reading minds."

"What does that mean?"

"Think about it. In a way, it's what you do for a living. That's what action empathy is all about. It's about using the information you gather from a person to project yourself into his mind and predict what he will do. Emotional empathy is the same, only different. You're still gathering information. It's just a different kind of information. And you're gathering it for different reasons: not to predict what a person will do but to understand what that person is feeling—and not so much to achieve your own objectives as to help the other person."

"But how am I supposed to do that if I don't know how?"

"We teach you."

"Yeah? How?"

"We re-socialize you."

Dave let out a bark of a laugh. "Ha! Yeah, sure."

We May Be Emotionally Out of Touch Now, but We Didn't Start Out That Way

I understood Dave's skepticism. As a former anthropologist he knew full well that socialization—the conditioning process by which human beings are trained to think, feel, and behave in ways deemed appropriate by their culture—begins at the moment of birth. And he was right: These patterns aren't easily changed. But that doesn't mean men can't work around them. They can—by adapting their highly developed action-empathy skills to the emotional-empathy arena.

Men often do react skeptically when I tell them this, convinced that what I'm suggesting would require the expenditure of a whole lot of energy for embarrassingly little return. After all, how good can the results possibly be? It's as if males think emotional empathy is, at core, some sex-linked genetic trait that they were simply born without. Which it isn't. Most men are born with the potential for developing emotional empathy. In fact, when you compare the potential males and females are born with, in some ways males have an edge. It's hard for a person to empathize with other people's feelings unless he or she is capable of feeling emotions. Or, to put it another way, the greater the capacity to feel emotion, the greater the potential for developing emotional empathy. That's where males have—or at least had—an advantage. Hard as it may be to believe, it's a pretty well documented fact that males are born more emotionally reactive and expressive than females.

Credit for calling attention to this intriguing fact goes to psychologists Jeannette Jones Haviland, of Rutgers University, and Carol Zander Malatesta, of the New School for Social Research.* In a 1981 review of data from twelve different studies of male and female infants, Haviland and Malatesta found that male infants startle more easily, become excited more quickly, have a lower tolerance for tension and frustration, become distressed more quickly, cry sooner and more often, are more irritable and less easily soothed, and fluctuate more rapidly between emotional states. And the fact that all but one of these studies were based on observations of infants who were only days old strongly suggests that these differences are innate.

Observations of older infants have turned up similar findings. In a 1992 study of male and female six-month-olds, psychologist Marta K. Weinberg, of the University of Massachusetts, found that males continue to out-express females at this key developmental stage—the age at which babies begin to crawl and sit up. Far from being distracted from the world of emotions by their fascination with their budding motor skills, six-month-old boys, Weinberg reported, continued to exhibit "significantly more joy and anger, more positive vocalizations, fussiness and crying, [and] more gestural signals directed towards the mother . . . than girls." This finding led

* Researchers are identified throughout this book by their university or hospital affiliation when the cited research was published.

her to conclude that boys are "more affectively reactive and socially directed than girls."

During babyhood, that is. Later on, boys change.

Male Emotions: Somewhere Way, Way Back, They Got Thoroughly Squelched

Haviland and Malatesta called the finding a paradox. "Boys," they wrote, "appear to start out in life as more emotionally labile than their sisters, but end up less expressive. This turnabout provokes the question of how such radical change takes place. The crossover in emotional expression . . . is one factor that is not accounted for in current developmental theory."

Haviland and Malatesta proposed some partial explanations as to how this "radical change" comes about. Piecing their theories together with my own research findings and those of other investigators, I've formulated a more comprehensive theory to explain how males' natural emotionality—the crucial precursor to emotional self-awareness and emotional empathy—gets squelched so early and so thoroughly that they later have trouble believing it was ever part of their makeup at all. Put simply, three powerful influences—mother, father, and peer group—work together to block this emotionality and rechannel it along three separate streams: one flowing into action empathy; one forced down into subterranean depths of emotional numbness; and one spilling out into the catch-all emotion of anger.

Mothers Favor Babies Who Make Mothering Easy—And Boy Babies Don't

All mothers want to keep their infants calm and contented. (Dads, too, now that fathers are taking on more child-care responsibilities. But we're talking here about the way our parents parented us, and when we were babies, dads had little to do with infants.) The more temperamental and unmanageable a baby is, the harder a mother will work to keep that baby soothed. And, here, as Haviland and Malatesta pointed out, is where the squelching of the male infant's emotionality begins. In their own laboratory studies, they found that while mothers of six-month-old infants of course smiled at their babies when their babies smiled at them, they smiled in response to a boy baby's smiles more consistently than they did to a girl's—perhaps, the researchers suggested, because "mothers are trying harder to strengthen positive affect" (i.e., happy emotion) in their more temperamental boys. Mothers were much less inclined to mimic their babies' expressions of unhappy emotion—especially if the baby was a boy. When girl babies expressed pain, mothers responded approximately 22 percent of the time. But when boy babies expressed pain, mothers ignored them!

Mothers' responses to their babies' expression of interest, surprise, or joy also varied according to the baby's sex. If the baby was a boy, the mother was more likely simply to mimic that expression rather than risk overstimulating her infant by responding with a different expression that might upset what Haviland and Malatesta called his "more fragile emotional equilibrium." If the baby was a girl, the mother was more likely to respond with a different positive expression—in part, the researchers theorized, because the mother has learned through experience that her less excitable girl baby is more likely to find this stimulation pleasant, and in part because she's also learned that her girl baby is more likely to hold her gaze and reward her by trying to mimic that new funny face, sound or gesture. As Haviland and Malatesta wrote: "When ability to share is measured by a matching . . . response . . . girls 'win' hands down. . . ."

In short, female infants make a better audience for a mother's expressive play. Mothers figure this out, of course, and, without necessarily realizing they're doing so, they play to that audience—exposing their female infants to a greater variety of emotional expressions and teaching them, in the process, to become more astute perceivers and decoders of emotional cues, which facilitates their development of emotional empathy. Male infants don't get this training. Rather than engage them in the same kind of play, mothers of sons are more likely, wrote Haviland and Malatesta, to "go to special lengths to ensure that their sons remain contented." Instead of stimulating a son's emotionality, they take pains to control it, to modulate it, to keep it tamped down. Unable to distinguish between himself and his mother during his first months of life, the male infant feels his emotionality being dampened and enfolds this feeling into his sense of self: He is a being who holds his emotions in check.

Mothers aren't solely responsible for training males away from emotional reactivity and expressiveness, however. Dads take an active role in this training process, too. They come next.

When We Started Walking, Our Dads Made Sure We Started Walking Like Men

Again, parenting practices are changing now, but we're discussing the way our folks parented us. And, a generation back, most fathers didn't much notice or bother with their sons until they were approximately one year old. Infants held no fascination for them. What could a father do with an infant besides hold him? Later, when his child progressed to a wide-eyed, spittle-mouthed crawler, a father might plop down on the rug to play with him now and again—but still more out of a sense of obligation than any real interest. It wasn't until a son pulled himself upright and began bumping around on his own chubby legs that his dad really noticed him. Then he was no longer a baby. He was a boy—a boy who would someday need to know how to pitch a ball, stand up to a bully, tune up a car, hold down a job, support a family. It was when he began taking his first tentative, independent steps out into the world that a boy became his father's son. And that's when his father came into his life, determined to rescue him from the feminizing influence of the females of the household and teach him how to be a man.

In a 1977 longitudinal study designed to investigate how mothers and fathers interact with their babies, research psychologist Michael Lamb, of the University of Utah, found that, whereas mothers were fairly equitable in the amount of attention they gave sons and daughters, the attention a son got from his father increased significantly during his thirteenth month of life. At that point, dads went from uninterested to extremely interested in their baby boys—so interested that they now began interacting with their sons twice as much as they did with their daughters and twice as much as mothers interacted with sons or daughters in an equivalent period of time.

And not only do fathers interact more with boys than they do with girls aged one year or older. They also interact differently—their agenda being to channel their sons' natural emotionality along what they consider acceptably masculine lines. Fathers are very concerned about that. It's very important to them that their sons be masculine—much more important to them than it is to mothers. And they tend to work a lot harder than mothers do to force-fit their kids into stereotypically masculine and feminine molds once their children start walking and talking. In a 1987 review of thirty-nine separate studies on how fathers and mothers socialize older children, psychologist Michael Siegal found that while all these studies taken together reported relatively few differences in the ways mothers treated daughters versus sons, twenty noted significant differences in the ways fathers treated sons versus daughters. And much of that differential has to do with teaching boys to stifle their expression of emotions—especially their vulnerable and caring ones.

Pain ranks high among the vulnerable feelings fathers teach sons not to express. Dave remembered learning this lesson at age seven. "We were having a barbecue in my aunt and uncle's backyard," he recalled. "My cousin and I were batting a ball around. He hit a high one, and I jumped up against their chain-link fence to catch it, and, when I came down, I ripped the heel of my hand on a broken link. It was a pretty bad gash—lots of blood. I screamed and ran to my dad. He was across the yard, standing at the grill with my uncle. When I got to him, he grabbed my wrist, looked at my hand, saw it was a bad cut and yelled to my mother to bring him a towel. He was holding my hand, putting pressure on the cut to stop the bleeding, and I was crying real hard, and he gave me this really stern look and said, 'Hey. What's this? You want people to think you're a baby? Stop that crying. Big boys don't cry.' " Dave chuckled softly. "That came as a shocker, boy. I'd never heard that before."

"So you stopped crying?"

"Yeah, I did. It wasn't easy, but I did. And my dad said, 'That's more like it'—which was high praise, coming from him. And then we piled into the car and drove to the hospital. And all the way to the hospital I kept saying, 'See, Daddy? I'm not crying.' And he'd pat my leg and say, 'That's good, son.' " Dave smiled. "I can still feel his hand on my leg. It made me feel so proud. I'll tell you, the lesson really took, too. I used to hurt myself a lot as a kid. But I hardly ever cried after that."

Fear is another vulnerable emotion. Another client remembered being terrified of escalators as a kid—until his father found out about his fear. "We went to visit a museum one Sunday, and my dad headed for the escalator," he said. "And my mother said, 'No, let's take the stairs. Paul doesn't like escalators.' My dad stopped, turned around, frowned down at me and said, 'What's this? My son is afraid to ride an escalator?' I didn't dare say I was, so I said, 'No, Daddy. I can ride it.' And he said, 'That's my boy. Come on, then.' " Stepping onto the first moving stair was the worst part, he recalled. "But once I got past that, it was fun. I loved riding escalators after that. He used to do that a lot. I could probably think of a dozen things like that—where he got me past my fear of something by making it harder on me to be afraid than to just do whatever it was I was afraid of."

Fathers also teach sons to suppress what I call the caring emotions—the ones that get expressed through gentle, nurturing, affectionate behaviors. Another client recalled being very attached to his teddy bear as a child and also being keenly aware that his father disapproved of the attachment. "Whenever he saw me with it, he'd get a disgusted look on his face, and I'd get embarrassed and put it away," he said. "I remember we were leaving for a vacation once, and I came running out of my room with my teddy bear in my arms, and he just looked at me, and I went and put it back. It disappeared a little while later."

Loving a teddy bear and playing pretend-mommy or pretend-daddy to a doll are some of the ways children practice nurturing behaviors and the expression of caring feelings. But because these forms of play are considered feminine, most fathers discourage their sons from engaging in them—much more actively than mothers do. As the results of my study indicate, that's still true of fathers even today. The men in my study agreed, for example, that "boys should prefer to play with trucks rather than dolls" and that "boys should not throw baseballs like girls." In a 1980 study, psychologists Judith H. Langlois and A. Chris Downs, of the University of Texas at Austin, found that mothers' biases tended to be mild and they tended to communicate them gently, by positively reinforcing a son's or daughter's gender-appropriate play. Much stricter referees, fathers communicated their biases both through positive reinforcement and through punishment: by signaling disapproval to, or withholding affection from, their children—especially from older boys—when they witnessed gender-inappropriate play.

Indeed, withholding physical affection from sons is one of the primary modes through which fathers teach sons to inhibit affectionate behaviors. Dave recalled, for example, that he and his father used to roughhouse a lot, "but there wasn't much kissing and hugging. My sister got a lot more of that than I did."

"Did that ever bother you?" I asked.

He was silent a moment, then nodded. "Yeah," he said. "It did."

That's not an easy thing for men to admit. Some men have so internalized this prohibition against expressing caring feelings that they can't acknowledge, to themselves or anyone else, how much they hungered for their father's affection and how much the denial of that affection hurt. Sadder still, some men are so imprisoned by this conditioning that they can't help repeating the pattern with their own sons—withholding affection just as their fathers withheld it from them.

"I don't think that's true of me," said Dave. "I hope not, anyway."

"But you have daughters."

"True. But I have nephews, too. And I'm pretty affectionate with them. So's their father, actually." Dave grinned. "It's really great to watch. He's this big bruiser of a guy, and he's always grabbing them up in these big bear hugs. They're sports nuts, all three of them—very macho in some ways. But there's a lot of physical affection there, too. I remember one time when I was visiting, we were all sitting around watching a movie on the VCR, and I looked over, and there was my brother-in-law on the couch with one boy on either side of him. He had an arm around each of them, and they each had their head against his chest. And they were just watching the movie that way, like it was the most natural thing in the world." Dave smiled. "Something tells me those boys aren't going to have any trouble expressing affection to their kids."

I smiled, too. "Something tells me you're right."

"So, okay," said Dave in a back-to-business tone. "We've got vulnerable emotions and caring emotions closed off. So what's left? Anger?"

"Not a bad guess," I said. In some ways, fathers do encourage sons to express anger, but not as an end in itself. What fathers are really trying to teach sons is how to assert their will and make their own way in the world, how to be active agents in life: how to be strong, aggressive, self-reliant, courageous. We were lucky that way, we males—much luckier than our sisters. Our dads taught us all kinds of invaluable lessons in how to push past fear, take on challenges, wrestle with and solve problems—all "manly" skills that served us well as we grew up and moved out into the world. Our sisters were perfectly capable of mastering these skills, but our dads didn't teach them to our sisters.

In six separate studies published between 1972 and 1981, researchers found that when fathers were placed with their kids in situations designed to elicit teaching behavior, they proved highly adept at teaching these skills to sons and downright incompetent at teaching them to daughters. Instead of offering just enough instruction and guidance to keep daughters plugging away at a challenging task, they offered too much help, none at all, or assistance that was discombobulated. Instead of encouraging daughters to persist at a task in the face of setbacks and frustration, they quickly stepped in to try to make the task more pleasant. Instead of allowing daughters to bump up against failure and then encouraging them to try again, they rushed in to protect them from failure by doing it for them—unintentionally sapping their initiative and undermining their faith in their ability to do it themselves.

Girls may receive more affection, but boys get training in how to achieve. Fortunately, fathers are now more aware of these biases, which means they're better able to guard against them. But men still tend to be more protective of daughters than of sons. They let boys climb trees or go run in the woods, but they see girls as more fragile—a stereotype that's partially reinforced by observable differences in the ways boys and girls play.

No Girls Were Allowed in Your Clubhouse? Guess What? They Didn't Want In

Any parent who's ever watched a group of young children in unstructured play can attest that, left to their own devices, girls prefer playing with other girls, boys with other boys. This may rankle—concerned as many parents are today with fostering more egalitarian gender attitudes in their kids. Parents may try to counter that impulse—for example, by conscientiously balancing a child's same-sex and mixed-sex play dates. But, as Stanford University's preeminent developmental psychologist Eleanor Maccoby confirmed in a 1990 research review, like it or not, that's the way kids are. Maccoby was also intrigued by the distinct kinds of play and modes of interaction that characterize these two groups. Why these differences exist is still an unanswered question. What is clear is that, within these sex-segregated societies, boys and girls require, and are required by, other members of their group to master very specific social skills—the net effect being that the peer group joins forces with Mom and Dad in encouraging girls' acquisition of emotional empathy and boys' mastery of action empathy.

On the whole, girls' play is more intimate. Given a choice between an open and an enclosed space in which to gather, they're more likely to choose the enclosed one. Given control over the size of their play group, they'll usually keep it small—often as small as two or three friends. Given a range of amusements, they'll usually gravitate toward the ones that draw participants close together—close enough to whisper and giggle and smile and share secrets. For girls friendship is paramount—and they gear their behavior toward fostering warm ties. When they must give directions, they give them softly, couching them as suggestions so that friends feel consulted and involved. Loath to risk sparking resentment by insisting on their way, they achieve the same end—just as effectively—by enlisting cooperation through persuasion. If conflict arises, they try to smooth it over in the interests of maintaining goodwill. All this relationship finessing requires keen skills, of course, at reading and responding to someone else's feelings. Girls in groups refine and polish these skills by constantly practicing them on one another—having no choice but to master these skills if they wish to achieve and maintain social success.

Boys' play is a different realm entirely. Boys like to congregate in bigger groups, in more wide-open spaces that allow plenty of room for running and throwing and tackling and yelling and just generally whooping and roughing it up. Aggression and dominance are what boys' play is all about. It's about who's bigger, better, stronger, faster, braver, tougher, cockier. Boys don't suggest. They order. They don't persuade. They impose. Instead of trading confidences, they trade taunts and boasts. Instead of smoothing over conflicts, they try to win them—through the use of threats and force if need be. And, of course, instead of expressing feelings, they squelch them: "This three-inch gash in my knee? Nah, I don't even feel it." Self-assertiveness, self-confidence, performance ability, and stoicism are what win a boy admiration from other boys.

Dave recalled witnessing an example of this truth while watching the way the boys at a company picnic made clear their admiration for an athletically gifted ten-year-old named Ethan. "He was the kind of kid who made everything look easy," said Dave. "A real laid-back kid, too. Everything was 'yep,' or 'nope.' Talk about charisma. The other boys followed him around like puppies. Then there was this other kid, Mark, who was overweight and kind of uncoordinated. The other boys didn't want anything to do with him, but Ethan adopted him as his sidekick, so they had no choice but to include him in their games." Dave smiled. "It really made me admire Ethan. That was an extraordinarily sensitive thing for him to do."

"Action empathy at its finest," I said.

Dave looked quizzical. "Action empathy? How do you figure?"

"Look at what Ethan did. He assessed the situation, didn't like what he saw, and immediately devised and implemented a strategy for achieving a more desirable outcome. By making a point of befriending Mark, he did a strategic end run around the other boys' resistance to including Mark in their games. That's a perfect example of action empathy. That's where males shine."

What males lack is emotional empathy. Given how early and thoroughly they're trained in one skill and away from the other, they can't help but lack it. In one 1976 study, psychologists Martin L. Hoffman and Laura E. Levine, of the University of Michigan at Ann Arbor, found that even young boys manifest this lopsidedness. Hoffman and Levine asked a group of four-year-old boys and girls to look at a series of slides depicting children in various life predicaments and then describe what the children were feeling: "The girl is sad." "The boy is afraid." Girls took to the assignment naturally, but boys were all but incapable of following these instructions. Asked to describe what the children were feeling, they instead offered suggestions as to what the children should do to solve their problem. Asked to respond in emotional-empathy mode, in other words, they consistently responded in problem-solving mode instead—a pattern that suggests, wrote Hoffman and Levine, that boys have a tendency "to act rather than to feel."

LEARNING
EMOTIONAL EMPATHY

Problem-solving has its place, of course. But sometimes that's not what the other person wants—or, at least, not right away. "That's why Joyce got angry at you," I told Dave, returning to the topic of the telephone conversation that had gone awry. "She was upset, and she wanted you to care that she was upset. She wanted some soothing, some emotional empathy. Had you given her that, she might then have been ready to discuss her problem in action-empathy terms. But she needed that emotional empathy first. When you failed to give it to her, it made her feel as if her emotions didn't matter to you. And that made her feel angry and hurt."

That's a classic conflict between men and women. Partly because men are uncomfortable with emotions and partly because their orientation is toward action, when a woman gets upset about something, a man immediately tries to solve the problem, never realizing that's not what she wants. She's not asking him to fix anything. She's asking him to recognize and respond to her feelings. When he fails to do that, she gets angry. He thinks he's being supportive and helpful. She thinks he's being insensitive and cold.

"Okay, I get the point," said Dave, sounding irritated. "But that still leaves us with one small problem."

"Which is?"

"Which is, how am I supposed to respond to her feelings if she won't tell me what the hell they are?"

"We teach you how to figure them out."

Dave snorted. "Oh, right. I forgot."

"I think you're going to find it's a lot easier than you expect." I pulled a printed sheet of paper out of my desk drawer and handed it to him. He sat for a moment, reading it over. The words *Learning Emotional Empathy* were printed at the top of the sheet. Beneath were three exercises:

1. **Develop a lexicon, or vocabulary, of emotions,** placing special emphasis on the vocabulary of vulnerable emotions ("hurt," "sad," "disappointed," "afraid,") and caring emotions ("affectionate," "warm," "fond," "loving"). Add at least five new words to your lexicon each day. Practice using this vocabulary to describe the emotional states of others.

2. **Study the way actors and actresses communicate emotions.** While watching television or a movie, pay attention to how they use tone of voice, phrasing, facial expression, physical gestures, and body posture to express feeling. Use your lexicon of emotions to name the feeling being expressed.

3. **Apply what you've learned from watching television or films to real-life situations.** When conversing with, listening to, or observing other people, pay attention to the way they also communicate emotional states through tone of voice, phrasing, facial expression, physical gestures, and body posture. Use your emotional vocabulary to name the feeling being communicated or revealed.

Dave grunted. "Homework, huh?"

"Yep."

"That's what I was afraid of."

He was half joking, half serious. Like most men I counsel, Dave usually responded well to homework assignments. Still, a certain amount of initial resistance is to be expected. It's one thing, after all, to talk ideas and theory—quite another to be asked to do something specific in the way of actual change.

"I was thinking you might enjoy this assignment," I said. "You're a Katharine Hepburn fan, aren't you?"

He narrowed his eyes at me. "You *know* I am."

"Well, there's a Hepburn festival coming up at the Brattle next week. I was thinking you might want to do the second exercise there."

"Well, I'll be away on business for a few days—I told you
that, right? But if the festival doesn't start until next week . . .''

Fine Tune Those Sensors, and It's Amazing What You Pick Up

"Well?" I asked as Dave settled in for the start of our next
session two weeks later. "How'd the homework go?"

He smiled and shook his head, weary amusement in his
eyes. "Talk about timing."

"Oh? What happened?"

He had patched things up with Joyce after our last session—he apologized for hurting her feelings, she apologized
for snapping at him—and they had begun making plans, before he left on his business trip, to spend an upcoming holiday
weekend together in New Hampshire. Joyce knew of a charming inn a few blocks from an art gallery her former college
roommate had opened a year ago. Dave's former dissertation
adviser and his wife lived just a few towns over. "So I thought,
'Great,'" said Dave. "'We can see her friend Gail early Saturday and drive out and have dinner with Hank and his wife
Saturday night.' So, while I was away, I called Hank to make
sure they were going to be around, and he said Saturday would
be fine." Dave sighed. "So I called Joyce from my office the
morning after I got back. I'd invited her to come with me to
the Brattle that evening—they were showing *Pat and Mike* and
State of the Union, and she'd never seen either one. And I mentioned that I'd set up the dinner with Hank. And she said,
'But Gail's having an art opening and jazz recital at the gallery
on Saturday evening.'"

"She'd just found that out?"

"She said she'd mentioned it before I left."

"So then what?"

"Well, I had to get off the phone then—you know how
crazy things are the first day back from a trip—so I said I'd

call her later. And then I thought, 'Well, if I pushed back the dinner, we could stop by the art gallery for a while and see Hank and his wife a little later.' So, first chance I got, I called Hank to see if that would be okay with him, and he said, 'Sure.' And then I called Joyce and said, 'Okay, it's all fixed.' "

"Uh-huh. And was she pleased?"

"Pleased? No, I wouldn't say she was exactly pleased. Try angry, annoyed, furious, really pissed off." He smiled wearily. "As you can see, I've been practicing my vocabulary."

"Did she explain why she was angry?"

"If by explaining you mean spewing venomous epithets about my being exactly like her self-centered, controlling jerk of an ex-husband—then, yes, she explained."

"Ouch."

"Yeah. It wasn't pretty. So then I got angry and said, 'Well, maybe we should just cancel the weekend. Maybe we should just forget it.' And then she said, 'Well, while we're at it, maybe we should forget about tonight, too'—which was really a low blow. I'd really been looking forward to taking her to see those films, and she knew it. So I said, 'Fine. I'll probably have a better time by myself.' And she said, 'Fine.' And we hung up."

Hardly in the best of moods, Dave had taken himself to the Brattle. "So, I was sitting there, studying Hepburn." He smiled. "She's such a great actress. And I realized that one of the things that makes her so appealing is the way she makes you feel like you're seeing right through her act. There's her crisp, opinionated, New England Brahmin exterior, and just beneath it there's this quivering vulnerability that you feel she's always trying but not quite managing to conceal. So I got all caught up in trying to figure out how she did that—how she communicated that vulnerability. And that was really fascinating, because the more I studied her, the more I realized that it's all in these tiny little things she does—a slight stammer in her speech, or the way she'll take a step or reach out to touch something and then hesitate, or the way she fiddles with her shirt collar or lowers her head and averts her eyes."

"And you were able to pick up on that. Nice work."

After the double-feature, Dave stopped in for a drink at a restaurant-bar near his home. As he settled in with his drink on a barstool, his attention was caught by a well-dressed couple just entering from the street. He watched them scan the lounge. "Then she pointed to an empty table for two against the wall, and they walked over and sat down. She took the banquette seat, and he took the outside chair. Then the waiter came over and took their drink order, and then she excused herself—to go to the ladies' room, I guess. As soon as she left, the guy twisted around in his chair and started looking around the room. I thought he was looking for the waiter. Then he stood up, picked up her coat, walked over to an empty table for four against the opposite wall, laid her coat across the two outside chairs and slid into one of the two banquette seats."

"So he could sit next to her instead of across from her?"

"That's what I figured. So then the woman returned and saw him waving to her from the other table. And she stopped still for a moment, and I saw her mouth go tight."

"That's very observant."

"It was really interesting, actually. At first I really identified with this guy. Here he is with this attractive woman in this cozy room, and he ends up having to sit across the table from her? I'd probably have done the same thing he did. But then when the woman returned and I saw her reaction, I realized, 'Uh-oh. Wrong. Bad move.' She was obviously not pleased."

"Obviously?"

Dave paused, considering. "That's interesting. Maybe it wasn't all that obvious. But it seemed obvious to me. Anyway, then she walked over to him, and I saw that he had his arm draped over the back of her seat. And I thought, 'Oh. Maybe she knew that if she sat next to him, he'd try to get too friendly.' And then, instead of admiring him, I started disliking him. I mean, I could understand his wanting to get closer to her. But still. To just get up and change tables without even consulting her? That's kind of a stupid move. I didn't blame her for being pissed." He paused. "That's when the bomb dropped. All of a sudden, I thought, 'Hey, wait a minute.

That's just what I was doing when I pushed back the dinner date with Hank. I was trying to make things more pleasant, too. And I didn't consult Joyce, either. Well, look at that—I'm as big an asshole as he is.' " He glanced up at me. "It wasn't a very pleasant realization, I can tell you."

"Did you tell Joyce that?"

"Yes, I did."

He called her when he got home, told her about the scene he'd witnessed and the realization it had led to and apologized for appointing himself chairman of their weekend plans. "So, look," he said. "If you want, I'll call Hank and tell him I screwed up and ask if we can have brunch on Sunday or something."

Joyce thanked him for the offer. But she'd been thinking, too. Her friend Gail would be busy playing hostess during the art opening, and they wouldn't be able to talk to her during the recital. "So how about if we have brunch with her on Sunday?" said Joyce. "She'll be more relaxed then, and we'll have more time to talk."

"So you worked it out."

Dave nodded. "We worked it out."

The next day, acting on an impulse, Dave had a dozen long-stemmed yellow roses delivered to Joyce's office, with a card enclosed that read simply, "Looking forward to N.H." The roses arrived shortly before noon. Joyce called immediately, catching Dave on his way out to lunch.

"I love roses," she said.

"I know."

"I love yellow."

"I know."

"I love you."

"I'm batting a thousand."

Their holiday weekend went well. Dave especially enjoyed the art opening, he told me later—not so much because of the art, which he thought mediocre, but because of the opportunity it gave him to practice his people-watching skills. "It's amazing what you can pick up about people when you really pay attention," he said. During the next few weeks, he continued practicing the exercises I'd assigned and soon found, as many men do, that they served him well not only in his personal life but also at work. The more skilled he became at picking up on the physical cues with which people communicate emotions and identifying the emotions being communicated, the more he was able to use these skills, for example, to detect when a client was feeling some unexpressed worry about a proposal he was presenting and ferret out and address that worry in order to keep things moving ahead. With practice, he also learned to check his impulse to immediately begin offering advice when someone came to him with a problem and first take time to express concern for that person's feelings by saying something as simple as "That's rough" or "That must've been upsetting." This change paid dividends not only in his interactions with Joyce and his daughters but also in his interactions with the people on his staff, who began to feel more recognized as human beings.

"I guess we all like to have our feelings acknowledged," Dave said during a subsequent session. Exactly. The more skilled men are at sensing and honoring other people's feelings, the smoother and more satisfying all their relationships become. But a man can progress only so far in developing emotional empathy unless he knows what it's like to feel emotions, which many men don't. And his relationships can improve only so much unless he's able not only to feel emotions but also to express them, which many men don't know how to do. In the next chapter, we'll look more closely at some of the causes and consequences of this common male problem and discuss how men can overcome emotional numbness.

CHAPTER THREE

Overcoming Emotional Numbness

THE COMMON PROBLEM WITH THE FANCY NAME

There's a word for the inability to identify and articulate one's own emotions. That word is *alexithymia* (literally, "without words for emotions")—a fancy name for a condition so common among men that they don't even think of it as a condition. They think of it as just the way men are. Men don't think their inability to express emotion is a problem. They see the women in their lives as the problem. If women would stop pushing men to be more emotionally expressive—in other words, more like them—everything would be fine.

But, in fact, men's inability to know and name their emotions is a problem—in some cases, a very serious one. Men don't realize it, but to live life incapable of feeling and expressing emotion is to live life in isolation—alienated not only from those they love but also from themselves.

Consider, for example, the divorced father who, during a meeting of one of my Fatherhood Project workshops, told of having arrived at his ex-wife's house the Saturday before to pick up his son for a father-son hockey game only to learn that, apparently having forgotten their date, his son had gone off to do something else. And how had he felt, I asked, when he realized his son had stood him up? "Oh, he shouldn't have done that," he said. No, I corrected. I hadn't asked whether he thought his son should or shouldn't have done what he did. I'd asked how he'd felt when his ex-wife told him his son wasn't there.

Felt? He looked at me blankly.

Trying another approach, I asked this man if he'd be willing to re-enact the incident, with another group member playing his ex-wife, while I videotaped the exercise to play back to him afterward. He agreed. On completion of the exercise, I again asked how he'd felt when he'd learned he'd been stood up. Again, he had no answer. I then played back the video, stopping the tape at the point where he'd learned his son wasn't home. "There," I said, drawing his attention to the way his expression had fallen slightly. "What were you feeling just then?" He studied his own image, frowning in concentration. "I guess I felt . . . I must have felt disappointed," he said.

"I guess I must have felt"—and this only after much coaching. Compare that to how a woman who'd had a similar experience—say, of being stood up by her daughter for a shopping date—would likely respond if asked what she'd felt at the time: "How did I feel? Well, at first I was surprised—it's not like her to forget a shopping date. And then I felt angry at being stood up. I was hurt, too, that she'd acted with so little concern for my feelings. And I was worried that maybe she was upset with me about something and that this was her way of telling me. And I was also disappointed and annoyed. I'd really been looking forward to our date—I'd planned the whole day around it. And now the day was ruined."

Well, of course a woman would carry on that way, some men might argue. That's the difference between males and females. They're more emotional by nature. Men don't have the same range and intensity of emotions that women do.

Wrong again. Men do have them. They've just been so thoroughly socialized to suppress them that, by adulthood, they've forgotten how to feel them. That's what alexithymia is all about. As psychiatrist Henry Krystal, of Michigan State University, wrote in 1979, alexithymia is "a disturbance . . . [in which] emotions are not differentiated and are poorly verbalized. . . . When alexithymic patients do mention having a feeling and are questioned about it, they are generally not able to describe what they are experiencing. . . . At best they become aware of physical sensations. . . . [These patients] often cannot tell whether they are sad, tired, hungry or ill. Occasionally, some become aware of a vague physical distress in situations where an emotional response would be expected. . . ."

Like research-psychiatrist Peter E. Sifneos, who first coined the term *alexithymia* in 1967 to describe symptoms he'd observed in a group of men suffering from psychosomatic disorders, Krystal was also describing symptoms seen in severely disturbed patients: shell-shocked war veterans and other men suffering from severe post-traumatic stress disorder; men suffering from psychosomatic illnesses; men caught in the grip of chemical dependencies. Among the other symptoms Sifneos and Krystal described: blank, stonelike facial expression; rigid body posture and wooden movement; lack of awareness of the physiological concomitants of emotion (changes in heartbeat, breathing, body temperature), or fear of these physiological changes accompanied by efforts to block awareness of them through use of drugs.

Most men balk at the suggestion that they have anything in common with these severely disturbed patients. But, in fact, these patients aren't as different from most men as one might think.

Imagine: A man comes home from a rough day at work, having been called on the carpet that morning for a screw-up he's been warned could cost him his job if repeated. He grabs a beer out of the fridge, sinks into the couch, flips on the television and stares at it, blank-faced, all circuits down. "You all right?" his wife asks, concerned, noticing that his jaw is clenched and his leg is twitching. "Yeah, sure," he mutters, eyes never leaving the TV. "I'm just beat."

Or: A man comes home from a good day at work, having just learned his promotion has come through. He grabs a beer out of the fridge, sinks into the couch, flips on the television and stares at it, blank-faced, all circuits down. "Well?" his wife asks tentatively, searching his face but finding no clues. He shrugs. "I got it," he says, eyes never leaving the TV. She lets out a whoop. "Oh, honey! That's great!" He nods. She's confused. "That *is* good, isn't it?" He nods again. "Yeah. That's good." Good? That's all he can say? He shrugs again. "I said it's good. What else do you want me to say?"

Or: A man comes home from an average day at work, grabs a beer out of the fridge, sinks into the couch, flips on the television and stares at it, blank-faced, all circuits down. Entering the room a few minutes later, his wife finds him sitting there, untouched beer still in hand, head fallen back against the couch, sound asleep. "You feeling okay?" she asks gently, never having known him to snooze through the news before. His eyes flicker open. "Huh? Oh. Yeah. Sure. I'm just tired." She puts a hand to his forehead. It's hot. "I think you've got a fever," she says. Huh? "Naaah," he says, shifting onto his side and closing his eyes. "I told you. I'm just tired." She fetches the thermometer from the medicine cabinet, sticks it under his tongue, waits three minutes, takes it out. "A hundred degrees! Honey, you're sick. Come on, you're going to bed." She hauls him up off the couch and leads him to the bedroom. "I'm okay," he says. "I just need to sleep a little." He's out the minute his head hits the pillow and doesn't wake until morning.

Obviously, these are examples of a milder form of alexithymia than that observed by Sifneos and Krystal in their severely disturbed patients. However, like others of my colleagues who specialize in counseling men, I'm continually amazed and saddened by how prevalent this milder condition is among men—and how unaware they are of its symptoms and the toll it takes on their ability to experience life fully.

Imagine if you were to wake up one day and discover that your fingertips had lost some of their sensitivity, your hearing had become weaker, your vision slightly dimmed. In a way, that's exactly how mildly alexithymic men do live life—every day. As a man in one of my Fatherhood Project workshops said, comparing his experience of life before and after he'd learned how to feel and express his emotions, "It's like, before, the world was a black-and-white movie, and now it's in full color." As Krystal wrote, "The patients who do not experience . . . their emotions . . . fail to attain a sense of aliveness. . . . Since they do not have affective [i.e., emotional] signals to guide them . . . they have to depend on reasoning."

Not that there's anything wrong with reason. We'd have a hard time navigating life without this critical faculty. But if reason is our chart book in life, emotion is our radar. When we navigate without it, we end up running onto emotional shoals not accounted for in our chart book—again and again and again.

How Many Shoals Can You Detect in This Tale?

There's a limit to how much of this kind of beating a man can take. Randy had reached that limit. A national supervisor for a highly respected accounting firm, he sat across from me during our initial session looking as weathered as the broken-in chinos, faded blue Oxford shirt, and scuffed Bass Weejuns he wore. Of average height and build, with brown hair and eyes, he looked to be in good muscular condition, but there was an air of exhaustion about him that made me think, "Running on empty." His complexion looked pale, and there were faint bags under his anxious-looking eyes.

He'd said when he called two days earlier to set up our appointment that he wasn't exactly sure why he was calling or what he thought I could do for him, but that he figured he better talk to someone because it was getting to be too much.

"What's getting to be too much?" I asked.

A silence, and then, "The pressure," he said. "Just . . . all this pressure."

"Can you be more specific?"

No, he couldn't.

"Do you know where it's coming from?"

No, he didn't.

"How long have you been feeling this pressure?"

He wasn't sure. Awhile. But it had been getting worse lately. He was having trouble sleeping. And he was having headaches.

Randy had never been to a psychologist before, he said now, shifting nervously in the overstuffed chair he occupied and gazing around my office. I asked him to tell me about himself. He was forty-six, married for twenty years. His wife, Lisa, was a children's book editor. They had a sixteen-year-old son named Jed. Randy had been with the same accounting firm for twelve years. As a national supervisor, he functioned primarily as a trouble-shooter and crisis manager, traveling extensively to regional offices in small and medium-sized cities around the country.

"You just came back from a trip," I said. "Tell me about that. What was this last one like?"

He dropped his head against the back of the chair, puffed his cheeks and exhaled through pressed lips. "The usual," he said. The trip had taken him to Ohio first, where, as usual, one of the regional reps had met him at the airport and driven him to his motel, making a lot of intimate conversation along the way.

"What kind of intimate conversation?"

"Divorces, problems with kids—you name it, I hear it all. This time it was the guy's recent gall-bladder surgery. I don't know why these guys think I want to hear about this stuff."

"You don't?"

"Not especially. But, you know, you can't be rude."

Eventually—again, as usual—the intimate talk had given way to a discussion of "the problem." There was always some problem, said Randy. This time it had been a $50,000 discrepancy in a client's books that local supervisors couldn't resolve. They were sure it could be resolved but they hadn't yet located the problem. That's where Randy came in.

Arriving at his motel and finding himself with an empty evening ahead of him, he'd headed down to the motel restaurant, where he'd eaten too big and too heavy a meal. Afterward, he'd returned to his room, scanned the listing of the evening's pay-per-view movie offerings and, finding none that appealed, had settled back on his bed with a Tom Clancy paperback. "That's one good thing about these trips, at least," he said. "I get a lot of reading done." Later, he'd called home to check in with Lisa and let her know his plane had arrived safely. As usual, she'd asked how he was feeling. As usual, he'd answered, "Tired. Tense." As usual, she'd urged him to "try to relax. Get some rest. You'll feel better in the morning." And, as usual, for some reason he couldn't put his finger on, her attempts to be soothing had failed to have the desired soothing effect. Still wide awake after he'd hung up, he'd flipped on the TV and channel-surfed for a while, looking for some program or movie in which to lose himself and, again finding nothing, had flipped off the set and turned in. After a fitful night's sleep, he'd awakened the next morning feeling unrested and downed a quick breakfast while waiting to be picked up at the motel. "Mornings are the worst," he said. "All I want to do is get in there and get working. And all I can do is sit there, drinking coffee."

"How'd it go once you got working?"

"It was tricky. It took the better part of the day to figure out where the screw-up was, but I found it. After that, it was just a matter of straightening out the figures."

"Sounds complicated."

"Well, I actually like that part. I enjoy the challenge. Once I've got my bearings, it's like solving a puzzle. I know the answer's there somewhere. It's just a matter of finding it. Once

I get into it, I completely lose track of time. One minute, it's nine A.M., and, the next time I look at the clock, it's three in the afternoon—and I have no idea where the time's gone."

"That's pretty intense concentration."

"Well, as I say, I enjoy that part—the actual wrestling with the problem. But it does leave me pretty wiped by the time I'm through."

"And then you flew home?"

"No, then I flew to Kentucky and then to New Jersey—those were just check-up calls—and then I flew home." He dropped his head against the back of the chair again and pulled a hand down over his face, as if wiping it with a towel.

"Was something wrong at home?"

He sighed. "No, not really. I mean . . . Oh, I don't know."

As usual, Lisa had welcomed him back with cheerful affection, full of news about all that had happened while he'd been away and eager to hear the details of his trip. "Which is just what I don't want to do when I get back, is talk."

"Did you tell her that?"

"No. I didn't have to. She usually gets the idea pretty quickly. Usually what I do is fix myself a drink and take it into the den. And she'll come in and sit down to talk, and I'll just kind of listen without saying much. And then, after a while, when she realizes I'm not responding, she'll go start dinner or something and leave me alone." He shook his head and snorted. "Which is usually when Jed comes bursting in with another one of his welcome-home stories."

"What kind of stories?"

Randy's face clouded with anger. "It's always the same. He's always screwing up something and then coming to tell me he's screwed up but that, really, it's okay, Dad." This time Jed had borrowed Randy's tennis racquet and had accidentally left it on the bench at the neighborhood court overnight—in a rainstorm. But it was okay, Dad. The guy at the shop had said the strings hadn't been ruined—just the paint. Hearing Jed's tale, Randy had exploded. "Damn it, Jed! Don't you ever think?" Jed had tried to explain, but Randy had cut him off.

"I don't want to hear explanations. I'm sick of your screw-ups. Enough!"

The family had eaten dinner that evening in a heavy silence broken only by occasional requests to pass the salt. After dinner Randy had returned to the den to read and watch the news. Later, exhausted and still in a sour mood, he'd gone up to bed. Lisa had followed, slipping into bed beside him and signaling with a touch that she wanted to have sex. He'd told her he was too tired. She had sighed. "Know what, honey?" she'd said softly. "Seems like, lately, you're always too tired."

Emotion: The Mere Mention of the Word Can Send a Man Running for Cover

I was beginning to understand where some of the pressure Randy felt was coming from and told him that his ability to feel it was a good sign—some men can't feel even that much. In order to relieve that pressure, however, we would have to go deeper and identify the unfelt emotions that were causing it.

"The what?" said Randy.

"Emotions. You know—happy, sad, angry." All human beings have these emotions. The problem is that males are so thoroughly trained not to express them that, as a safeguard, they train themselves not to feel them. But this self-protective mechanism often proves men's undoing—because if they don't know they're having an emotional reaction, they can't identify and correct the problem that's causing it. "That's what's happening to you," I told Randy. "You're feeling the pressure of your emotional reactions but you're not feeling the emotions themselves. We have to sleuth them out. For example, can you tell me what you were feeling as you waited to be picked up at your motel?"

Randy frowned, shrugged. "Pressure," he said. "I don't know how else to describe it."

"Do you remember any physical sensations? Queasy stomach? Tightness in the jaw?"

"Headache," he said. "I remember a kind of pre-headachy feeling."

"Anything else? Any vague sense of physical discomfort?"

He shook his head. "No. Why?"

"That's often the way unrecognized emotional reactions come through to men—as a kind of vague, physical buzz." By the time males reach adulthood, many are so accustomed to this buzz that they don't even notice it. It seems as much a part of them as does their ability to suppress emotions, which males seem to master by the age of six.

Internalizers, Externalizers, and the Birth of the Buzz

Born champion emoters, males continue to communicate emotions clearly until around age four. Then they begin to change. In a 1977 study designed to measure nonverbal expressiveness in children, psychologist Ross Buck, of the University of Connecticut, assessed the ability of mothers of four- to six-year-old boys and girls to accurately identify their child's emotional responses to a series of slides simply by observing their child's facial reactions on a television monitor. Buck found a negative correlation between age and expressiveness among his male subjects: The older the boy was, the less his responses showed, and the harder it was for his mother to tell what he was feeling by looking at his face. Buck found no such correlation among girls: They rated high in expressiveness no matter what their age. Between the ages of four and six, Buck concluded, "boys apparently inhibit and mask their overt response to emotion to an increasing extent, while girls continue to respond relatively freely"—suggestive evidence that "adult sex difference in expressiveness is based on social learning."

Why the pace of this learning should accelerate so markedly during this two-year span is a question Buck didn't address. Other research suggests, however, that, this being the age at which children start school, stepped-up pressures from teachers and peers to conform to gender-appropriate behavior is a powerful influence. In a 1985 review of the research literature psychologist Leslie Brody, of Boston University, cites a host of studies documenting the degree to which cultural "display rules" about the "quality and intensity of emotions that can be expressed in different contexts" work to discourage boys from expressing those emotions deemed inappropriate for males. With those display rules now boxing them in on all fronts—at home, at school, and in their same-sex play groups—boys learn quickly to suppress and deny these "unacceptable" emotions.

In a 1989 study of fifth-, seventh-, ninth-, and eleventh-grade boys and girls, Janice C. Stapley and Jeannette M. Haviland, of Rutgers University, found that while girls readily admitted to feeling sadness, shame, shyness, guilt, and surprise, most boys did not report experiencing these emotions. Long before they reach adulthood, it seems, boys and girls are handling these feelings in much the same way as psychologist Susan Nolen-Hoeksema, of Stanford University, theorizes that male and female adults do. Her theory, based on her own investigations of adult emotional response patterns: Females ruminate on these feelings while males distract themselves from them. A ten-year-old girl who learns she hasn't been invited to a classmate's birthday party, for example, is likely to retreat to her room to pore over her feelings of hurt, sadness, and humiliation; confide them to her best friend; or spill them out in her diary. A boy, in contrast, is likely to feign indifference to the slight; devise some distraction ("Hey, I bet I can hit that can with this rock!") when the subject of the party comes up among friends; or make sure he has something else to do on the day of the celebration, which he lets everyone know he'd much rather do than go to any stupid old party.

Both are simply doing as they've been taught. Other studies have found, for example, that mothers talk to girls about sadness and the experience of emotions (thus encouraging them to do the same) but tend to talk to boys about anger and the consequences of emotions (thus encouraging them to keep their emotions in check). Fathers also talk about emotions with girls but are more likely to engage boys in verbal roughhousing. The end result is that school-aged boys expect their parents to react negatively to expressions of sadness. So, instead, they deny it and distract themselves from it.

Now, distracting isn't always a bad coping strategy—nor is ruminating always a good one. As Nolen-Hoeksema points out, too much ruminating can leave a person vulnerable to depression. Distracting, when done in healthy ways, can help lift spirits and generate a more positive mind-set with which to tackle problems. But girls' way of handling emotion does offer two major advantages over boys'. In the process of ruminating, girls become intimately acquainted and comfortable with the full range of their emotional responses and receive invaluable training in identifying and articulating these feelings. Taught to distract themselves from feelings, boys, in contrast, remain estranged from and uncomfortable with their emotional responses and are denied the opportunity to develop a vocabulary of emotions.

The fact that males aren't aware of their emotional reactions doesn't mean, however, that they don't have them. And the fact that males don't express them overtly doesn't mean they don't get expressed. In a 1974 study of college students similar to the one he conducted a year later with children, Buck and his colleagues found that while females outperformed males in communicating their responses to emotionally charged slides both in words and through facial expressions, males had more intense physiological responses as measured by monitors lightly attached to the skin. When males viewed the slides, their heartbeat speeded up, and their galvanic skin response (a measure of skin-surface conductivity) increased—even as, verbally and facially, they revealed nothing. Females, on the other hand, registered very little change in heartbeat and galvanic skin response. Their emotional responses were so freely discharged through verbal reports and facial reactions that little of this effect was left over to seek discharge through internal outlets.

UNLEARNING ALEXITHYMIA

I have a file cabinet full of case histories of clients whose chronic backaches or jaw pain or indigestion eased up and sometimes disappeared once they learned to recognize these symptoms as the internal discharge of emotions and learned to identify and handle emotions in healthier ways. Randy is one of these clients. He was experiencing this internal discharge of emotions as pressure and, lately, as headaches and trouble sleeping. Not knowing what else to do about these symptoms, he'd simply been doing his best to distract himself from them—usually by trying to lose himself in a book or a movie, when he could find a movie worth watching on TV. He told me during our first session that he also played squash twice a week when he wasn't traveling. "And I'm a fly fisherman, too," he said. "Not a bad one, either, if I do say so myself." He smiled. "Not as good as my dad was, though. He was the best. I must have been five or six when I first started fishing with him. I remember standing beside him in the stream, and I'd just study and imitate everything he did. The way he stood. The way he held his rod. The way he tossed his line. We didn't talk much. We'd just stand there for hours, listening to the stream and the birds and the wind in the trees and the insects buzzing around . . ." He fell silent, lost in thought.

"What are you thinking about?"

"Oh, I was just thinking about my dad." He shook his

head. "Talk about pressure. There were six of us in the family—me, my two sisters, my parents, and my dad's mom. She came to live with us after my grandfather died. My dad had to work two jobs to support us. During the day he worked as a customer-service manager at a bank, and then, at night, he worked as the maître d' at this seafood restaurant he owned a part of. Can you imagine? Having to be nice to people that many hours a day? And then, when he was home, which wasn't often, he'd have to play go-between for my mother and my grandmother, who were always bickering. And then, of course, there were us kids always clamoring for his attention." He shook his head again. "No wonder he loved fly-fishing so much. That was probably the only time he got any peace and quiet. But, you know, I don't think I ever once heard him complain. Not once. He'd get kind of sullen and moody sometimes." He smiled. "Things would get real quiet in the house when he got that way. My mom would make us kids go play outside for a while, and she and my grandmother would go into the kitchen and leave him alone in the living room. But it's understandable that he'd get that way. I mean, I get that way, too, sometimes, and I don't have things nearly as rough as he did." He glanced at me. "That's pretty normal for a man. To get that way. Isn't it?"

"Normal in the sense of common, yes. It's quite common among men. Usually it's a sign that we're just about at the limits of our ability to keep our emotions in check. Push us beyond that point, and we explode." In fact, this explosive tendency is another of the symptoms Krystal found to be common among alexithymic men. "The final characteristic pattern," he wrote, "involves sudden outbursts of . . . strong emotions: for instance, rages. . . ."

But men wouldn't have to reach that explosion point if they had other ways of handling these pent-up emotions. "Your dad didn't know any other way except to keep them pressed down," I told Randy. "But that doesn't mean you have to follow in his footsteps. There is a better way. The more you're able to identify these emotions, the more you'll be able to figure out what's triggering them and deal with the problem at its source. That way you prevent them from ever building up in the first place. I can teach you how to do that, if you're interested."

Randy weighed my offer. "I don't know," he said guardedly. "What does it involve?"

"Nothing you're not already good at. There's a vocabulary-building exercise—a kind of word game you play against yourself. But the rest is just observing, record keeping, and quantifying. Then we analyze the data you collect to see if it tells us anything about cause and effect."

"If I say yes, how long am I in for?"

"Only a week. After that, you decide. If you feel it's helping you, we keep going with it. If not, we drop it." I opened a desk drawer, took out a printed exercise sheet, and handed it to Randy. "Here. Take a few minutes to read this over." The sheet read as follows:

LEARNING HOW TO KNOW YOUR EMOTIONS

1. **Build a vocabulary of emotions**—particularly the vulnerable emotions (hurt, sadness, disappointment, rejection, abandonment, fear) and the caring emotions (warmth, affection, closeness, appreciation). Sit with pen, paper, and wristwatch and write down as many emotion words as you can think of in two minutes. Repeat this exercise once a day for a week. See if you can list four times as many words by the end of the week as you did the first day. This exercise will develop both your emotional vocabulary and your emotional awareness.

2. **Keep a daily log of each time you experience the physiological component of an emotion (a "buzz") during the course of the week**.

a. *Buzz-detect.* Be on the lookout for: tightness in the throat or chest, clenching of the gut, teeth grinding, difficulty concentrating, antsiness, etc. Put a hand-mirror face-up in your top desk drawer or somewhere else you can glance at it easily and discreetly. Check your reflection in it periodically for signs of emotion in your face.

b. *Buzz-tally.* Keep a numbered listing in your log of each "buzz" you experience in a day. Briefly describe the physical sensations or symptoms of each "buzz."

c. *Put the buzz in context.* Next to each "buzz" listed, enter the *time* it occurred; the event, or *cue*, that triggered it; and/or the *context* in which it happened—i. e., what you and the people around you were doing when you became aware of it. Don't spend a lot of time trying to figure out a deep, hidden reason for your "buzz." Just jot down whatever comes immediately to mind as the possible triggering event. For example: "Boss slapped report on my desk." "Co-worker mentioned sales meeting." "Client didn't take call." "Office mate turned on radio."

Here's how a sample page in your Emotional Response Log might look:

Monday, August 10

BUZZ		TIME, CUE, CONTEXT
1. Trouble breathing	10:15 a.m.	Colleagues talk about new Lexus
2. Pit in stomach	11:20 a.m.	Cold calls to Denver clients
3. Tightness in face	2:20 p.m.	Executive meeting rescheduled
4. Grinding teeth	4:40 p.m.	Talk w/boss about monthly figures

The purpose of the vocabulary-building exercise is to help men familiarize themselves with the rich variety of words that exist to describe emotional states, in preparation for learning to use these words to identify and name their own emotions. But before men can learn to name their emotions they first have to learn how to become aware that they're having an emotional reaction. That's where the Emotional Response Log comes in. It's unrealistic to expect men who have been trained to internalize their emotions to suddenly be able to know and name them, so I break the process down into steps. First I ask a client simply to pay more attention to the various symptoms of physical unease he experiences through the course of a day and jot down what was happening when he became aware of these symptoms. This first step is the data-gathering stage in learning to know emotions. Once that data is gathered and after a client has had some time to build up a basic vocabulary of emotions, we go back over the data and try to attach the appropriate emotion words to the physical symptoms he noted.

"Well?" I asked Randy. "What do you think? Want to give it a shot?"

He considered for a moment. "Okay. I'll try it."

The First Step in Tuning into Your Emotions—Tuning into Your Body

Randy walked into my office at the start of our next session slapping a pocket-size notebook against the palm of one hand. "Well, Ron," he said, settling into a chair. "I gotta hand it to you. You're right. Those are some interesting exercises."

"How'd it go?"

"Well, the first day I did the vocabulary exercise I only came up with twelve words—well, two, actually. The other ten I took from the sheet."

"What were your two?"

"Anger and impatience." He shrugged. "I couldn't think of any vulnerable or caring ones. But it was interesting. I think that kind of tuned me in. I never really paid much attention to emotion words before. But after doing that first exercise I kind of started watching out for them, so I could add them to my list." He smiled. "I never realized there was so many. Once I started watching out for them, it was like, 'Oh, there's one.

Oh, there's another one. Oh, that's a good one—I have to remember that one.' I usually forgot most of them by the time I sat down to do the exercise. But still. Yesterday, I was up to . . ." He consulted his notebook. "Fifteen."

"Fifteen of your own?"

"Yep."

"That's really good. What about your Emotional Response Log? How'd that go?"

He shifted in his chair. "Well, that was interesting, too. 'Enlightening' is probably a better word." During the course of the week, Randy had made thirty-two "buzz" entries in his notebook—far more than he'd expected. "I thought I'd catch one, maybe two a day, tops." He shook his head. "That mirror suggestion is a good one. I propped one up against these manuals I keep on my desk, where nobody could see it. I kept forgetting it was there, and then I'd be going over a report or something and I'd glance up and catch myself . . . grimacing, I guess is the best way to put it—almost like I was in pain." A pause. "It kind of shocked me, to tell you the truth. And then I'd realize I was clenching my teeth." He dropped his gaze to his notebook. "I do that a lot—grind my teeth." He glanced up, the expression in his eyes one of frank concern. "I didn't know that. I never knew that about myself."

"But you know it now," I said. "That's the important thing. It's not a pleasant discovery, I realize, but it's a crucial one. Remember, most men aren't aware of these physiological buzzes. That's the whole point of these exercises—to help you become aware. Sounds to me like you're doing well. Anything else you noticed?"

"Well, that pre-headachy feeling I told you about—that happened a lot. And a kind of tightness in the back of my neck. I hadn't been aware of that before, either. Sometimes it would happen with the headachy feeling, and other times it would just happen by itself. My stomach felt kind of queasy a few times, too, like it does after I eat too big a meal when I'm traveling—which makes me wonder now if maybe it isn't only the food."

"Do you want to keep going with this for a while to see if anything else turns up?"

"I was thinking it might be interesting to keep with it during this trip I leave on tomorrow."

"Fine. But, for now, let's see what we can learn from the data you've already collected. Remember, these buzzes are usually signs that some kind of emotion is going on inside you. What we want to do now is try to identify and name the emotion itself. That's where the notes on time, cue, and context come in. Those are our clues. We can use that information to try to figure out the emotion that triggered the buzz."

I opened the notebook at random to a page marked *Friday* and read the fourth entry on that day's list. "Okay. 'Face constricts'—that's the buzz symptom. 'Call from travel agent'—that's the cue. So, why did your face constrict? The travel agent told you the flight you wanted was booked?"

"No," said Randy. "It was just being reminded of it."

"Reminded of what?"

"Of this trip I'm leaving on tomorrow. She was calling to tell me she'd booked my flight for the Tulsa leg of the trip. One of our clients out there is really unhappy with the way the local guys have been handling his account—with good reason, too. Turns out the guy in charge of his account is a total incompetent who's made a real mess of things. The client is threatening to take his business elsewhere unless everything gets straightened out pronto. So the local guys started waving my name around, saying I'd see to it personally—no problem. So, of course, now, that's what I have to do."

"And being reminded of all that made you feel what?"

"Pressure. A lot of pressure."

"Anything else?"

He thought for a moment. "Yeah. Anger."

"Anger. Anything else?"

He thought again, shook his head.

I suspected that beneath the anger lay fear—that he just might not be able to pull the reps out of the mess they'd created. In fact, I suspected that fear of possible failure was probably a constant companion on these trips. Because it makes men feel so nakedly powerless and vulnerable, however, fear is one of the emotions they bury most deeply. I wasn't surprised, then, that Randy didn't connect it with the buzz he'd experienced while talking to his travel agent. Nor did I suggest this connection to him. He'd make it himself, when he was ready.

"You've done good work," I said. "Since you've decided to keep going with this, I'd like you to add another step. Before you go to bed each night, take a few minutes to review that day's log and see what emotion words you can attach to each buzz—the way we did now. Don't spend a lot of time on it. Just jot down whatever pops into your mind. We'll go over what you come up with the next time we meet."

Those Buzzes Aren't Just Noise—They're Trying to Tell Us Something

Once men move on to this second step of attaching emotion words to the physical buzzes they experience they almost invariably find that it prompts them to begin asking why a certain situation triggered a certain buzz and emotion—in other words, "What's wrong with this picture and how can I fix it?" Randy was no exception. He returned from the Tulsa trip in the same exhausted, strung-out state as he had from his earlier trip to Ohio. Again, he reported, he'd exploded at Jed, who'd come bursting into the den, this time to explain that he'd accidentally dumped one of Randy's spread-sheet files while writing a science report on their home computer—but that it was okay, Dad, because he'd found the hard copy and was half through reentering the data. Again, Randy had also avoided Lisa, who, this time, instead of reaching out to touch him when she slipped into bed, had silently turned her back to him and settled into sleep. But all was not exactly as it had been during and after his Ohio trip. The vocabulary building and buzz tallying were paying dividends. This time he returned to my office eager to discuss what he'd discovered about possible reasons he returned home in such an exhausted, strung-out state—and he'd discovered a lot.

The list of buzzes Randy had tracked during this ten-day, three-city trip was extensive. His log was filled with entries of face constricted, grinding teeth, stiff neck, headache, pit in stomach, tightness in chest, and trouble breathing—none of which, he'd noticed, ever occurred during the hours he spent actually wrestling with the particular problem at hand. Our in-office review of his log confirmed something else he'd begun to see that he hadn't been aware of before—that it was the bombardment of intimate conversation to which he was subjected by the reps and the thinking he did about a problem before he'd actually taken its measure that triggered most of these buzzes. He had also done well at matching emotion words to these buzzes. Next to the ones he experienced while thinking about an unmet problem, he'd jotted pressure, anger, anxiety, and tension. Next to those he experienced while riding in cars with too-talkative reps, he'd written embarrassed, taken advantage of, trapped, overwhelmed, on guard, resentful, and angry.

"This is good material," I said. "Let's work with it. We now know that you experience a fair amount of physical discomfort during these car trips, and that this discomfort is triggered when these men start telling you the intimate details of their lives, and that the reason these confessions trigger discomfort is because they arouse all these unpleasant emotions you've described. So we've isolated the trigger. In other words, we've identified the problem. Now, the next step is to—"

"Solve the problem. Yeah, I've been thinking about that."

"You're ahead of me, then. Want to tell me your thoughts?"

"Well, like I said before, I don't want to be rude to these guys. But, on the other hand, I don't want them giving me headaches, either. So I was thinking—most of these guys have tape decks in their cars. Maybe what I could do is carry along a few of my favorite classical-music cassettes. Then, when we get in the car, I can say something like, 'Boy, you know, these plane trips really wipe me out. Mind if I pop this cassette in? Classical music really helps me relax. I think you'll enjoy it, too. Here, give a listen.' " He looked at me expectantly. "What do you think?"

"Not bad. What if you also tried to steer the conversation away from their personal lives—keep them talking about something else?"

He considered my suggestion. "Like sports. That might work. Most of these guys are real sports buffs."

With two promising strategies now mapped out for deflecting the reps' intimate conversation, I turned our attention to the second major source of Randy's buzzes: his own thoughts about an as-yet unmet problem. "I see a lot of 'thinking about problem—pressure, tension, anxiety,' " I said, watching his face go tense.

"Yeah," he said guardedly. "I know."

"Looks from these entries like this mainly comes up in the evening, after you arrive at your motel, and in the morning, when you're waiting to be picked up. So, we've identified the problem—"

"No, we haven't," he said forcefully, casting me a challenging look. "That's just it. I don't know what the problem is yet. That's the problem."

"That's what's causing your anxiety—you're right. And, no, there isn't anything you can do about that. But there are things you can do to relieve the tension."

"Like what?" he said, angrily. "Read a book? Watch television? Call home and ask Lisa to make it all better? I've tried those things, remember? They don't work."

I let his words hang in the air for a moment. "Is that what you expect from your wife? For her to make it all better?"

He shifted in his chair, his face reddening. "No. Of course not." A silence. "I don't think so, anyway." Another silence, this one longer. And then, "I don't know. Maybe it is. Maybe that is what I expect." Another silence. "If it is, it's pretty stupid."

"No, it's not. It's pretty common, actually. We're talking about emotional needs here. We all have these needs—to feel loved, appreciated, competent. And we all look to our partners to satisfy these needs. Sometimes they can. Sometimes they can't."

A silence. "And when they can't, we get angry."

"Sometimes. Why? Have you been feeling angry at Lisa?"

Another silence, and then a nod. "Yeah. I think I have been."

"Can you tell me why?"

He frowned, studying his hands. "I'm not sure. Maybe that is it—or part of it, anyway. We always talk every night when I'm traveling. And she's never anything but supportive. It's always, 'How was the flight?' 'How's your room?' 'Did you have a good meal?' 'Is your bed comfortable?' She's always telling me how much she loves me and misses me and believes in me. . . . It should make me feel better. . . ." He shook his head. "But it doesn't." He glanced up at me. "And I guess I resent her for that." A pause. "So when I get home and she wants to talk or . . ." He looked down. "Or have sex . . . I just turn off." He fell silent again, drifting off into private thought. I waited. "Hunh," he grunted softly.

"What was that?"

"Oh, I just had this crazy flash."

"Of what?"

"Of me talking on the phone to Lisa."

"What were you saying?"

"Well, it's funny. I mean, it's not like I've ever actually said this to her." He shook his head, lips crooking into a faint smile. "I don't think I've ever even said it to myself, come to think of it."

"What's that?"

He glanced up at me. "This is kind of embarrassing." He looked down. "I was telling her I was scared."

"I'm scared." Potent words for men, who are trained all their lives not to speak them.

Having finally said them, Randy now said them again. "It's true—I am scared," he said, his voice sounding deeper, fuller, his whole body relaxing now that he'd unlocked and released this secret he'd been holding inside. "That's what's really going on when I think about these problems. I'm thinking, 'Well, this could be it. This could be the one you don't pull off.' " He shook his head, the expression on his face a mixture of sadness and wonder. "Here I am, a national supervisor, twelve years with the company, the best record in the firm, and I'm afraid of screwing up. You'd think I was some kind of rank beginner or something. I mean, nobody pulls it out a hundred percent of the time. Nobody. I know that. And yet it's like I think I have to—like, one strike and I'm out. It's like I have to be invincible or something."

I wasn't surprised that Randy felt this way about himself. Most men do. Nonetheless, as I told Randy, "That's a pretty rough standard to hold yourself to."

Randy let out a snorting laugh. "You're telling me."

"Who was like that? Who did seem invincible to you?"

His answer was instantaneous. "My dad." He smiled. "I mean, I know he wasn't, really. But when I was a kid? He was God. Just to stand beside him in that stream . . . I wanted to be just like him. I wanted to be that perfect." He turned serious again. "But this isn't about him. I know he was human, too. But that doesn't stop me from worrying about falling on my face. I mean, I'm already feeling tense about this trip to Montana I've got coming up."

"What's this one about?"

"It's this federally funded anti-drought project we've been handling the books for. It's turned into a real hot potato. Looks like a whole lot of money hasn't gone where it was supposed to go, and nobody knows where it did go. And now this fat-cat bureaucrat down in Washington who was one of the original sponsors of the project is pointing fingers at our guys to save his own hide."

"And you're supposed to save the local reps' hides."

Randy nodded. "And, I'll tell you, I've got doubts about this one."

"But you always have doubts."

"No, this is different. This one really is serious. We just had a big meeting about it yesterday. My boss is already telling me, 'Look, just do what you can do.' "

"Where will you be staying?"

He shrugged. "Some motel."

"Have you thought about booking yourself into a better hotel? Maybe one that has a health club with a squash or handball court?"

He looked slightly stunned. "I never thought of that. I could do that. It'd cost more. But, God, to be able to go play squash instead of sitting in my motel room? That'd break the tension. I always feel better after a game. Maybe I could play in the morning, too."

"Or go for a jog, or take a walk."

"Or take a walk. I don't know why I didn't think of that before." A silence. And then, "Geez," he said softly, shaking his head.

"What?"

"Traps," he said. "All these traps I've got myself in." A pause. "That I've got myself in," he said, jerking a thumb toward himself. "And I didn't even see them until now."

You Gotta Know What Feels Bad before You Can Make It Feel Better

That's the ultimate payoff of overcoming emotional numbness. Once men become aware of their emotional reactions, realize that these reactions are telling them something important, and learn to heed the flags that indicate something's wrong, they become much more skilled at identifying and devising ways out of all kinds of traps they didn't know they were in.

Randy had much news to report the next time we met. The mystery of the missing anti-drought project funds had proved even more difficult to solve than he had anticipated. For the first time, his log contained entries of buzzes experienced while actually working on the job, accompanied by jottings of emotions he'd been able to connect to these buzzes: anger at the local guys for screwing up; feelings of inadequacy for not being able to untangle their screw-up on the first try; resentment over having the problem they'd created tossed in his lap. "So I decided that instead of trying to straighten it all out myself, which is what I usually do, I'd throw it back at them for a while," he said. "So I mapped out a half-dozen problem areas, made sure they understood what needed to be done, and then basically said, 'Adios. See you in two weeks. When I get back, I want these problems resolved.' "

His cassette-tape strategy had also worked—for a while. "It turns out that Jay, the guy who met me at the airport, loves classical music as much as I do, which was a nice surprise. So there we were, driving along, listening to Bach—and then, all of a sudden he said, 'Did I tell you my wife and I are separating?' And I thought, 'Oh, God, here we go again.' So I said, 'No. I'm sorry to hear that.' And then he started in telling me the whole story. And I could feel my head beginning to throb. So I thought, 'Okay, what's the choice here? Either I listen and say nothing, and end up with another headache. Or I say something and risk insulting him.' " He glanced up at me. "I have to admit, I almost decided to go with the headache. But then I thought, 'No, that's ridiculous. If I do that, I've got no one to blame but myself.' So I took a deep breath and said, 'Know what, Jay? I really am sorry about you and your wife. And I understand your wanting to talk about it. But I really don't think I'm the person you should be talking to. I mean, that's pretty private stuff. I think it'd be better if we talked about something else.' "

"How'd he react?"

"I think he was a little miffed at first. He got quiet for a while. But then he said, 'You're right. I'm sorry. I shouldn't be laying my problems on you. So, tell me, who're you rooting for in the playoffs?' So then we started talking sports, and it turned out he's a squash player, too. So when we got to my hotel, I invited him to come up with me to the health club, which had a court. So we had this great game, and then we had dinner together. He turned out to be really good company."

"So you did book into a better hotel."

"Yeah, I did." He shook his head and chuckled. "What a difference." The difference was right there in his log, which contained far fewer buzzes noted during the evening and morning hours.

"What'd you do in the mornings?"

"Went for a swim."

The long-standing, unarticulated tensions between Randy and Lisa also seemed to be easing. "When we'd talk on the phone at night, it was . . . different this time. Easier, somehow. It didn't make everything go away—you know, the headaches and the trouble sleeping and everything. A lot of that was still there. But talking to her was just . . . better. It felt better. I think maybe that's because I wasn't expecting so much anymore." He smiled sheepishly. "I think, before, I really was expecting her to make everything all right. I mean, I didn't realize it, but I think I was." He shook his head. "And, there she was, trying to do exactly that. . . ." He smiled. "And not doing all that bad a job at it, either, I have to say. The truth is, I do feel better after our conversations. I didn't see that before, either. I didn't realize how much comfort I really do get from talking to her."

"How were things between you when you got home?"

"That was better, too. I was still pretty wiped when I got back. But this time I didn't freeze her out the way I usually do. I think realizing how much I do get from our telephone conversations really helped. It's hard to explain, but I think it made me feel more like giving something back. I couldn't do it the minute I walked in the door. I still needed some quiet time first. But at least this time I knew I wanted to do it. So when she came into the den, I said, 'Know what, honey? How about I take fifteen minutes to unwind, and then we'll talk.' I don't think she believed me." He smiled. "Can't say I blame her. She went into the kitchen to start dinner and just kind of stayed there. So, after fifteen minutes, I went in and asked her about this new series of kids' pop-up books she's been working on." He chuckled. "You should have seen her expression." He glanced up at me. "I brought her a present, too—a pair of turquoise earrings. I had them in my pants pocket. So after we'd talked awhile, I said, 'Oh, by the way, I brought you something.' And I handed them to her."

"Did she like them?"

"Oh, yeah." He smiled. "I haven't done that in a long time—brought her a present." He shook his head. "Such a little thing . . . I'd forgotten how small things like that really please her."

"And what about Jed?"

"Well, he came bursting into the den, as usual, ready to spill another story. But this time I stopped him. I said, 'Jed, whatever it is, I think it'd be better for both of us if you held off telling me until I've had a chance to unwind a little, okay?' He looked a little surprised, but then he said, 'Yeah, okay. Sure, Dad.' So after I'd given Lisa the earrings I went into the living room, where Jed was watching TV, and said, 'Okay, what is it this time?' "

"What was it this time?"

"He'd used my power saw but hadn't cleaned it."

"Not a capital offense."

"No. I got a little angry. But not as angry as I usually do." He smiled. "Maybe because I didn't come home feeling as angry as I usually do." A pause. "I think maybe I've been taking some of that anger out on him—maybe being a little too hard on him. I mean, yeah, he screws up. But who doesn't?"

"Nobody I know."

Randy chuckled. "No, nobody I know, either. He does need to learn to think more carefully before he rushes into things—and to show more respect for other people's property. We had a talk about that. A calm talk. I think it got through to him. But I have to give him credit, too. He does screw up—a lot. But when he does, he always takes responsibility for setting things right again. And that's an admirable trait."

"You told him that?"

"Yeah, I did."

"How'd he respond?"

"I think it made him feel better. I know it made me feel better—to be able to pay him a compliment and not just dump a lot of criticism on his head. I think it made it easier for us to talk about the things he needs to work on."

All in all, Randy felt that he now had a much better handle on things. His insomnia and headaches were subsiding, and he was feeling much less tense and pressured in general. We agreed that there was no need to meet again. Five weeks later, I received a postcard from him. On its face was a full-color photograph of a fisherman standing knee-deep in a sun-dappled stream, his body arched backward, his rod bent under the weight of the fat trout caught flapping in the air at the end of his line. On the back of the card, in an accountant's neat hand, he'd written: "Ron. Got Montana straightened out. We're up in Maine on vacation. No more headaches. Thanks. Randy. P.S. Jed's got a new passion—fly-fishing!"

There Are Words for What You're Feeling. Learn Them—and Use Them

It's hard to know what you're feeling if you can't name what you're feeling—if you can't find and speak the word that captures and expresses the emotion causing a physiological buzz. Naming an emotion helps to clarify it. The more emotion words you know the better you'll be able to identify and verbalize your feelings—to externalize them instead of internalizing them. Here are some words with which to start building your own vocabulary:*

abandoned	distraught	ignored	petrified
amused	disturbed	imposed upon	pleased
angry	eager	impressed	pressured
annoyed	ecstatic	indifferent	proud
anxious	edgy	infatuated	rejected
ashamed	empty	infuriated	relieved
bashful	enchanted	insecure	reluctant
bitter	envious	inspired	remorseful
blissful	exasperated	intimidated	restless
blue	excited	isolated	sad
bored	exhausted	jealous	scared
burdened	exuberant	jittery	screwed up
calm	fearful	joyous	silly
capable	fed up	jumpy	sorrowful
cheated	flustered	left out	spiteful
cheerful	foolish	lonely	tender
childish	forlorn	low	tense
combative	frightened	mad	thwarted
confused	frustrated	melancholic	trapped
contemptuous	furious	miserable	troubled
contented	glad	nauseated	uneasy
contrite	gloomy	nervous	unsettled
crushed	grieved	offended	upset
defeated	guilty	ornery	vulnerable
delighted	happy	outraged	wary
desirous	helpless	overwhelmed	weary
despairing	homesick	pained	wistful
diminished	hopeful	panicked	worried
discontented	hurt	persecuted	

* Adapted from *Men and Feelings: Understanding the Male Experience*, by David J. Kundtz (Deerfield Beach, FLA: Health Communications, Inc., 1991)

CHAPTER FOUR

The Gathering Storm

THE DYNAMICS OF ANGER AND AGGRESSION

When I lecture on the subject of men, anger, and aggression, I often begin my talk by offering examples of the many ways in which men use angry outbursts as a way to express other emotions. Here are three such examples, taken from the case histories of couples I've counseled.

- A man and his wife return to his parents' house from the cemetery, where his family has just buried his mother. He has not yet cried over her death. As they pull up to the house, they encounter a group of neighborhood boys playing a subdued game of roller-hockey in the street. The man gets out of the car and explodes at them: "Get the hell outta here! You want me to call the police? Go find a playground!"

- A woman is in her newly unemployed partner's kitchen, fixing him dinner at the end of a day during which none of the people he called about job leads called back—a washout of a day he has shrugged off as no big deal. "Honey, where's your salad bowl?" she calls out to where he sits in the living room, reading a magazine. He slaps down the magazine. "Jesus!" he spits acidly. "Are you that helpless? Check the dishwasher for Chrissake."

• A man tells his wife about a face-off he had at work that day with his supervisor. He'd gone to him for advice in handling a troublesome employee, but instead of offering advice his supervisor said, "Well, I've heard some complaints that you're too autocratic." Taken aback, he retorted, "Yeah? Well, I've heard complaints that you're not a very supportive boss." His wife's mouth drops open. "You didn't say that," she says. "Oh, yes I did," he says. "I just gave it right back to him."

Sound familiar? Anger—oh, yes, males are good at that. In study after study, researchers have found that whereas females excel in expressing most other emotions, males lead by a wide margin in expressing anger. It's unclear whether males experience anger more intensely or more frequently than women do. What is known, however, is that when they do feel anger, females are more likely to cry or attempt to avoid or reconcile the conflict, whereas males are more likely to express it through an act of aggression. And, as demonstrated above, men also express a range of other feelings as anger and aggression.

On this point the research is clear. In their comprehensive 1974 review of the research literature on gender differences of all kinds, developmental psychologists Eleanor E. Maccoby, of Stanford University, and Carol N. Jacklin, of the University of Southern California, found reliable evidence of only a handful of gender differences, one of which was aggression—for which the evidence supporting greater aggressiveness among males was substantial. Since then, other researchers have confirmed that when it comes to behaving aggressively, males have it all over females—both as children and as adults.

In his 1976 survey of ethnographic data from various societies worldwide, anthropologist Ronald P. Rohner found evidence of much greater aggressiveness among boys than among girls in ten of the fourteen societies studied. (In the other four, boys and girls rated equally aggressive.) In a 1984 review of 143 studies on gender differences in children, psychologist Janet S. Hyde also found that boys were more aggressive than girls. In their 1989 study of fifth, seventh, ninth, and eleventh graders, Janice C. Stapley and Jeannette M. Haviland found that girls reported experiencing more surprise, sadness, self-loathing, shame, shyness, and guilt, but boys reported experiencing more contempt. In a 1977 review of the research literature on adults, psychologists Ann Frodi, Jacqueline Macaulay, and Pauline R. Thome, of the University of Wisconsin at Madison, found that men were much more likely than women to become aggressive without provocation and were more likely than women to resort to verbal and physical aggressiveness when provoked. And, finally, in their 1986 review of sixty-three studies on adult aggression, psychologists Alice H. Eagly and Valerie J. Steffen, of Purdue University, found that men were more aggressive than females in general and were also far more likely than females to resort to physical aggression.

So it seems well established that males are more aggressive and express anger more aggressively than females. The question is why. In their 1974 literature review and again in a 1980 paper, Maccoby and Jacklin expressed their belief that this gender difference is innate. But to attribute this gender difference solely to differences in male-female biology is to overlook the powerful shaping influence of gender-role socialization. If male aggressiveness is so innate, Rohner should have found, for example, that males—especially testosterone-rich adult males—were uniformly more aggressive than females in all societies studied. But he didn't. Examining the data on adults, he found that men rated as more aggressive in only six of thirty-one societies studied, with women rating as more aggressive in five and men and women rating as equally aggressive in twenty. Consider also that Frodi, Macaulay, and

Thome found that, when provoked, women could become both verbally and physically aggressive. Clearly, then, it's not beyond the power of women to behave aggressively—as it would be were aggressiveness purely biologically based. So why don't they? Frodi, Macaulay, and Thome's theory: Women may very well have the same aggressive impulses men have, but—except when provoked—their guilt and anxiety about acting aggressively and their empathy with the target of their anger cause them to inhibit their aggressive impulses. In their review of the literature on adult aggression, Eagly and Steffen found evidence to support this theory. Women, much more than men, expressed concern about the guilt and anxiety they'd feel, the harm they might cause the other person, and the harm that might come to them were they to behave aggressively—particularly if they were to engage in an act of physical aggression. The reason females are less aggressive, in other words, is because they learn to consider the consequences that could befall them and others if they acted on their aggressive impulses.

And what do males learn? Not to empathize with an adversary, that's for sure—and certainly not to feel guilt, anxiety, or much of any other emotion. Males learn to be tough, unfeeling, assertive, aggressive. From childhood on, they learn that it's through fighting, conquering, dominating, and intimidating that they earn the respect and approval of other males. This traditional male norm of aggression may be changing now. The results of my study suggest that men are becoming more discriminating in their sense of what is and isn't healthy use of aggression and that they're thinking more carefully about just how much they want to encourage aggressiveness in their sons. But back when they were growing up, the traditional norm of male aggressiveness still ruled, and they were trained to adhere to it. When something happened or was done to males that made them feel alarmed, afraid, frustrated, fearful, or nervous, their task was to suppress and deny the feeling and come out angry and fighting. To do anything less was seen as unmanly. And that, in turn, resulted in shame—

the most intolerable feeling of all. As psychologist Steven Krugman, of Harvard Medical School, wrote in a 1991 paper, "Shame is the emotional response to feeling exposed as inadequate, insufficient, dirty, vulnerable and helpless. Male culture can be said to be shame-phobic in that men will go to great lengths to avoid feeling ashamed." Indeed, shame is so excruciating to men that it can drive them, as Krugman wrote, to instantaneous explosions of rage and violence—anything to expunge these unbearable feelings.

If a man were able to identify these feelings as he's having them—to experience them and name them—he might be able to find a less destructive way to manage or relieve them. But most men can't do that. By the time they reach adulthood, they're so numb to their emotions that they often aren't aware these emotions are present and building inside them until, suddenly, they explode. Instead of feeling and expressing vulnerable emotions, men compress them and transmute them into anger: an unruly emotion that too easily shades into rage and too often results in violence, not because men are inherently more violent than women but because, unlike women, men learn that violence is acceptable—even laudable. As men's studies scholar Harry Brod wrote in his 1987 book, *The Making of Masculinities*, when one looks "specifically at *male* socialization," what emerges is "a picture of considerable socialization toward violence. Whether learned in gangs, sports, the military, at the hands (often literally) of older males, or in simple acceptance that 'boys will be boys' when they fight, attitudes are conveyed to young males ranging from tolerance to approval of violence as an appropriate vehicle for conflict resolution, perhaps even the most manly means of conflict negation." In a recent review of the research literature psychologist Leslie Brody, of Boston University, concludes similarly that sons are still being socialized by parents to view retaliation as an acceptable way to express anger.

When Males Get Angry, Females Get Hurt

And who are the primary victims of male violence? Women. Statistics compiled by family-violence researchers are graphic:

- One-eighth of all husbands in the United States engage in one or more acts of physical aggression against their wives every year.

- Between three and four million women are battered each year, and some two million of those batterings are severe.

- Wife-beating results in more injuries serious enough to require medical attention than do rape, car accidents, and muggings combined.

- More than half of all women murdered in the United States during the first half of the 1980s were killed by their present or former male partner.

Indeed, so substantial is the evidence that men are the main perpetrators of violence and women their main victims that, in her 1991 book, *Men Are Not Cost Effective*, psychologist June Stephenson proposed that a $100 "user's fee" be added to every man's income tax to cover the cost of running the criminal justice system.

Outrageous as it's obviously intended to be, Stephenson's proposal still rankles many men: Is she saying that all men are guilty of violence toward women? What kind of male bashing is that? Sure, there are men running around loose out there, committing these appalling acts. That much we'll grant. But to judge all men guilty by gender association—of course we're offended. After all, we're talking minority here—not majority. We're talking about an unfortunate subset of men who clearly suffer from some serious problems—men like Jack.

A thirty-four-year-old automotive engineer, Jack paid one

visit to my office three years ago in the company of Sue, the thirty-two-year-old executive secretary with whom he was living. It was obvious the moment they entered the room that Jack didn't really want to be there. Silent and brooding, he sat slouched in his chair as Sue answered my get-acquainted questions. As she spoke she monitored Jack's reactions, as if watching for any sign that she was edging near something she shouldn't. After soliciting the same background information from Jack, who answered my questions tersely, I asked them to tell me why they had come. "Sue, why don't you answer first."

She glanced nervously at Jack. "Well, I . . ."

"I drink," said Jack, cutting her off. I glanced at Sue. She remained tense.

"I'm not clear what you mean by 'drink,' " I said to Jack. "Could you be more specific?"

He regarded me stonily for a moment, then slid his eyes away. "I get drunk sometimes," he said.

"How often?"

The question seemed to surprise him—as if he'd been braced for an attack. He sighed, relaxing a little. "Too often," he said. He used to drink only after work and on weekends. But, lately, he'd started drinking during lunch, sometimes taking the rest of the afternoon off. His boss had warned him that he was putting his job in jeopardy, and that had shaken him enough to try to quit, but he couldn't.

I turned to Sue. "And what's it like for you when Jack gets drunk?"

"It's . . . hard," she said softly.

I had a strong hunch she was saying that when Jack got drunk, he got violent. But she hadn't said it. She seemed to be waiting for him to say it—fearing, perhaps, that if she revealed his secret, he might punish her when they returned home. How to handle this? I chose the direct approach. "Sometimes, when people get drunk, they lash out at those around them," I said to Jack. "I'm wondering if that's true of you."

He looked down. "Yeah," he grunted. "Sometimes I kind of push her around a little."

"No!" Sue said forcefully. "That's not true. If you're going to tell him, tell the truth. You don't just push me around a little. You've slapped me, punched me. You've given me black eyes."

Jack glowered at Sue for a moment, then looked down and sighed—a long, heavy sigh. "I don't mean to," he said. "I just . . . I don't know. It's like something snaps, and I lose control."

Had we been further along in therapy, I might have asked Jack why he hadn't broken a few of Sue's bones while he was at it. A horrifying question—as it's meant to be. When I pose one like it to men who are violent with their partners, they usually recoil in horror, demonstrating, as I point out, that, although they claim to be out of control when they turn violent, they are in fact still enough in control to set limits on their violent behavior—a crucial point we'll return to later.

But I didn't know Jack well enough to risk confronting him with this question. And there were other issues to address—such as whether he was serious about wanting to quit drinking. In the discussion that followed it emerged that Sue never knew whether he would come home drunk or sober until he walked in the door—by which time it was often too late for her to leave. Then she would protect herself from his blows as best she could until she was able lock herself in the bathroom, where she'd stay until he left or fell asleep, then flee to a friend's house. The next day he'd telephone her at work, repentant and promising it would never happen again, and, within a day or two, she'd come back. Things would be good for a while. And then he'd come home drunk, and the nightmare would begin again. She'd thought of leaving him. But she still loved him and wanted to help him. She'd urged him to go to Alcoholics Anonymous, but he'd resisted, insisting he could quit drinking by himself.

I turned to Jack. "Are those still your feelings?"

He was silent for a long while. "I don't know," he said finally.

"Would you consider entering a rehabilitation program?"

Another long silence. "I'm not sure."

We left it that he'd think about it while I looked into treatment options and that we'd discuss these options when we met again in four days. I asked Sue where she'd be staying in the interim.

"At home," she said.

"Is that safe?"

She glanced at Jack. "Yes, I think so."

I turned to Jack. "What do you think?"

He frowned. "She'll be okay."

I wish this story ended happily. It doesn't. Jack and Sue didn't keep their next appointment. Sue called a week later to say that on the day of the appointment Jack had gotten drunk and beaten her again. "I've left him," she said. "This time I'm not going back." I never heard from them again.

Men Who Lose Control Want Control— and Use Violence to Get It

I often tell Jack's story during workshops and lectures to illustrate how three powerful forces often converge and conspire to propel men into committing violence against women. Clearly Jack was a troubled man. But rather than confront and deal with his troubles, he was driven by gender-role socialization to numb himself to his emotions and their accompanying physiological "buzzes" (force number one). Some men accomplish this end through relatively harmless means, such as zoning out in front of the television. Others, like Jack, turn to mind-altering substances such as alcohol—which, in loosening inhibitions, also loosen the cap on anger, increasing the danger that it will spill out as violence.

The second and third of these forces are so closely intertwined that they're almost inseparable. The second is fusion; the third, control. Long before he learns to walk or talk, a male learns that being male means having to be separate from his mother. As a result, he comes into adulthood with a host of unmet dependency needs that he then transfers onto his female partner—unconsciously trying to re-create with her the state of blissful oneness, or fusion, he didn't get enough of in infancy. Unconsciously, he may relate to his partner not as a separate being but as an extension of himself and expect her to do for him as his mother did before he was required to separate from her: to anticipate and satisfy his every physical, psychological, and emotional need. When his partner fails to do that—whether by forgetting to restock the refrigerator with beer or by falling short in her ability to shore up his flagging sense of self-worth—he gets angry. Sometimes he gets furious. And sometimes he turns violent—especially when under the disinhibiting influence of alcohol or drugs.

He loses control, he tells himself. But he doesn't really. In fact, he is very much in control and is using anger or violence to control his partner. When she isn't there for him, doesn't do for him, or otherwise fails to anticipate and satisfy his needs, he uses anger or violence to punish her and bring her back under his thumb—and keep her there, right where he wants her.

When I tell Jack's story during workshops and lectures, I always gaze around the room to see how the men listening to it are responding. Usually what I see is a roomful of middle- to upper-middle-class men sitting with arms folded across their chests, looking detached, impassive—sometimes smug. Their expressions say it all: Why am I telling them about Jack? What does he have to do with them? Jack's got serious problems. They're educated, civilized guys.

"Maybe you'll find it easier to relate to this next story," I'll say then. And then I might tell them about Kurt, a forty-three-year-old airline executive who was unfailingly polite and charming to associates and friends and who put great store by making the right professional and social impression—so much store that he would blast his wife with tirades of verbal abuse that reduced her to tears if she so much as set the dinner table with the wrong linen or fetched him the wrong cufflinks when he was dressing for an evening out. Or I might tell them about Andrew, a thirty-seven-year-old newspaper editor who took great pride in his intellect and ability to tell an entertaining story—so much pride that he would viciously attack any opinion his wife expressed that contradicted his own until he succeeded in silencing her and would turn red-faced with fury and bellow at her for ruining his story if she interrupted with a question or comment while he was telling one. Or I might tell them about Eric. On its surface, Eric's story seems very different from Jack's—which is why I like to pair them. Men usually find it easy to relate to Eric. They relax, open up. As I speak, I watch their faces, waiting for the moment when they come to realize that the two stories are very much alike.

SOLUTIONS

Eric was a trim, slightly built, forty-eight-year-old pediatrician who kept himself impeccably groomed and favored tweeds in his casual attire. His wife, Laura, was a thirty-eight-year-old registered nurse. Presenting problem: marital ennui. An anxious, plump, pleasant-faced woman, Laura explained during our first session that the problem was really hers. "I feel like I'm having some sort of midlife crisis," she said, smiling nervously at Eric, who sat beside her on the couch with one arm draped protectively behind her. In the fifteen years they'd been married, she'd gained thirty-five pounds and couldn't seem to lose them. She felt listless and fatigued much of the time, had lost interest in cooking and homemaking, and, with their eight-year-old daughter, Lizzie, now in school, she felt a void in her life that her work didn't fill. She'd enrolled in a few advanced nursing courses on Eric's recommendation—she smiled at him as she said this, and he smiled back—"but then I lose interest or confidence or something," she said, "and end up quitting." She looked up at her husband, whose face showed concern.

"I try to encourage her," Eric said to me. "I bring home brochures from Northeastern, B.U., and Brigham and Women's and point out courses I think might be of interest, but . . ." He shrugged, his expression perplexed, glanced down at Laura, gave her a little hug. "It's hard to go back to school at this stage in life, I know," he said, looking from her back at me. "Believe me, I give her credit for even making the effort. And what with everything else she has on her plate— working full time and taking care of Lizzie . . . But I'm willing to help in any way I can. I've told her that."

Watching their exchange, I thought to myself, "There's something wrong with this picture." Eric was too much the loving, concerned, supportive husband; Laura, too much the anxious, depressed, incompetent wife. No individual human being, male or female, is either so all-endowed with character virtues or so totally lacking in endowments—we're each a mix of weaknesses and strengths. What I saw before me, I strongly suspected, were not two separate people but the end-product of fifteen years of unconscious marital fusion during which Laura had surrendered all her strengths to Eric and he had transferred all his weaknesses to her—a heavy burden that might very well be connected to her physical weight-gain. I suspected, indeed, that, for all Eric's apparent support of his wife's efforts to better herself, over the course of their marriage he had, in fact, encouraged not her strengths but her weaknesses—in direct proportion to the degree he suppressed any awareness of his own.

To test my hunch, I asked Eric to tell me more about his work. He was an assistant professor of pediatrics who also had a private practice. Most of his patients were children of low-income families on Medicaid—a fact in which he took pride.

"It's exhausting," he said. "But it's much more satisfying than some cushy practice would be. I'll never be rich. But at least I feel I'm making a contribution."

Impressive. But if Eric was really so proud of and satisfied with his work, why the frown on his face? Might it be that, for all the pride he expressed, he was, in truth, neither as proud of nor as satisfied with his career as he wanted me to believe—as he wanted himself to believe? The harsh fact is that within the medical profession, pediatrics is considered one of the lower-status specialties, and Medicaid pediatrics lower still. The other harsh fact is that, in the world of academia, the rank of assistant professor is also considered low-status—and to have risen no higher by age forty-eight is to be considered an also-ran by one's peers.

It seemed to me there was a pebble lodged in Eric's shoe: a compressed, hard pebble of vulnerable feelings that he'd been walking on for years—unconsciously reacting to, without consciously experiencing, the pain. The picture of the couple seated across from me was now coming into clearer focus, and I was beginning to discern a not uncommon marital pattern:

1. Alexithymic man is unable to identify, experience, or express vulnerable feelings.

2. Man fuses with female partner, charges her with responsibility of assuaging his vulnerable feelings, bolstering his self-esteem.

3. Man uses anger/abuse to control his female partner, insure that she continues to satisfy his unconscious needs.

4. Pattern escalates and relationship deteriorates unless man is able to identify, acknowledge, and own his vulnerable feelings.

From what Eric and Laura had said and shown me thus far, it seemed fairly clear that the first two steps in this pattern were very much present in their relationship. The task facing me now was twofold: to uncover steps three and four; and to guide Eric and Laura in exploring the hidden dynamics of their relationship so that, if they were willing, they could also become aware of this pattern and take steps to bring their relationship into healthier balance.

They were willing—a testament not only to their individual strength and courage, but also to the strength of their love for and commitment to each other. Let's face it: It's not easy to change patterns laid down over many years of marriage—in part because these patterns are often maintained by the interplay between individual character traits that initially attracted each partner to the other and now repel. As one wife said of the husband she was considering divorcing: "I married him because he was as solid as a rock, and now I want to leave him because he's as cold as a stone." Eric and Laura worked very hard over the course of the next year to identify and change this pattern—beginning in our second session, during which, searching to find steps three and four in the pattern, I asked them each to tell me what annoys them about the other.

"Gee, not much, really," said Laura, glancing at her husband. (For this session, I'd asked them to take separate chairs.) "Eric's pretty perfect." She thought for a moment. "His fastidiousness, maybe. He's extremely fastidious—much more so than I."

"True," said Eric, frowning. "Laura's extremely messy. I find that very annoying. She's always taking books from the bookshelf and leaving them wherever she puts them down instead of putting them back in the right place. And the brochures I bring home for her are scattered all over the coffee table. I keep telling her to put them away somewhere, but she doesn't. It drives me crazy."

We were on to something. Both of Eric's examples sounded like the kind of normal, everyday behavior that would be distressing only to someone with a need to control—someone who might be compensating for a sense of lack of mastery in life by exerting obsessive control over the small things he felt he could master. When Laura upset the orderliness of their house, threatening his sense of control over his home environment and over her, he became angry—and expressed that anger in ways unconsciously intended to intimidate ("She's extremely messy"; "It drives me crazy") and make her toe the line.

True to form, once this pattern had been established between them, Eric's use of verbal intimidation as a means of controlling Laura had escalated during the years of their marriage (step four)—as became apparent during our third session, when a conversation about the emptiness Laura had been feeling since their daughter started school looped back to a discussion of a conflict that had arisen between husband and wife when Laura had been pregnant.

As soon as she'd learned she was expecting, Laura had embraced the La Leche League philosophy of long-term breastfeeding. Eric had been against it. The arguments had started before Lizzie's birth and had continued through the six months after her birth that Eric considered a suitable amount of time to breastfeed. Laura had wanted to continue breastfeeding until Lizzie weaned herself—for as long as three years, if necessary. Eric had declaimed vociferously, in private and in the presence of family and friends, that the idea was disgusting and that only someone really twisted would consider it. He'd won. Laura had weaned Lizzie at seven months.

"*Disgusting* and *twisted*—those were your words?" I asked Eric.

"Well, I . . . I don't remember exactly," he said, his tone professorial. "It was so long ago, after all."

"I remember," Laura said softly.

"I used those words?" he said, looking mildly astonished. "Oh, but, if I did, I'm sure I didn't mean them the way you took them. I'm sure I was just trying to make my point."

Laura looked at him for a long moment but said nothing. She dropped her eyes, looked up at me. "Actually, that's when my weight problems began," she said. She remembered experiencing deep sadness over weaning Lizzie so early. "I just ached," she said. She looked down, embarrassed. "I guess I tried to smother the ache by eating." She kept trying to lose the weight she'd gained during pregnancy, "but I just couldn't seem to do it," she said. Instead, she'd gained more. A silence. And then, softly, "Eric didn't like that, either."

He looked stunned. "When did I ever say that? When have I ever said one word about your weight?"

"You've said things," Laura said softly, not looking at him. When she was breastfeeding Lizzie, she remembered, he often greeted her when he returned home in the evening with "How's my little cow today?"—a greeting he maintained he'd meant affectionately. During heated arguments, she said, he sometimes made comments about her "fat ass"—which he didn't recall making but insisted must have been made unthinkingly in the heat of anger. He also tried to monitor what she ate, she said. "Like when we go out to dinner and I order something he'll say, 'Sweetheart, are you sure you really want to eat all that? Maybe it would be better if you just had a salad.' "

"He says this before you order?" I asked.

"No, when I order. He says it in front of the waiter. . . ." A pause. "And whoever we're having dinner with."

"That's not fair," said Eric, indignant. "You make it sound as if I'm being cruel." He turned to me. "Laura's the one who's always saying she needs to lose weight. I'm just trying to be helpful."

"Do you find Eric's remarks helpful?" I asked Laura.

She looked down. After a moment of silence, she shook her head. "No," she said softly.

"What effect do they have?"

Another silence. And then, "They hurt."

"Do you tell him that?"

Another silence. She shook her head. "No."

"Why not?"

Another silence. And then a shrug. "Because I know he's right, I guess. And because I know he really is trying to help.

It's like when he brings home those brochures." She glanced up at Eric, looked down. "I know he's doing it for my own good. It's just . . . some of the things he says."

"What does he say?"

"Well, there was this course I wanted to take in obstetrical-care nursing. This was years ago. Actually, that's how the whole idea of my going for advanced training got started. A friend of mine had signed up for the course—that's how I found out about it—and I really wanted to take it." She smiled. "I really love babies." Her smile faded. "But when I told Eric about it, he said, 'Oh, but, darling, that's an awfully demanding course, and you're not exactly spilling over with motivation, now, are you? I think perhaps you're setting your sights a bit high. You don't want to embarrass yourself by taking on more than you can handle. Why don't you let me look around for something easier.' " She fell silent.

"And?"

"And, that was it."

"You didn't take the course?"

Laura shook her head. "No. A couple of days later he brought home a bunch of brochures, and I enrolled in something else." She shrugged. "I don't even remember what it was. I quit after a few weeks."

"Well, but you see?" said Eric, coming to his own defense. "That's the point. If you couldn't stick with an easier course, what makes you think you'd have stuck with that one?"

Laura looked down at her hands. "Maybe because that's the one I really wanted to take," she said softly.

The Words We Speak
Can Do Violence, Too

It's usually at around this point in my recounting of Eric's story that the men listening to it start looking uncomfortable. Yes, they see themselves in Eric. And they don't like what they see.

Here's a man who seemed very different from Jack but turned out not to be so different after all. Both were alienated from their emotions and unconsciously fused with their partner. The difference is that instead of using physical violence to control his wife, Eric used psychological and verbal abuse to achieve the same end.

Men tend to think of verbal manipulation as women's terrain. And it's true that women can be master verbal manipulators when they choose to be, using their facility at articulating emotions and keen insight into other people's feelings to play upon the emotions men are less capable of expressing until they achieve their desired outcome or until their partner becomes so frustrated, confused, and defensive that he lashes out in anger. Women are also capable of intentional and unintentional verbal cruelty, of course. I think, for example, of the way a former client's girlfriend announced to him that she wanted to get married. She wasn't very skilled at stating her desires directly, in the form of "I want." So instead she said, "You know what my father says about you? He says you're a Peter Pan—that you're never going to grow up and settle down." But men are not as much the innocent victims of verbal manipulation as they sometimes like to think. They have their way with words, too—and it can be a cruel way when they want it to be. As psychologist Don Long, cofounder of Rape And Violence End Now (RAVEN), noted in a 1987 book chapter, "Three out of four men use verbal abuse (psychological violence) as a mechanism of control in their homes."

The rest of my third session with Eric and Laura was devoted to helping them understand and acknowledge to themselves and each other that his angry remarks, "helpful" comments, and "affectionate teasing" were, in fact, deeply hurtful to her. It took a while for Eric to accept this. "Perhaps I have been blunt," he said. "But I certainly never meant to be hurtful. I guess I didn't realize Laura was so sensitive."

"I'm sure you didn't," I said, meaning what I said. Numbed to their own emotions, many verbally abusive men honestly don't realize how much pain they're inflicting on their partner—anymore than they're aware of the pain buried inside them that causes them to lash out at her. "I'm thinking it might be helpful if you and I met for a few individual sessions to explore what prompts you to make these remarks," I said. "Then, once we've got that sorted out, the three of us can meet again. What do you think?"

He frowned, considering. "Yes, well. Perhaps that would be useful."

When We Find and Feel
Our Own Hurt—*Then* We'll Stop
Hurting Our Partner

Eric and I met for ten sessions. Our first task was to help him learn to identify his emotions and track them to their source, in order to find better ways to manage and express them than by becoming verbally abusive with Laura. Toward that end I assigned Eric the same vocabulary building and emotional response log exercises that had proved so helpful to Randy. To his credit, Eric embraced the assignment, and by our third session he'd begun discerning a pattern to his verbal abusiveness that he hadn't seen before. When he'd spent a busy, satisfying day at his office, treating the young patients about whom he genuinely cared, he'd return home feeling good, and his interactions with Laura would be warm and affectionate. But on days when he'd had to leave his practice to teach or attend meetings at the medical school, he'd return home in a sour mood and begin insulting and belittling his wife— "trying to make her feel bad because I feel bad, I suppose," was the way he put it. But why did he return home from a day at the medical school feeling so bad? It took two more sessions of delicate probing for Eric to find the answer. The reason: Time spent at the medical school was time spent interacting not only with students but also with professional colleagues who, because of their more prestigious areas of specialization and more advanced academic rank, accorded one another more status and respect than he felt were accorded to him. "It's an old-boys' network," he said bitterly. "And I'm not one of the boys. I'm seen as deficient in some way—as not quite good enough."

"Have your colleagues said things to indicate they feel that way?"

"Well, no, not in so many words. But they don't have to. You know how it is. Some things you just know."

I didn't doubt that Eric was being subtly slighted by his colleagues. Rank and pecking order and in-groups and outsiders are a harsh reality of academic life, as they are of any organization made up of more than one person. But I sensed in Eric a degree of sensitivity to these slights that I suspected had as much to do with how he saw himself as it did with how his colleagues saw him.

It wasn't until our sixth session together that the painful pebble finally popped out of Eric's shoe. We were talking about his passion for his profession when he mentioned that he'd fallen in love with it at age seven, the first time he'd accompanied his father to the university hospital where he'd taught.

"Your father was a doctor?"

"Yes."

"You haven't mentioned that before."

"No?"

Retired now, his father had enjoyed a medical career studded with accomplishments and honors. A full professor and chair of his hospital's department of pathology at the time of his retirement, he'd earned a far-reaching reputation as one of the best research physicians in his field. "That's why I don't speak of him often," he said. "The last thing I need is for people to know I'm his son."

"Why wouldn't you want people to know you're his son?"

He glared at me. "Do you have any idea what it's like being the son of a well-known father? The minute people make the connection it's, 'Oh, you're *Sam's* son. Fine man, your dad. Wonderful doctor, your dad.' "

"You sound pretty angry."

"I am," he shot back.

"Why's that?"

"Because I don't need that," he said, furious. "I may be his son but I'm not him, and I'm never going to be him. I don't need anybody comparing me to him. Not strangers, not colleagues, not students, not you, not anybody. Is that clear enough?"

"Who's comparing you?"

"Are you being insulting?"

"No, I'm asking a question."

"Who's comparing us? You want a list? Why, well—" His words broke off. He frowned, shifted in his chair. "Well . . ." He shifted again, frowned harder. A silence. And then the frown softened into an expression of sad surprise. He sat for a long moment, gazing at nothing. "I am," he said then. "I guess I am."

We were getting close now. The pebble was out. Now we had to probe to its core. The suddenness and intensity of Eric's anger had already led me to suspect that beneath the anger lay shame. It seemed a safe guess that the source of this shame was Eric's deeply buried sense of inadequacy over not measuring up to his dad.

My hunch proved correct. During our next session it emerged that, as a boy, Eric had dreamed of growing up to be just like his dad, but it hadn't happened. Thrilled that Eric had decided to follow him into medicine, his dad had urged him to become a surgeon. Eric had tried it, thinking he might specialize in pediatric surgery, but he hadn't liked it, had found himself fighting nausea every time he entered an operating room. He'd stayed with it for a year out of a desire to please his father, who was mightily disappointed when Eric finally told him he'd decided to go into pediatrics instead.

"What did he say?"

"Not much. We were in his study. He just looked at me

for a long time with this crestfallen expression on his face. Then he shook his head and said, 'Pediatrics. And I had such high hopes.' And then he got up and left the room.''

Prior to that brief conversation, Eric and his dad had spent many a long evening in his dad's study, talking medicine—their mutual passion. After Eric's announcement that he was dropping surgery, their evenings together had dwindled to a halt. "It was just too uncomfortable," said Eric. "Too . . . stilted." Eric had thought that, perhaps somewhere down the road—when he'd finished school, established his practice and begun rising in his own field—his dad would come to respect his choice. "But things didn't quite work out that way," he said.

It took two more sessions, both emotionally fraught, for Eric to fully acknowledge and experience his shame and grief over having failed to measure up to his father. From there it was a comparatively small step to recognizing his attempts to bolster his own shaky self-image by keeping his wife in a many-steps-down position. He began to see that he'd been using verbal abuse to erode Laura's self-confidence and maximize her insecurities, in order that his would seem negligible in comparison, and to get her to feel and express the shame and inadequacy he'd been unable to feel or express himself. "I don't just do it with words, either," he said. "I do it in other ways, too."

"For example?"

"Well, for example, I bring a lot of sweets into the house—ice cream, cookies, things like that. I always say I'm buying them for Lizzie, but Lizzie's not big on sweets. It's usually Laura who ends up eating them. I think I do that on purpose to keep her from losing weight. I think I've been afraid that if she lost weight she might start feeling too good about herself."

"Have you told her that?"

He shook his head. "No." A silence. "But I think I should."

When Eric and Laura returned to my office the following

week, I noticed a change in both of them. Eric's manner toward his wife seemed less paternalistic and more respectful. Laura seemed a little less beaten down. With my help, they spent the next year examining the dynamics of their relationship and practicing healthier ways of relating. More self-aware now, Eric learned to catch most of his hurtful comments before they came out of his mouth. Laura, in turn, learned to cut him short when he did let one slip by responding with a calm, forceful, "I will not hear that, Eric."

By the end of the year, each with the other's support, Eric and Laura had made other positive changes. Laura had lost ten pounds and had enrolled in a nursing-skills refresher course in preparation for taking a course in obstetrical-care nursing when it was offered again the next fall. Having finally confronted his own sense of failure at not having measured up to his father, Eric had finally been able to put down that burden. With more energy freed up, he'd begun taking steps to actualize a dream he'd had for some time: to form a consortium of like-minded colleagues and raise funding to purchase, equip, and staff a mobile medical van with which to deliver medical care to the children of families living in inner-city welfare hotels.

"You know how it is when you start talking to heavyweights about funding a project," Eric said during our last session. "Word travels fast in those circles." It had traveled back to his father, who'd called two nights before to say, "I hear you're up to something interesting." They'd talked for an hour about Eric's project. His dad had offered some good suggestions and asked if there was anything he could do to help.

"I don't think so, Dad," Eric had said. "But I appreciate the offer."

"Well, if there's anything, anything at all."

"Thanks, Dad."

"My pleasure, Son. I have to say, it's about time somebody did what you're doing. Hell, I'd come up and work as a volunteer if I weren't such an old geezer. Anyway, just wanted to say I'm proud of you, Son. Keep me posted. And keep up the good work.''

Bottom Line: There Is No Excuse for Abusiveness

If, like many men, you are prone to angry outbursts, verbal abusiveness, or physical violence, be aware that you can change these patterns and that help is available—in the form of individual and group counseling and peer-support groups. An effective anger-management program will help you to do the following:

1. **Recognize that you're angry and identify the cause of your anger as it's happening.** Because men are so numbed to emotion many are oblivious to the countless irritations they deal with in the course of a day that cause anger to accumulate and build. Meanwhile, like a rubber band being pulled back slingshot-style, their ability to maintain their equilibrium is being stretched tauter and tauter until finally one last, often minor, irritation causes them to snap—and explode. If this is your pattern, you might want to assign yourself the exercise of keeping an emotional response log in order to become more aware of these minor irritants and deal with each as it comes up.

2. **Express your irritation calmly and directly—to the person causing it.** Many men think it's not manly to complain. Instead of voicing irritation—say, at a wife who habitually keeps them waiting twenty minutes when they agree to meet her somewhere—they contain their anger, letting it seep out in the form of subtle or not-so-subtle verbal abuse, or letting it accumulate until they become furious and sometimes violent. If this is true of you, you might want to experiment with expressing your

irritation calmly and directly. For example, you might say, in a calm tone of voice, to a habitually tardy wife, "You know, I really don't like being made to wait twenty minutes. If you'd told me you were going to be late, I could have worked a little longer at the office, or I'd have brought along something to read. I'd appreciate your not doing that again. If you're going to be late, please let me know." You'll feel an immediate sense of relief simply for having expressed your annoyance rather than having contained it, even if your wife doesn't apologize. The likelihood, however, is that she will, which will relieve your irritation even more.

3. **Keep in mind that when someone does something that makes you angry, you might be misinterpreting his behavior.** We all misconstrue other people's actions—especially when they do something that triggers our own deepest insecurities and fears. When that happens we feel anxious and ashamed—intolerable emotions that can trigger an immediate rush of anger. If you find that a particular kind of behavior on the part of another person invariably sparks your anger, stop to consider that this behavior may be touching one of your sensitive spots and that, because it is a sensitive spot, you may be misinterpreting and overreacting. Instead of holding fast to your interpretation, make an exercise of coming up with other plausible explanations for that behavior. For example, perhaps you know you get anxious when you have to call a client to find out if it's a go or a no-go on a proposal you've submitted for her approval. You place the call. Her assistant takes a message. At the end of the day she hasn't called back. You're enraged. Recognize that you may be angry because you're thinking, "She hasn't called because she doesn't like the proposal and doesn't want to say so." Consider the possibility that she hasn't yet read the proposal, she's been tied up all day in meetings, or she's read and loves the proposal

and is waiting to get the go-ahead from her boss before giving it to you. You'll learn which is the truth soon enough. Keeping these other possibilities in mind in the meantime will ease your anxiety—and your anger.

4. **Understand that you *are* in control.** If you have a tendency to turn verbally or physically abusive when upset or angry, stop telling yourself that you lost control. It's a lie—plain and simple. The truth is that you are very much in control and are using anger or violence to control your partner. Men who beat their wives are often extremely calculating in their abuse. They choose when to hit, how to hit, and where to hit (where the bruises won't show when their wife goes to work the next day). Other men are equally shrewd in their use of verbal abuse and other tactics designed to dominate and intimidate. If your need to control or fear of losing control of your partner often incites you to verbal abuse, you should seriously consider seeking professional counseling. If that same need or fear has prompted you to strike your partner even once, you can't afford to think about seeking professional help. *You must get help now.*

The most effective way to short-circuit anger, of course, is by learning to feel, identify, and express a full range of human emotions—including the vulnerable ones such as anxiety, inadequacy, and fear that men are taught to consider shameful and which are therefore most likely to trigger angry outbursts. It isn't pleasant to feel these emotions. But it's much more freeing, humanizing, and potentially healing than keeping them locked up inside or venting them in the form of anger, rage, or violence.

In the next chapter we'll take a look at some specific kinds of vulnerable feelings that men often keep locked up inside and examine the early-life experiences that are the source of these unresolved feelings, which often lead to personal and relationship problems that can't be corrected until men attend to these long-buried hurts.

CHAPTER FIVE

Men's Wounds

THE FATHER WOUND

I wasn't surprised when the painful pebble in Eric's shoe turned out to be his unresolved feelings of inadequacy in relation to his dad. Get a man to the point where he's willing to begin excavating long-buried feelings, and the Dad issue usually is the first one he hits. Many of the men who participated in my Fatherhood Project workshops freely admitted that they were there because they didn't want their sons to grow up feeling as bad about them as they did about their dads. Again and again these men confessed feelings of anger, hurt, grief, and regret about never having been close to their fathers; about never having felt loved by their fathers; about having been raised by distant, demanding, difficult dads who were never there for them, physically or emotionally, and for whom their best never seemed good enough.

The "father wound," Harvard psychologist Samuel Osherson calls this painful mix of emotions so many men feel toward their dads. It used to be men didn't talk much about these feelings. What was the point? Distant, demanding, difficult—that's just the way fathers were. So why are men confronting this issue now? The answer, I think, is that, until recently, men had no reason to think their relationship with their fathers could be other than it was—and now they do. Now, just as men of the Baby Boom generation are becoming fathers themselves, they're being told that everything they learned about fathering from their own dads—that a father is someone who works hard, who isn't around much, who criticizes more than he compliments, who doesn't show affection or any other emotion except anger—no longer applies. Instead, men are supposed to be sensitive, caring, enlightened dads who are really there for and involved with their kids. Makes sense. Beats the way they grew up. The only problem is many men don't know how to be that kind of father, for the simple reason that their own dads weren't that kind of father to them. That's the painful part. Struggling to learn how to give what they never received, many men are beginning to see just how much they missed.

Bury These Feelings, and You Bury All Feelings

Jim didn't need help tracing his concerns about what kind of father he'd be back to the kind of fathering he'd had as a boy. "I mean, it's not like I had the greatest role model in the world," he said dryly during his first visit to my office. It was his total lack of feeling—positive or negative—about the approaching birth of his first child that had brought him to see me. A thirty-five-year-old financial analyst, he and his thirty-three-year-old wife, Nora, a clothing designer, had waited five years to start a family. He'd been excited when she first announced that she thought she was pregnant. "But then, when she called to tell me her doctor had made it official, it was like—I don't know, it was like all my excitement drained away, and I just went dead. I don't know how else to describe it. I mean, in my head I know I want this baby, but I don't feel that anymore. At first I thought, 'Well, it's just a stage.' But it's been like that for four months now, and it's really starting to worry me, and it's starting to upset Nora."

For the rest of the hour, we talked easily as Jim filled me in about his work (challenging and satisfying), his marriage (solid) and his family background: oldest of two children; only son; upper-middle-class upbringing; mother, a full-time homemaker, still living in his hometown in Indiana; father, owner and president of a local newspaper, now deceased.

"When did he die?"

"Eight years ago."

"So you were twenty-seven. That's fairly young."

"Is it? I guess." When it came to Dad, that was as expressive as he got.

During our next session, I elicited a sketchy portrait of his father as a hard-driving businessman who, even when he was home for an evening or weekend instead of traveling or working late, was usually closeted in his den with paperwork or tied up in meetings with community leaders who were always paying late-evening calls. "It's funny the way things worked out, though," he said. "After his first heart attack his doctor told him that if he didn't throttle back he'd be dead in a year, and after that he was a changed man. He'd call just to talk, and he'd ask when I was coming home to visit. And I'd say, 'I don't know, Dad. I'm pretty busy.' And then he had the second heart attack, and . . ." He shrugged. "That must have been weird, though—always running at full speed and then being told to slow down. I wonder what that was like."

We were getting somewhere. Though Jim's tone was still detached, his shift from disinterest in, to mild curiosity about his dad was progress. The lid he'd screwed down on his feelings about his father was coming loose.

"It seems you have some questions you'd probably want to ask your dad if he were still alive," I said.

A nod. "Yeah, I guess."

"I'd like you to think about these questions. Write each

one down on a separate index card. We'll go over them the next time we meet. If you've got any old family pictures, bring those in, too."

He looked skeptical, but he agreed—and I knew that, as with most men I counsel, so long as I wasn't pushing too hard too fast, I could count on him to carry out the assignment even if it made him uncomfortable.

Three days later, Jim entered my office carrying two manila envelopes. "Questions," he said gruffly, tossing one envelope down on the table. "Pictures," he said, tossing down the other. Then he sat down heavily and began massaging his forehead with one hand. "Yeah, I've got questions," he said. "I'd have written more, but I ran out of cards. It doesn't matter though, because you know what I realized? If you take all my questions and roll them into one, what you come up with is that I don't know a damn thing about my father. And you know why?"

"Why?"

He waved a hand at the envelope of pictures. "After our last session, I went home and began looking through old photographs. I must have gone through them three times, looking for pictures of me and my dad. The only ones I found were shots of Nora and me posing with both sets of parents at our wedding—none from when I was a kid. I figured, 'Well, Mom must've kept them.' So I called and asked her to send me a couple. But she said she wasn't sure she had any either—she'd have to check." He shook his head and laughed a hard-edged laugh. "It fits, see?"

"What does?"

"The photos, the questions." His face was flushed now. "Of course I don't know anything about my father. The bastard was never there! He was always too busy with more important things—anything except spending time with his own son. And then, later, when he did have time, it was like, 'Fuck you. I can be busy, too.' And then—" His voice cracked. He gazed out the window, tears welling in his eyes, lifted a hand to his face and began to cry.

He didn't cry long—a few minutes, no more. Then he

pulled out a handkerchief and wiped away the tears. "I don't believe it," he said, half chuckling in surprise and embarrassment. "I haven't cried in . . . Well, not in a long time."

"You didn't cry when your father died?"

"No."

"How are you feeling now?"

"A little strange. Kind of embarrassed. But better, I think. Kind of relieved."

We spent the remainder of that session and most of the next going over some of the questions Jim had written down and exploring ways he might get them answered. He didn't feel comfortable going to his mother. "But I have to be in California next week and I've got an aunt there."

"Mother's side or father's?"

"Father's. His only sibling. My Aunt Millie. Maybe I'll give her a call."

Your Dad May Have Seemed Like a Monster, But He Wasn't Really

Settling in for our first session after his return, Jim reached inside his jacket pocket, pulled out what looked like an old snapshot, placed it gently on the table in front of him, and stared at it for a moment before starting to speak. He'd seen his Aunt Millie, had dinner at her house.

"And did she answer any of your questions?"

He chuckled softly. "Oh, yeah," he said, sliding the snapshot closer with one finger. "Yeah, she did."

They'd been sitting around the table having an after-dinner coffee when Jim had casually mentioned that he'd been thinking about his dad lately, realizing he'd never really known him all that well. His aunt's eyes had lit up. "Then she got up, left the room, and came back with all these photo albums and boxes of old letters and stuff—stuff I never even knew she had." He wanted to know about his dad, her beloved older brother? "It was almost like she'd been waiting for me to ask." They'd spent the rest of the night sifting through his aunt's trove of memorabilia and talking. "She talked. I listened." He shook his head. "All this stuff—all this stuff I never knew."

He'd known his father's own father had died when he was six and that he and his aunt had been raised by a stepfather. He hadn't known the stepfather had been a drinker who beat his wife and stepchildren until, at age twelve, his father had put a stop to the beatings by shoving the man against a wall and threatening to kill him if he laid a hand on them again. He'd known this stepfather had died when his dad was fifteen. He hadn't known his dad had quit school then to get a job to help support the family, and that he'd finished high school and put himself through college by working days and taking classes at night. He'd known his dad had built his business from scratch. He hadn't known that, at one point early on, he'd had to start over from scratch after his first business partner ran off with all his savings. He'd known his dad had always managed money wisely. He hadn't known that, when his parents married, his dad had put the money his in-laws had given him toward a down payment on a house into college savings bonds for his future children instead. He'd known his dad as an aloof, unavailable, taciturn man who never showed emotion. He hadn't known that his dad actually had shed tears once—the first time he held his newborn son in his arms.

And the snapshot? A present from his aunt—of his father at age two. He picked it up, held it cupped in one hand. "I'd never seen a picture of him as a baby before." Smiling, he passed it to me. "It's uncanny, really. Even Nora says so. If I didn't know better, I'd think it was me."

Tricky stuff, this business of uncovering long-buried feelings and experiencing the pain of the "father wound." Once we begin this "descent into the ashes," as poet Robert Bly calls it, we're likely, at some point, to find ourselves awash in feelings such as rage and grief. The trick is not to get stuck there. Freeing up these feelings is the first step. The second step is to flush them out, to feel them and let them go, by making peace with our fathers and accepting who they were. Few of our fathers were ideal dads. Many fell far short of the mark. But to see them only as imperfect dads is to fail to see them fully and realistically. The reality is that, given their upbringing, the times in which they were raised, and the very different standard of appropriate fathering that held sway then, most of them were doing the best they could.

This is why I encouraged Jim to learn more about his dad. Were his father still alive, I might have suggested a series of visits or phone calls. Sure, I could have talked these ideas to him—and then kidded myself we were getting somewhere by having him parrot them back to me: "Angry at my dad? Nah, I see now that he was doing the best he could." But it doesn't work that way. Real understanding and forgiveness doesn't come from grasping concepts intellectually. It happens in our hearts, when we're finally able to see and accept our fathers for who they really were—no more and no less than flesh-and-blood human beings.

I handed the snapshot back to Jim. "My aunt told me something else," he said. "She said my grandmother had two miscarriages. My mom had one, too. You don't think that's something Nora and I should be worrying about, do you?"

That wasn't for me to say. But it was for me to help Jim deal with the fears that were surfacing now that his emotions were coming unblocked. I suggested he might want to discuss this question with Nora's doctor.

Jim and I met four times after that. During our next two sessions he remained preoccupied with worries about the baby. Then, gradually, his anxieties gave way first to anticipation, then to excitement—and our sessions came to an end. Basically in sound psychological health, Jim had sought my help in resolving a specific problem. Having resolved that problem, we shook hands and wished each other well. Two months later I received a birth announcement in the mail. He and Nora had had a healthy baby boy. In the lower left corner of the announcement Jim had added a handwritten note: "He looks just like me! Baby, mother, and father doing well."

THE MOTHER WOUND

When I'm helping men excavate long-buried feelings, I deal first with what comes up first. And what usually comes up first is Dad, because Dad issues are more accessible. A man doesn't have to dig very far down to reach them. Most of the time, they're right there, just beneath the surface, waiting to be tapped. You have to dig down through more layers to reach the Mom issues.

When a man has chronic difficulties getting along with male authority figures or maintaining male friendships, it's often a sign that he needs to do some work on the Dad issue. Problems in intimate relationships, on the other hand, often indicate that he needs to look at the Mom issue. I can't count how many single, married, and divorced men I've counseled who came to me seeking help for relationship problems that were inextricably bound up with their unexamined and unresolved feelings about their mothers. One former client wanted help figuring out why he was invariably attracted to women who deprived him of sex and affection. Another wanted to know why he always got involved with women who were overly fragile, clinging, and dependent. Another had finally become concerned about his pattern of bolting from a relationship as soon as it started getting serious. Another was spilling over with anger at what he saw as his partner's selfishness and insensitivity (translation: her refusal to cater and kowtow). And so on. Even when a man's relationship problems are severe and chronic, however, he may have difficulty connecting these problems to his unresolved feelings about his mother because these feelings are buried so deep. Many men, in fact, don't even begin to look at the Mom issue until their relationship problems reach crisis state.

This was true of Bruce. Then an assistant sales director for a publishing house, Bruce first came to see me at age thirty-two after being passed over for promotion to associate sales director for reasons having to do with what his boss described as his "difficulties getting along with male superiors." We worked together for six months, during which time Bruce came to see that his attitude problem was directly linked to his unresolved anger toward his father—a high-ranking telephone company executive who had died ten years earlier and who, like Jim's father, had given little time or attention to his son. Working first with what came up first, Bruce and I focused on resolving these painful feelings, which he was able to do in much the same way Jim did—by learning to accept his father as an imperfect human being and by finally allowing himself to feel and express the pain of never having felt loved by his dad. By the end of those six months Bruce's attitude problem had improved to the point where even his boss remarked on the change, saying that if things looked as good in another six months, he'd reconsider Bruce for promotion.

I didn't hear from Bruce again until five years later, when he called asking for another appointment—this time to discuss a problem he was having with his wife, Janet. Entering my office, he plunked down on the sofa, his whole manner tense and agitated.

"Janet's moved out," he said tersely.

"When?"

"Ten days ago."

Could he tell me why?

Yes and no. There'd been friction ever since she had returned to teaching a year earlier, three years after the birth of their second son. (Their older boy was six.) But he'd chalked it up to mutual exhaustion and the fact that they didn't spend much time together now that she had to be up and out early and he seldom returned home until late. (He had since been promoted to sales director of his publishing house.) She'd become impatient and short-tempered, too. "And our sex life hasn't been all that hot," he said. "She's always 'too tired,' which usually leads to a discussion of how she needs more help around the house. Which she does. I agree. But I don't know what she expects me to do about it. I'm working my butt off, too, and I already help out a lot."

Hearing the anger in his voice, he stopped and took a breath. "So anyway, a few weeks ago, she said she wanted to take the boys and go to stay with her sister for a while. Her sister's divorced, lives on the other side of town. She said she thought we needed to take a break for a while to sort some things out. 'Like what?' I said. 'Well,' she said, 'like how much this marriage means to you and how much you're willing to change to preserve it.' "

And so, telling the boys they were going to visit their Aunt Linda, Janet had taken the kids and left. For the first few days Bruce had been too angry to feel anything except "good riddance." Then the anger passed. "And then, I don't know. It was like I began coming apart." It wasn't a matter of needing Janet to cook and clean for him. Those things he could do for himself. "It's more like—I don't know how to describe it. It used to be that I'd come home after work, and she'd be there. We'd have a glass of wine, and I'd tell her about my day, and she'd laugh or sympathize or get angry for me. And then I could just let go of it. It was a real release. And now I don't have that. We still talk. I call every evening. But it's not the same. It's like when I was a kid. Sometimes I'd come home from school and my mother wouldn't be there, and it would be a shock. It's like that. Only it's day after day, and it's really starting to get to me. I'm starting to snap at people, flub things at work. That's why I called you."

None too soon, either. Our first order of business was to get Bruce venting some of the pent-up emotion he'd relied on Janet to help him process until now. I told him that, beginning that same day, I'd like him to start keeping an emotional response log. Every evening, he was to spend thirty minutes going over the log—just as he used to go over his day with Janet—adding any emotion words that came up as he reviewed that day's entries. I also said his description of feeling like a boy coming home to a motherless house was probably more on-target than he knew—that, last time we'd worked together we'd examined his relationship with his dad but hadn't looked at his relationship with his mother, which might be contributing to his marital problems.

Why Feel Feelings When You've Got a Wife to Do It for You?

When Bruce returned for his second session, he seemed slightly less tense. "At first I felt silly scribbling notes in a notebook twenty times a day," he said. "But I have to admit, I'm learning some things about myself. Yesterday, for example, I almost snapped at my assistant just for mentioning Janet's name. I wouldn't have made that connection if I weren't keeping this log."

"So it's helping."

"Yeah. Surprisingly enough."

Not so surprisingly, I said. Like a lot of men, Bruce was accustomed to relying on his emotionally skilled wife to help him sense, name, and interpret his feelings. When she moved out, taking these skills with her, he was left with no way to get to his emotions and no way to get them out. The purpose of having him keep the log was to show him that he needn't remain in this emotionally helpless state—that, with practice, he could develop these skills himself.

"I suppose," he said with a lack of enthusiasm that didn't surprise me. Showing a man that he can give up his emotional dependence on his wife is one thing. How he feels about giving it up is another. Most men come into marriage with a host of dependency needs that have their roots in a man's early relationship with his mother. Tinkering with the way those needs get played out in a man's marriage inevitably stirs up painful memories of the unfulfilled yearnings that gave rise to these needs—an experience most men would rather avoid.

"So you're saying my missing Janet has something to do with my feelings about my mother?" Bruce asked skeptically. "I don't get the connection."

"That's okay," I said. "Your conscious mind may not get it, but your unconscious does. Just let what I've said percolate awhile and see what comes up."

A dream was what came up. "More of a nightmare, really," he said, settling in for our next session. He dreamed he was in a rowboat on a lake or pond. His mother was a little way off, standing calm and still waist-deep in water, sinking slowly beneath the surface. "I was trying to row over to her, but I could hardly move the oars," he said. "By the time I got to her, she was about a foot beneath the surface. I could see her looking up at me. I reached down, and she reached up. But as I tried to grab her hand, it slipped away, and I realized, 'She's gone.' And then I woke up in a cold sweat." He wiped a hand across his forehead. "I'm sweating right now, just talking about it."

"Keep talking," I said. "In the dream, what did you feel?"

"Panic. Real terror. And fury. I wanted to scream at her, but when I opened my mouth, nothing came out."

"What did you want to scream?"

"I wanted to scream, 'Come back! Don't do this! Don't leave me! You can't just—' " And then suddenly he broke into sobs. I sat quietly until the sobs subsided. "I'm stunned," he said softly, reaching for a tissue and wiping his eyes. "I don't even know where that came from. I haven't cried like that since I was a little boy." He was quiet a moment. "Funny. That's just how it felt, too. I felt just like a frightened little boy, crying for his mommy." He frowned. "But that doesn't make sense. I haven't lost my mother. She never abandoned me or . . ."

"Or what?"

"I don't know. There's something there. But I can't quite get a handle on it."

Boys Will Be Boys, Whether They Want to or Not

I wasn't surprised by the content and timing of Bruce's dream. Unpleasant as it may have been, I explained, the dream had been a gift: a freeing up of the deeply stored memory and pain of traumas experienced so early in life that dreams are often the only access to them. He'd said that, while crying, he'd felt like a frightened little boy. In fact, the pain and fury he'd re-experienced in his dream dated back much farther.

A baby is born. Helpless, dependent, it exists for the first months of life in a state of undifferentiated oneness with its primary nurturer—which, in our society, is still almost always the mother. The baby has no awareness of its gender. But the mother does. And as sociologist Nancy Chodorow argues in her seminal book, *The Reproduction of Mothering: Psychoanalysis and the Sociology of Gender*, from the moment of the baby's birth, the mother's relationship with her baby is unconsciously influenced by that awareness. If the baby is a girl, the mother experiences a sense of "same" that fosters and prolongs the state of oneness between mother and child. The mother feels and subtly communicates to the baby that the baby is not only like her but is in some sense an extension of her. If the baby is a boy, on the other hand, she experiences a sense of "different" that disrupts this state of oneness. She feels and subtly communicates that the baby is "separate" and "other." She also recognizes her baby as "male," which causes her to interact with him and shape him in ways that have less to do with his needs and personality than with the assumptions about maleness she has absorbed from her culture—for example, that boys are more independent.

No wonder males take less naturally to nurturing, Chodorow argues. If a mother's "sense of oneness and continuity" with her female infant "is stronger and lasts longer" than it does with a son, it follows that girls "emerge from this period with a basis for 'empathy' built into their primary definition of self. . . ." Boys, in contrast, "are more likely . . . to have had to curtail their primary love and sense of empathic tie with their mother. . . . A boy has been . . . required to engage, in a more emphatic individuation and a more defensive firming of . . . ego boundaries. . . ."

Note Chodorow's wording: "had to curtail"; "required to engage." No boy baby looks down at himself and thinks, "A penis! That means I'm a boy. I better start pushing away from Mom." He doesn't choose to leave this tranquil state of one-ness with his mother. He's pushed out of it—a highly stressful experience that psychologist William Pollack, of Harvard Medical School and McLean Hospital, calls the "traumatic abrogation of the holding environment." The baby's stress and shock might be lessened if his father were there to catch him as he falls out of this cradle of oneness with Mom. But, until recently, dads didn't do that. End result: Denied nurturance by his mother and his father, the boy baby finds himself in the untenable position of hungering for the closeness and attachment he once knew while also sensing that these needs are wrong. The only way out of this painful predicament is to make these needs go away. So he drives them underground, only to have them resurface years later in the form of unconscious dependency on his wife.

Like many men, Bruce had some trouble accepting that this early forced separation from his mother had had such a deep and lasting effect on him. "But it could have, I guess," he said. "And it would explain a lot, wouldn't it? I mean, the dream and everything."

We spent our next session going over his log, which he was still keeping and which seemed to be helping. He was feeling much calmer, he said. "I still worry about what's going to happen with me and Janet. I want us to work things out. But I don't feel so desperate anymore. I don't feel like I'm going to die without her, which I did at first."

When he arrived for his next session, his agitation level had again risen. This time, however, the agitation was eager, not desperate. He and Janet had had a long talk the night before. "She says I'm easier to talk to now, that I listen better," he said. "She thinks maybe we could actually sit down and try to work out some of our differences, and she suggested coming in for a joint session with you. I told her that sounded good to me but that I'd have to ask you."

I was glad he and Janet were talking, I said. And, yes, I do counsel couples. But I really couldn't counsel the two of them because my relationship with Bruce would probably bias me in his favor. "What I could do, however," I said, "is have both of you come in for a few consultation sessions. Then, if it seems you'd benefit from couples therapy, I can refer you to someone else."

"How Often Do I Have to Ask You?" (How Often Has Your Wife Asked That?)

A pleasantly attractive woman, Janet impressed me during our first joint session as a woman who was essentially at peace with herself. It also seemed obvious that, whatever the problems troubling their marriage, she and Bruce still loved each other very much.

I began by filling her in on the work Bruce and I had been doing. She listened intently, frowning when I got to the part about a man's early relationship with his mother. "I have two reactions to that," she said. "On the one hand I think, 'That sounds right.' I've always felt that the problems we're having have something to do with Bruce's relationship with his mother. She's a lovely woman—don't get me wrong. But the way he walls me out when I try to talk to him, and this attitude he has that he shouldn't have to help with the house and kids—I've said to him, 'You know, you're not treating me like a wife. You're treating me like I'm your mom.' "

"And your other reaction?"

"Well, as you know, I'm a mother of sons. And the mother in me wasn't buying any of it. You know, me push my sons away? But who knows? Maybe I did."

Janet had already raised what I knew was one of their main points of contention—her feeling, unshared by Bruce, that he wasn't carrying his weight around the house. "Let's talk more about that," I said. "I'd like you to pick an example of how this causes problems between you, and then I'd like you each to tell me your side."

They settled on Saturday house cleaning, and as they spoke, I found myself listening to a variation on a theme of marital miscommunication that I've heard countless times before. She says, "You know, the house really needs cleaning this Saturday." He says, "Okay." She thinks she has just asked for and received a promise of help. He thinks he's simply acknowledging her statement of fact. Saturday arrives. She's in the kitchen, scrubbing counters. He's in the living room, watching the game. Containing annoyance, she calls out to him, "Honey, would you mind stripping the beds?" He hears a question, at most a suggestion he feels free to postpone acting upon—"In a minute"—if not completely ignore. Half an hour later she sees that the beds haven't been stripped. Furious, she begins yanking the sheets off herself. "Thanks for the help," she spits as she passes through the living room with an armload of dirty linen. Huh? What's she so ticked off about? "I asked you to strip the beds half an hour ago!" No she didn't. She asked if he'd *mind* stripping them. And he'd said he'd do it. He just hadn't done it yet.

"I'm not saying Bruce is an innocent victim here," I told Janet. "I'm saying that as long as there's room for him to misinterpret your requests for help, we can't know how much of the problem is simple miscommunication and how much is genuine unwillingness to do his share."

She mulled that over. "Okay. I can accept that. So what do I do?"

"I'd like you to write out a list of exactly which tasks you want Bruce to take off your hands. We'll go over it the next time we meet."

"Great!" said Janet enthusiastically.

"Oh, great," Bruce groaned.

Settling in for our second session, Janet looked like a woman eager to get down to business. Bruce looked like a man about to be sentenced.

"Okay," she began. "I started making a list. But it just got longer and longer. And I realized, 'This is ridiculous.' Let's say I do make a list. And let's say I accidentally leave something out. Then it's my fault if Bruce doesn't do it because I forgot to write it down. I'm still responsible. And I'm tired of always being responsible. I want him to share the responsibility." She turned to her husband. "Can you understand that?" she asked gently. "I'm tired, honey. I can't do it anymore. I need help."

She turned back to me. "So I've given this a lot of thought. And I realized that the worst time for me is mornings. There's Bruce taking a leisurely shower. And there I am rushing around like a madwoman, trying to get the kids up and dressed and fed and into the car and dropped off at school and at day care in time to make it to my school before first period. So I've decided that what I want—what I need, really—is for Bruce to take over the morning shift with the kids. Getting them up, dressed, fed, packing their lunches, dropping them off—everything. And that includes checking the day before to make sure there's bread to make sandwiches and running a load of laundry if they're out of clean underwear. I don't even want to think about it. I want him to do it all."

Bruce exploded. "You can't be serious!"

"Oh, but I am," Janet said calmly.

"That's ridiculous! How the hell am I supposed to do all that when I'm already working my butt off."

"I do it."

"That's different. It's—" He stopped himself.

"It's what?" Janet asked, looking daggers at him.

"Nothing."

"No. Say it. It's what? It's my *job*?"

"Okay, let's slow it down," I said. "That's not going to get us anywhere. Janet, you've made a clear proposal. Bruce, not only do you find that proposal unacceptable, but it makes you furious."

"You can say that again!"

"Okay. Bruce, I think the next step is for you and I to go back into individual sessions for a while to see if we can figure out what it is about Janet's proposal that you find so unreasonable. Later, depending how that goes, I may want to see the two of you again."

So We're Not Being Fair. Let's Be Honest, Guys. The Truth Is, We Don't Care!

Bruce arrived for our next session loaded for bear.

"All right, let's hear it," I said.

Out it came: "Where the hell does she get off? Yeah, sure, she works, too. But I'm the one who brings in most of the money. And I work damn hard to do it. And it's not like I don't do anything around the house. I help out a lot—more than most men do. What she's asking is impossible. I'd have to totally reorganize my schedule. Take over the morning shift—give me a fucking break."

"Got everything off your chest?" I asked.

"No. Yeah. I guess so."

"Good. First. You're right. You do work hard. You do help around the house more than a lot of men do. And you do deserve credit for that. So I can see your side. What I want to know now is whether you can see Janet's side."

He thought for a moment. "No. I can't."

"Would you be willing to try an experiment that might help you see her side?"

He looked at me sullenly. "What kind of experiment?"

"Imagine Janet's been sitting there listening," I said, pointing to the chair she had occupied during our last session. "I'd like you to sit in her chair and pretend you're her. Then I want to hear you respond as you think she would."

He eyed me dubiously. "I don't know," he said, rising slowly from his chair. "Something tells me this is going to feel stupid. But if you think it'll help." He sat down in Janet's chair.

"Okay, you're Janet. I want her response to what you said."

"I'm Janet. Right. Okay, let's see. Hmmm." A long silence followed. Then came a grunt, followed by a soft, "Damn."

"What?"

He peered up at me resentfully. "Okay, okay. This isn't easy to admit. But I was just thinking she's got a point. Yeah, I earn most of the money. But she puts in just about as many hours as I do. And, yeah, I help out. But it's true. Compared to her, I do get off light—real light." He grimaced. "And yet, even as I say that, some other part of me feels like I shouldn't have to do as much as she does. I mean, I love her and I want her to be happy. But it's like, not if it means more work for me." He frowned. "I don't know. Maybe I'm just selfish."

"Maybe, maybe not. We can look at that in our next session. In the meantime, keep up with your log. I'd also like you to spend an evening looking through old family photographs, the way I had you do when we were working on your feelings about your father. Jot down any thoughts that come up as you look through them. Maybe it'll jog something loose."

Bruce arrived for our next session looking haggard. He'd begun looking through his photo albums the previous weekend and had been stopped by a snapshot of himself in his Little League uniform. "I hadn't thought about Little League in a long time," he said. "I was never a very good player, and I always blamed my father for that. I remember envying this other kid, Danny, who was really good. It seemed like every time I went to his house, he and his dad were out in the yard hitting the ball around. My dad never did that. I don't think he ever came to any of the games, either. My mom came, which always embarrassed me. But not my dad. He was always too busy working.'' He sighed. "So I started thinking about that. And it made me feel really down. I had a hard time falling asleep that night. I just lay there staring at the ceiling, and then I started crying again. It was like when I told you about the dream about my mother, except the tears felt different this time. Not so angry. Just . . . sad.''

Two days later he called his mother in Florida to tell her he'd be down her way on business in a few weeks. Before hanging up, he asked if she recalled whether his father had ever come to any of his Little League games. She'd have to think, she said. It was so long ago. Why did he ask? "No reason,'' he said. "Just wondering.'' He spoke to Janet a couple of times, too. She heard the weariness in his voice and asked if he was all right. Not really, he said. But he had a sense that whatever he was going through was something he had to go through. He wasn't sure why.

Okay, We're Selfish. That's Established. The Interesting Question Is, "Why?"

Bruce was right. His latest crying episode and the mini-depression it had triggered were things he had to go through. When he had cried while telling me his dream about his mother, he'd dealt with the long-buried pain and anger of having been forced to separate from her in infancy—just as he'd dealt with the pain and anger of feeling unloved by his father when we'd worked together five years before. This time he was finally experiencing and expressing the grief that attends the mourning of these early losses.

"Great,'' Bruce said wearily. "But why now? I thought the issue was whether I'm selfish.''

"It is.'' Being pushed out by his mother, denied closeness with his father—these were traumatic losses, I said. Psychologist William Pollock calls them "normative developmental traumas"—normative as in normal, meaning they're considered such an accepted part of a boy's development that they're not even recognized as traumas. But if an experience is considered normal, there's no reason to mourn it. And if men don't mourn these traumas, they don't get over them. That's how people recover from traumas—by mourning them. If they don't mourn, they don't heal. The trauma stays with them.

"But what does that have to do with my being selfish?"

"I'm coming to that. A psychiatrist named Ivan Boszormenyi-Nagy has proposed that, as we grow, we each develop a personal code of ethics that governs both how we treat others and how we expect them to treat us. He further proposed that when early traumatic losses don't get resolved, they can give rise to a skewed sense of relational ethics that he calls 'destructive entitlement'—an unconscious belief that it's okay to exploit people and take more than we give to make up for what we didn't get in childhood."

"I think I see what you're getting at. So you're saying that when I cried the other night, I was finally beginning to mourn these traumas."

"Right."

"And that it's because I never mourned them before that I've felt entitled to take advantage of Janet."

"Not consciously. I'm not suggesting that when you wake up in the morning you say to yourself, 'I think I'll exploit my wife today because I had a lousy childhood.' Remember, this is all unconscious. But think about it. These unresolved losses affect just about all adult men. And how many men do you know who don't feel entitled to this kind of unfair relationship with their wife?"

"Yeah, well, why do women put up with it? It takes two to tango."

"It goes back to their more highly developed emotional skills and greater need for connection. It's just easier for them to empathize with what someone else is feeling, and they're more inclined to adapt to another person's needs for the sake of preserving the relationship. But, usually, that's true only to a point. They'll give and give. But eventually, if they feel the kindness isn't being reciprocated, they'll put a stop to it—which can be a shock to a husband, who may have had no idea the change was coming."

Bruce snorted. "Yeah. Tell me about it."

By our next session Bruce's mini-depression had begun lifting. He'd spent another evening going through his old photo albums. "It was hard, looking at those pictures and thinking about everything we've been talking about," he said. "I teared up a couple of times. But it passed. And this time I didn't feel bad afterward. It was more of a peaceful feeling, like I was finishing something." During our third session he began reconsidering Janet's proposal and wondering aloud what kind of sacrifices it would entail. He'd have to get up earlier, and he'd have to give up breakfast meetings. "But I suppose I could live with that," he said. He thought for a while. "You know, I think I'm ready to give this another try. I'd like to have Janet come in so we can talk about how we'd work this out."

Three days later Janet and Bruce sat in my office, discussing the details of her proposal. Of course, he'd need some coaching for a while, Bruce said gruffly—until he got the hang of things.

"Of course," said Janet. "But you wait, honey. I'll bet you won't need nearly as much coaching as you think. A lot of it is just planning and organizing." She smiled lovingly at her husband. "You really mean it? You're willing to give it a try?"

Bruce nodded. "Yeah. I've been doing a lot of thinking, looking at some things I never looked at before. And I see now that I haven't been fair with you. What you said about me treating you like my mother—well, you're right. I couldn't admit it before, but some of the stuff I went through when I was growing up wasn't so hot. And I think I've been expecting you to make up for that. I don't have it all sorted out yet. But I see now that I wasn't being fair."

Janet's eyes glistened with tears. "You know," she said, "in all the years we've been married, I think that's the most feeling you've ever shared with me. And you know what that makes me realize?'' She wiped away a tear. ''It makes me realize how lonely I've been. I can't help thinking things wouldn't have gotten to the point where I felt I had to leave if we'd been able to talk like this. But you always had this wall up. No matter how I tried, I couldn't get past that wall. So, eventually . . .'' She smiled sadly. ''I just stopped trying.''

I Hear You Knocking, But You Can't Come In

That same weekend Janet and the kids moved back home, she and Bruce having agreed to postpone inaugurating the new morning regimen until after his trip to Florida. While there, he spent a day and a half visiting his mother—first sorting out her financial affairs, which she entrusted to no one but him, then talking. ''Just . . . talking,'' he told me, sounding surprised.

''Is that unusual?''

''It is for us. I mean, we talk. But we don't *talk*, you know? I hadn't even told her that Janet and I were having problems. But this time . . . I don't know if it was what Janet said about my not letting her in or what. But this time was different.''

He'd been sitting in the kitchen reading a newspaper while his mother cooked breakfast when she brought up his question about his dad attending his Little League games. ''What started you thinking about that?'' she asked. His first impulse, deeply ingrained through long years of habit, had been to deflect her inquiry with a terse, ''Nothing. It's not important.'' Instead, feeling as if he were taking a flying leap off a sheer cliff, he'd taken a deep breath and said, ''Well, Mom, I've been seeing this psychologist.'' He wasn't sure why that had been such a scary thing to do. ''But it was,'' he said. ''It was like I expected her to burst into tears or try to throw her arms around me or something.''

"And did she?"

"No. She didn't say anything at first. She just finished cooking breakfast, brought the plates to the table, sat down, and looked at me. You know that mushy look moms can get. And then she said, 'To answer your question, no, he didn't.' And then she said, 'It wasn't easy for you as a child. I know that. I'm glad you've found someone you feel you can talk to about it.' And then she was quiet for a moment. And then she said, 'Is there anything else you'd like to ask?' "

"And then?"

"And then we talked."

What could be more simple? It seemed so easy once he'd done it that he wondered why he'd never confided in his mother before. "I mean, I love her. She's a wonderful person. But I've always felt like I had to keep this distance. It's so weird. What was I afraid of?"

Two things, I suggested. Being abandoned—as he had been in infancy and as he'd re-experienced in his dream, when he'd felt fury and terror as his mother disappeared under the water. And being swallowed up. The first would hurt, I said. "But you've already been through that one. So, on another level, it would also feel familiar. It's the second one you're really afraid of."

"Yeah, it's true. It's like this fear of being suffocated. But I don't get it. My mother isn't the suffocating type. And what about all that stuff about my unfulfilled needs for closeness and my dependency on Janet? I thought I *wanted* closeness."

"You do. But you also fear it." I reminded Bruce of our earlier discussion of Chodorow's theory about boys being "required to engage in a more defensive firming of ego boundaries." The boy baby forms this first sense of himself as separate from his mother just as he's forming his first sense of himself as a male. So the two get linked. He doesn't realize he's being forced out of that early state of oneness with his mother. So far as he knows, he's doing this to himself. It all gets muddled into his sense of who he is. As Chodorow writes, "Masculine personality, then, comes to be defined more in terms of denial of relation and connection. . . ." Or, as she sums it up, "The basic masculine sense of self is separate."

Much as men desire intimacy, in other words, they also experience it as threatening. They want closeness. But if someone gets too close they freak: It feels too much like they're being sucked back into the original state of oneness with Mom that they had to give up in exchange for their male identity. On an unconscious level, many men feel they have to choose: intimacy or identity. And if that's the choice, they'd rather be alone.

That's not the choice, of course. In reality a man doesn't have to choose. But he thinks he does. So, to protect himself from too much intimacy, he adopts a stance that William Pollack calls "defensive autonomy"—allowing his partner to come only so close. If she tries to come closer, he pulls back. He pops a brew and zones out in front of the TV. He buries himself in the newspaper or in his work. He turns silent and sullen. He picks a fight. He falls asleep. Anything to re-establish distance—which is hurtful and frustrating to his partner, whose need and tolerance for intimacy is much greater than his.

"The wall Janet was complaining about," said Bruce.

"Exactly. And the kicker is that the more out-of-touch a man is with his dependency needs, the more he's going to fear intimacy and the more he's going to distance. He can't let anyone get even moderately close for fear that if he does, these needs will rise up and overwhelm him. He doesn't realize that's what he's afraid of, of course. If he did, he'd be less fearful. It's our unconscious fears that hold power over us. As soon as we bring them up to consciousness, they lose strength. So, you see, you're ahead of the game, because at least you know what you're struggling with."

"Struggling. That's the word, all right."

I laughed. "Speaking of struggles, how's the new morning regimen working out?"

He frowned. "It's rough—rougher than I expected. It's a lot of work—a *lot* of work. Janet says it gets easier with practice, but I don't know. Last night I really snapped at her about something. I don't even remember what. And I know it's because I'm feeling under so much pressure—like, what if I can't hack this? What if I blow it?"

"Did you tell her that?"

"Not right away. It took me a while to realize that's what was going on. And even then, part of me wanted to stay mad. It was like I didn't want to admit that I was—well, that I was feeling scared is what it comes down to."

"And that's what you told her?"

"Finally, yeah."

"And how did that feel?"

He laughed. "Scary. And good. It really meant a lot to her. She said, 'I know you're scared, honey. So am I.' I hadn't thought about that. It never occurred to me that she might be feeling the pressure, too. That was a relief. So then we talked, and she was really supportive. She said I shouldn't worry so much about trying to do everything perfectly because there's no such thing as perfect when it comes to raising kids. That helped. I think it made me feel less judged. And then she told me how much she appreciated what I was going through and how much it meant to her that I was willing to do it. She said it made her feel a lot closer to me—like we were more of a team. And that felt good. It made me feel like we were really in this together. I felt a lot better after that."

I was impressed, and said so. Bruce had come a long way—not only in resolving the long-buried hurts of his early upbringing and overcoming his unconscious dependency on Janet and his sense of entitled exemption from household duties, but also in overcoming the sense of defensive autonomy that had caused him to hold both his mother and Janet at an emotional arm's length. It takes courage for a man to let down his wall and allow his partner in close enough to see him as a human being capable of feeling fear. It spoke well of Bruce that he'd summoned the courage to do that—and well of Janet that she had responded by affirming how much she loved and respected him for it.

Bruce was a fortunate man. In exchange for taking his wife into his confidence she had offered him two valuable insights—that he was holding himself to an unrealistic standard of perfection, and that his fears of being judged according to this standard were unfounded. Many men do hold themselves to unrealistic standards—at work, at home, and in every other aspect of their lives. Like Bruce, many men are also loath to admit to the sense of inadequacy they feel when they measure themselves against these standards. So, instead, they keep these feelings to themselves, never realizing that these standards are unachievable. In the next chapter we'll take a closer look at some of the manhood ideals that rule men's lives and examine the price men pay for trying to live up to them.

CHAPTER SIX

Achieving Manhood: "The Big Impossible"

Back in the fifties, few husbands or wives would have thought to question a man's sense of entitled exemption from household and child-care duties. When men worked outside the home and women in it, these and other old-style male attitudes still satisfied the needs and expectations of both partners and contributed to the smooth functioning of a marriage. But that was before the social upheavals of the sixties and seventies led to the crisis in American manhood that now has men re-examining and reconstructing the traditional masculine code.

The purpose of this book is to help men figure out which parts of the old code to keep and which to replace. Thus far we've examined how the powerful early life influences of gender-role socialization and normative developmental traumas reinforced men's adherence to this code, the attitudes and behaviors that characterize that adherence, how these attitudes and behaviors work for and against men, and how men can change some of these patterns if they choose. It's time, now, to examine a third and even more powerful influence: the over-arching, culture-spanning beliefs about manhood from which our society draws the precepts that govern how males are socialized.

MANHOOD: UNENDING QUEST, UNATTAINABLE GOAL

In his 1990 book, *Manhood in the Making*, anthropologist David Gilmore, of the City University of New York, notes that nearly all cultures uphold sex-differentiated standards against which masculinity and femininity are assessed. In cultures ranging from hunter-gatherer to high-tech, men and women are expected to observe and conform to these standards. Male or female, in other words, we all get judged—but we get judged differently.

In most cultures, Gilmore notes, females are recognized as having attained irrevocable womanhood at the onset of menstruation. Once their bodies declare them capable of conceiving a child, their culture declares them women—simple as that. Of course, there usually exist other, often stringent standards of comportment to which females must also adhere—some of which approach or cross over into slavery. So no one's suggesting females have it easy. It is true, however, that females seldom have cause to doubt their essential womanhood and femininity—because in most cultures these are never in question. As Gilmore notes, females worldwide are expected to enhance their femininity through the use of "body ornament . . . or other essentially cosmetic behaviors." But womanhood itself is considered a given.

Not so manhood. Across cultures, writes Gilmore, "there is a constantly recurring notion that real manhood is different from simple anatomical maleness"—that it's not a natural condition that comes about through maturation but rather a precarious state that boys must win against powerful odds, "a critical threshold that boys must pass through testing. . . ." Unlike womanhood, in other words, manhood is viewed not as a given but as something that must be achieved through sometimes traumatic tests of bravery, endurance, strength, and skill. A "restricted status," the attainment of manhood, writes

Gilmore, "is doubtful," resting on demonstrated ability to meet "rigid codes of decisive action in many spheres of life: as husband, father, lover, provider, warrior."

Were we to reduce these codes to their fundamentals, we would be left, notes Gilmore, with three basic manhood requirements: ability to (1) impregnate women, (2) protect dependents, and (3) provide for kith and kin. It is no accident, then, that "manhood ideologies always include a criterion of selfless generosity, even to the point of sacrifice," writes Gilmore. "Again and again we find that 'real' men are those who give more than they take; they serve others. Real men are generous, even to a fault."

Nor, once attained, is a male's membership in the fraternity of real men ever assured—for no matter how many times he has proved his strength, skill, courage, and generosity, there are always more tests to pass. And, as Gilmore notes, "there are always those who fail." And with failure comes expulsion and ridicule. "These are the negative examples," writes Gilmore, the "men-who-are-no-men, held up scornfully to inspire conformity to the glorious ideal." Manhood ideologies "force men to shape up," he writes, "on penalty of being robbed of their identity, a threat apparently worse than death."

Manhood. The "Big Impossible," Gilmore tells us the Fox Tribe of Iowa calls it—which is, of course, exactly what it is. In cultures around the world, men's lives are characterized by this anxious uncertainty about their standing in a fraternity from which exile means shame and humiliation—this desperate struggle to retain a tenuous grasp on a status they can never fully claim.

But Our Ideas about Manhood Are Changing Now . . . Aren't They?

Gilmore notes that these "manhood codes" are most glorified and strictly enforced in societies in which harsh environment and meager resources make survival most difficult—and compliance to these codes most crucial. No surprise there. When I mention this fact in lectures or workshops, men usually nod sagely. Then, as they're about to drift off in imaginings of how vastly different their lives would be had they been born into one of these societies, I like to read them a brief quotation and invite them to identify its source. The quotation: "Nobody was born a man; you earned manhood provided you were good enough, bold enough." Taken out of context, the quote has the ring of a pronouncement made by a chief or warrior in some tribal culture. In fact the words are Norman Mailer's, taken from *Armies of the Night*, his 1968 book about the anti-Vietnam War movement's march on the Pentagon. They're an American male's succinct and accurate description of the "manhood code" with which he and most men were raised.

The results of my study indicate that this code seems to be changing in the wake of the social upheavals of the sixties and seventies, but the unanswered question is how much and how quickly? The fact that men now seem to be re-examining traditional male norms doesn't mean these norms don't still hold power over them. It's one thing for men to question or even reject these norms in the privacy of their own thoughts but quite another to actually behave in ways that violate these norms and risk the shame of being judged unmanly by other men.

To illustrate this point, I often ask men who attend my lectures and workshops to listen as I read off a list of norm-violating behaviors and ask themselves whether they'd be comfortable engaging in them. These behaviors include:

1. Taking up sewing or needlecraft as a hobby.

2. Crying in a public place other than a darkened movie theater.

3. Admitting to a male co-worker that they're worried about an upcoming job-performance review.

4. Passing up a chance to have a guaranteed-safe, guaranteed-secret one-night stand with a sexy woman out of loyalty to their long-term partner.

5. Confessing to their partner that they sometimes doubt their skills as a lover.

6. Telling their boss they can't work late to help meet an emergency deadline because they've promised their daughter they'd attend her dance recital that evening.

7. Getting roped into going out for a budget-breaking restaurant meal with their partner and another couple who insisted on treating last time and not insisting on picking up the check.

8. Getting lost while driving somewhere with their partner and being the first to say, "We're lost. I think we better ask for directions."

9. Walking away after being taunted or shoved by another man.

10. Telling a man that they think another man is good-looking.

This list usually takes a long time to read because I have to pause after reading each item and wait for the laughter to subside. "I take the laughter to mean that most of you can't quite see yourselves engaging in these behaviors," I'll say once I've finished, which usually brings more laughter. I'll then ask the men to think back to occasions when they could have behaved in these or other norm-violating ways and recall whether they even considered doing so. Glancing around, I'll usually see some men nodding and others shaking their heads. "For those of you who shook your heads," I'll say, "my question is, why didn't you consider it? And, for those of you who nodded, my question is, if you did consider it, why didn't you do it?" These questions are invariably met with silence, whereupon I offer what I believe to be the answers. "I suspect that the rea-

son some of you didn't even consider engaging in these behaviors is because it never occurred to you that these options
were available to you. And I suspect that the reason others of
you did consider it but didn't act on the thought is because
you didn't want to risk appearing unmanly. So, you see, either
way, these traditional norms win because we're still adhering
to them."

The truth is that most men don't realize how much their
lives are ruled by these norms. And until they become aware
of it they can't help but continue to live in accordance with a
code of behavior that, in many ways, no longer serves their
best interests. The only way men can break this pattern is by
learning to pause before speaking, acting, or deciding and ask
themselves to which they're being loyal—to this traditional
code of masculine behavior or to their own personal needs
and beliefs. A man doesn't always have to choose between one
or the other, but he often does. And when he does, he often
runs into trouble, because he's so conditioned to adhere to
these norms that he usually places loyalty to them above loyalty
to himself.

Men Can't Climb Out of the Box They're in Until They Realize They're in It

After reading off this list of norm-violating behaviors in workshops, I'll then invite participants to share their thoughts on
how traditional male norms influence their lives. The discussion that ensued during one recent workshop was fairly
typical.

"What you said about walking away when another man
taunts or shoves you," said one man. "My gut reaction was,
'No way in hell.' I'm not proud of that, but that's the truth.
It was just too drilled into me as a kid that you didn't ever

back down from a fight. But I don't know if that's true of all men, or whether that was just the neighborhood I grew up in.''

"What kind of neighborhood was that?'' I asked.

"Working-class Irish. My family was immigrant Italian, and I took a lot of heat for that. When I was in grammar school, two or three kids would gang up and follow me home, calling me names and shoving me around, and I'd either have to fight them and get my ass kicked, or ignore them and be humiliated.''

"What did you do?''

"I fought them. There wasn't any choice, really. The first time it happened I tried to ignore them. But when I got to school the next day, even my buddies wouldn't talk to me because 'nobody wants to talk to a sissy'—I remember one of my friends actually said that to me. So after that I started fighting, because it was either that or be ostracized, which was a lot worse than taking a punch in the nose. I got to be a pretty good fighter after a while, and after that they started leaving me alone. So, yeah, I fought. But only because I had to—that's the thing. It was this knowing that you had to—that's the part that sucked.''

Another participant recalled having to learn to fight, too, but in a different way. "I grew up in an upper-middle-class neighborhood and attended very academically oriented schools where kids didn't do a lot of physical fighting,'' he said. "It happened, but that wasn't how you proved yourself. You were supposed to be good at sports, but that was more part of the whole achievement thing. There was a lot of emphasis on that in my school: who made the dean's list, who made team captain, who made president of the student body—none of which I ever did, by the way. But we fought, too. We just didn't do it with fists. With us it was more verbal fighting. We beat up on each other with words. You were always trying to be faster, funnier, and more sarcastic than the next guy. And there was a lot of challenging each other to see who had the guts to do stuff that was going to get you in trouble, like wise off to a teacher or pull off some prank. And no matter how much you wanted to you didn't ever back down from a dare. It was better to get caught and suspended—which I was, a number of times—because if you chickened out you were mud. I still have a lot of that in me. I still have trouble backing down from a dare."

Another young man recognized this trait in himself. "Last summer my girlfriend and I went to the beach with this other couple," he said. "The ocean was pretty rough—too rough for me. I was going to stay out of the water, but then the other guy, Hank, said, 'Hey, how about we do some body surfing?' That was the last thing I wanted to do, but I couldn't say that because I didn't want to look like a wimp, so instead I went in. So we were in the water something like five minutes when this huge wave came along and slammed me good. It just threw me around and then flung me up on the beach. I came up coughing water, all scraped up along my left side. Hank and the two women come rushing over, and they're going, 'Are you all right?' And I'm going, 'Yeah, yeah, sure, I'm fine,' when the truth was I hurt like hell and I was so scared I thought I was going to puke."

Other men spoke of the pressure they feel to always appear competent and in charge—especially in the eyes of members of the opposite sex. A Hispanic man recalled the way his early social life suffered because of his lack of sexual sophistication. "I'd walk a girl home after a date," he said, "and we'd be standing there talking, and I'd be thinking, 'Kiss her. You're supposed to kiss her.' And it'd be obvious she was waiting for me to kiss her, but I couldn't do it. Or I'd make the mistake of asking permission to kiss her. Most of the girls I took out wouldn't go out with me a second time, and I'm sure it's because they lost respect for me when I didn't, you know, take charge of the situation."

Another participant talked about what he called "this responsibility I feel to always make everything right—even things outside my control." He told, for example, of the time he and his wife found themselves stranded at the airport late at night after returning from a vacation. "There were no taxis anywhere," he said. "I finally called a car service, but the waiting was hell. My wife was fuming—like it was my fault we were stranded. And the crazy thing is I bought into it. I felt like I'd fucked up."

Others spoke of the strain of trying to live up to the traditional male norm of being the good provider—which has become increasingly difficult to do now that women are also working. "That's a big point of contention in our house," said another man. "I'm an architect, and, as some of you probably know, most architects don't make a lot of money. My wife's in corporate law. She just got made partner—nice raise, big bonus and everything. So now she's got this bee in her bonnet about wanting to buy a bigger house, and I keep saying, 'No, we can't afford it.' Actually, we can now that she's pulling down the bucks. But the idea of buying a new house on her salary just rubs me the wrong way. Maybe I'm being old-fashioned—she keeps saying I am—but my feeling is that *I* should be the one who puts the roof over my family's head, and if we can't buy a new house on the money I bring in, we don't buy it at all."

Still others admitted to a deep unwillingness to violate the traditional prohibition against showing emotion. An African-American man told, for example, of how he struggled to control his pain and grief when his wife left him four years before. "No warning, no nothing," he said. "I came home from work one Friday and found a note on the kitchen table. She'd been having an affair with another man. She'd tried to tell me, but she couldn't. They'd decided to move away together. I should initiate divorce proceedings. She'd write and tell me where to send the papers. I could keep the house and the savings. She didn't want anything. She was sorry. She didn't mean for it to happen. I should try to forget her. Good-bye."

"How long were you married?" I asked.

"Fifteen years."

"And you didn't cry?"

"I did later, after I got myself into therapy. But not at first, no. Not for a long time, actually. At first, after reading the note, I was too numb to do anything. Then, around midnight I guess it was, I called my sister and said, 'Joan's left.' She said, 'What do you mean, she's left?' I said, 'She's left. She's gone.' And she said, 'I'll be right there.' She stayed with me for a week, and she kept a pretty close eye on me for the next few months, until she was sure I was going to be okay—which I wasn't sure of either, at first. It was the worst pain I've ever experienced. Ever. I felt like someone had hacked out my guts with an ax. But I never cried. I remember there were times when my sister and I would be sitting together on my couch, watching TV or something, and I'd feel my throat start to tighten and my eyes start to burn, and I'd push it all back down. I just couldn't let it out because I was ashamed to let my sister see me in tears—and I guess because I was afraid that if I did start crying, I might never stop. I wouldn't do that now. And, looking back, I'm sorry I did it then. Because it would have really helped to just let it out. It would have been a great relief to just give in to the grief and let my sister comfort me.''

MEN'S SECRET SHAME

These stories and countless others men have shared with me in workshops and counseling sessions illustrate what I consider to be four basic points about the nature of the quest for manhood. The first is that this quest is never-ending. The stories recounted here testify to that. All are stories of how men have responded at various times in their lives when they felt their manhood was being tested in one way or another—and all confirm the fact that these tests never cease.

Nor do men ever stop watching for and worrying about them. That's the second point. Men's grasp on this achieved state called manhood is so tenuous that many men feel they can't afford to fail so much as a single test. A man may become more confident with age that certain tests won't come his way again. If he has already fathered children or achieved financial success, for example, he may no longer worry about having to prove his manhood in these ways. But he'll continue to worry about having to prove it in other ways out of fear that if he fails to do so his past successes will be canceled out and his manhood will be revoked.

The reason men worry so much about failing these tests, of course, is because they know from experience that they very often do. That's point number three. Whether or not he admits it, there's not a man alive who hasn't flunked his share of these manhood tests and experienced the shame of being judged, and judging himself, unmanly.

That's the punishment for failing to meet these male norms—shame. And, as we touched upon earlier, men's aversion to shame is so intense that most men will do just about anything to avoid it. That's point number four—that it's men's fear of the shame attached to violating these norms that reinforces their power and keeps men complying with them.

One of the main ways in which men's shame-phobia works to reinforce these norms is by keeping men silent and secretive about their own failures to meet them. The result is that men have no way of knowing that other men are also having trouble living up to them. If they knew that they might be less inclined to blame themselves for their failures and more inclined to question these norms. But because they don't know that they do blame themselves. They heap on their own heads the shame they're convinced others would heap upon them if their failures were ever revealed.

One tool I use in workshops to help men break through this wall of silence is a variation on something called the Top Secret Exercise, which was developed by a psychiatrist named Irving Yalom as a way of getting at some of these secrets men usually don't talk about. Participants are given index cards and asked to review their own list of failures and write down the one they're most secretly ashamed of—the one they'd be least willing to share with the group. I then collect the cards and read the secrets aloud, asking the men to hold their comments and reactions until I've finished. The vast majority of the secrets revealed are variations on five basic themes:

1. **Fear of closeness to mother.** "The nasty way I treat my mom," wrote one man who participated in a recent workshop. "Seems I'm always pushing her away and putting her down. It hurts her, and I feel bad about that. But I keep doing it. I don't know why." "Being so close to my widowed mother," wrote another. "I took an apartment near her when my marriage broke up. I eat a lot of meals at her place, that kind of stuff. My friends razz me that I'm a mama's boy. I pretend to laugh it off, but the truth is it bothers me. I worry they might be right."

2. **The father wound.** "Hunger for my dad's affection," one man wrote. "It's like I don't even exist to him. He's never once told me he loves me, and the truth is that hurts like hell. I'd give anything to hear him say that—just once." "My hatred for my dad," wrote another. "He was a total bastard. Drank. Beat my mom. Used me as his punching bag—and threatened to beat me even worse if I cried. He disappeared when I was fifteen. Don't know where he is now. Dead, I hope. An awful thing to admit, but you wanted the truth."

3. **Hidden dependency.** "I'm ashamed of the way I let my wife baby me," one man wrote. "I pretend not to like it, but I do. The truth is, I love it. That's what scares me. I worry I'm letting her turn me into an infant." "Coming close to suicide when my marriage broke up," wrote another. "Total shock. She always complained I was too distant. But I never thought she'd leave. Always thought she was too dependent on me! Wrong! I'm in therapy now. It's helping, but I'm still shaky."

4. **Emotional numbness.** "Tension—I think," wrote one man. "Been waking up in the middle of the night in cold sweats. My doc said exercise might help. I tried it. It didn't help. I think maybe I need a shrink." "My whole life is a fake," wrote another. "I've got it all—success, money, beautiful wife, great kids. But none of it means anything to me. Nothing gives me any real pleasure. Most of the time I feel like a zombie—just going through the motions."

5. **Courage/cowardice.** "Ducking the Vietnam War," wrote one man. "Finagled a 4-F for asthma. Might not feel so bad about it if I'd been active in the anti-war movement—put my ass on the line in that way. But I didn't. Basically I spent those years partying while some of my best friends were getting killed." "The day a plane crashed near my house," wrote another. "A friend and I drove over. It was horrible—bodies everywhere, people pulling passengers out of the burning wreckage. My friend ran to help, but I couldn't. I was too scared. I'll always be ashamed of that."

When I finish reading these secrets, I usually look up to see a group of somewhat dazed-looking men staring back at me. "Reactions?" I'll ask. The responses almost invariably fall into one of three categories. Some men are astonished and relieved to discover that other men have been harboring a secret uncannily similar to theirs. As one man said, "I never expected that." Others are astonished and relieved by the lack of reaction from other men when their secret is revealed. "I was waiting for everyone to gasp," said another man. "But no one did." Others are amazed and relieved to learn that the secret they've felt so ashamed of is no worse than any of the secrets other men feel ashamed of. As another workshop participant said, "You know what I think after listening to all these deep, dark, horrible secrets of ours? I don't think they are so deep, dark, and horrible. I think we've been feeding ourselves a load of shit."

The bottom line is that every man has his share of deep, dark secrets—and every man thinks he's the only one who has them. What does that tell us about manhood? I'd say it tells us that it truly is the "Big Impossible." But many men never come to see that because the shame they feel over their failures to meet these manhood ideals keeps them silent about their failures—and their silence prevents them from discovering that other men have these secrets, too. Instead, many men walk around thinking they're the only ones who have reason to feel ashamed of themselves. And each time they fail another manhood test, they feel more ashamed. Not guilty—that's something else. Guilt a man can do something about. Shame he can't. That's what makes it so lethal. As psychologist Robert Karen writes, "Guilt is about transgression; shame is about the self. . . . Guilt is about behavior that has harmed; shame is about not being good enough."

To illustrate the difference, let's take a hypothetical situation. Let's say I find a wallet with a lot of money in it. It's got the owner's identification in it, too. But instead of trying to return it, I decide to keep it. The next day I feel guilty. I return the wallet and the money to the rightful owner. No more guilt. I've gotten rid of my guilt by making amends. Now let's say that, after returning the wallet, I berate myself for even having thought about keeping it. I tell myself that only a really rotten person would think of doing such a thing. It doesn't matter that I've returned the wallet. The fact that I considered keeping it convinces me that, at core, I'm a rotten person. That's shame. As Karen writes, "Shame is often triggered by behavior, but in shame, the way that behavior reflects on you is what counts. To be ashamed is to expect rejection, not because of what one has done, but because of what one is." Or, as psychologist Martin Wong writes in a 1992 paper, shame is "the felt variation between one's real self and one's idealized self. It is the feeling of not measuring up; that there is something wrong with you, and if it is exposed to others you will probably be ridiculed, rejected, and abandoned altogether."

Wong's writings on shame are based on his work at the

Veterans' Administration Hospital in Battle Creek, Michigan, where he works with Vietnam veterans suffering from post-traumatic stress disorder. In workshops I always make a point of telling participants something Wong has learned about these men. "A number of you wrote about feeling ashamed of failing to meet the male-norm requirement of fearlessness and bravery," I'll say. "It's interesting to note that Wong found that these men felt they had also failed to meet this requirement." Every Vietnam veteran he has interviewed, he writes, "has told me, in the confidence of the office, that he was terrified during much of his experiences in Vietnam. The shame associated with such secret fear . . . is immense in some of the men I've worked with."

Because so many men invariably write about feeling ashamed of their yearnings to feel loved, appreciated, and cared for or ashamed of the anguish they experienced when love either wasn't forthcoming or was offered and later withdrawn, I also always take time to explain how the combined influences of early life traumas, gender-role socialization, and traditional male norms work to instill this shame in men. It's as if men believe that a real man isn't supposed to want or need human connectedness—which is exactly what men have been trained to believe. Of all traditional beliefs, this one is the most insidious, because from it flow all the subsidiary beliefs that keep men so walled off from themselves and others (i.e., men should never feel or express vulnerable emotions; men should never ask for or accept help), and because males start to learn this one so early that they usually don't even know it's there inside, wreaking havoc on their lives. The result is that men are constantly at war with themselves. They want closeness and connectedness. Like all human beings, they need closeness and connectedness. But because they consider these needs unmanly, they fight them. They're always on guard, always struggling not to let anyone in too close, not to let themselves need anyone too much. And either they succeed in fending off closeness and lead lonely, barren lives, or they fail and feel profoundly ashamed of their failure. And most men do fail. Because even when they manage to conceal their need for closeness from those closest to them, the mere fact that they harbor this need makes them feel ashamed.

At this point I usually return to Karen's definition of shame being "about not being good enough" and explain that he is referring to what he calls normal shame—the kind most human beings experience at one time or another. I then offer his definition of a more crippling kind of shame, which he calls pathological shame. This shame, he writes, is "an irrational sense of defectiveness, a feeling not of having crossed to the wrong side of the boundary, but of having been born there." When I glance around a room after reading this definition, I usually see men shifting uncomfortably in their seats, which doesn't surprise me. Most men know that feeling. And the reason they do, I suggest, is because they've bought into a set of masculine ideals that teach them to see their essential humanness as a defect—because they're caught up in an impossible struggle to live up to an unattainable definition of manhood that requires they always be ashamed of, and at war with, their own human needs.

SELFLESS GENEROSITY: THE REQUIREMENT MEN FLAIL TO FULFILL

Let's return now to David Gilmore's observation that manhood ideologies invariably include a criterion of selfless generosity "even to the point of sacrifice"—that "real men" are defined by these ideologies as those who "give more than they take," who "serve others" and who are "generous, even to a fault." Many women and some men react with surprise when they hear the term "selfless generosity" applied to men because they're accustomed to thinking of females as the more generous sex. But they're usually thinking in terms of emotional generosity—of who does more of the intuiting and responding to another person's emotional needs. Women *are* more emotionally generous, for the simple reason that they're trained all their lives to be sensitive to their own and other people's emotions, and men aren't. Men are so thoroughly trained to suppress emotions that most of the time they can't even sense their own feelings, let alone someone else's. But that's not the kind of generosity Gilmore means. He's referring to a different kind of generosity—the more assertive, aggressive, action-oriented kind that isn't expected of women but is expected of men. He means a man's willingness to sacrifice his own comfort, welfare, and even his life to nurture and protect the material and physical well-being of those for whom he feels responsible. As Gilmore writes, ''Men nurture their society by shedding their blood, [and] their sweat . . . by bringing home food for both child and mother . . . and by dying if necessary . . . to provide a safe haven for their people.''

We're living in a time now, however, when there's less and less need, or opportunity, for men to demonstrate this kind of selfless generosity. In part because the needs of society have changed, and in part because these once exclusively masculine strengths are no longer exclusively masculine, men now find themselves living in a world that affords them little means to demonstrate their selfless generosity—which puts them in the demoralizing position of having little means for proving their manhood in these all-important ways. There may never come a time when men won't need to know how to fight, but the world's wealthier, industrialized societies are now gradually shifting away from the traditionally masculine ethic of win-lose contests and life-or-death confrontations toward the more traditionally feminine ethic of mutual understanding, compromise, and peaceful coexistence. And now that women have entered the work force, men are also being relieved of some of the responsibility and rights that once came along with the traditionally masculine role of good provider. As one recent workshop participant said, "I think it's great that women are out there working. It's only right—I can see that. But it's a change, no doubt about it. I can see how much happier my wife is now that she's working compared to the first seven years of our marriage, when she was home with the kids. And a second paycheck sure helps. But things are very different around our house now that she's working. It's like I'm not the big cheese anymore." He chuckled. "It's been an adjustment, let me tell you."

In Some Ways, We Men Had It Easier When We Had It Harder

In the next chapter we'll take a closer look at the centrality of work to men's lives and examine some of the positive and negative consequences that flow from their dedication to it— one negative being the confusion men are experiencing now that they're being forced to relinquish their traditional reliance on work as their primary source of identity and self-worth. For now, though, I want to focus on some of the specific difficulties men encounter when they try to uphold the traditional good-provider standard in a time when the possibilities of meeting that standard are becoming increasingly slim.

Few men in our society will ever know the feeling of indispensability and pride that Gilmore describes a hunter in some primitive culture experiencing when he returns from a hunt with just enough game to feed his tribe and abstains from eating in order that all others may be fed. Up until not all that long ago many men were able to know that feeling. But those days are gone—and not only because women are now working. There are other reasons as well. One workshop participant touched upon these reasons while fondly recalling how his father, who'd been a steelworker, often voluntarily went hungry so his children could eat. "He had an ulcer, so whatever my mother cooked, she had to make a special portion for him that didn't have any spices," he said. "My brother and sisters and I loved my mother's cooking, so we'd always scarf down whatever she cooked for us, and then, if my dad hadn't finished his portion, we'd ask for whatever was left. And he always gave it to us, even if all he'd had was a couple of bites. My mother would give him this look and say, 'Hen-ry.' And he'd say, 'No, it's okay. Let them have it. They're hungry.' She'd act annoyed, but you could tell she wasn't really. You could just see the love all over her face."

"That's a wonderful story," I said.

"Yeah, well, my dad was a wonderful man."

"He was a steelworker, you say?"

"Yeah. The mill's closed now—has been for years. There used to be a lot of factories in our town. They're pretty much all dead now."

That's the other big shift that's happened in the last few decades. Not only have women entered the work force in huge numbers, but the very nature of work itself has undergone radical change. It used to be that men could come home from a day at the steel mill or the mine or the factory feeling something akin to the hunter's sense of manly pride and satisfaction in having really sweated and faced danger to provide for their families. Not anymore. Now many of the jobs our fathers did are being done by machines that have thrown literally millions of men permanently out of work. And predictions are that in the years to come the problem of permanent, large-scale unemployment is only going to get worse.

You see where this puts men. They want to fulfill the male-norm criterion of being the good provider—not only to prove their manhood but also to prove their love. So to have this outlet closed off is deeply painful. The bottom line, however, is that this outlet is being closed off, which leaves men no option except to branch out. The challenge facing men now is to learn to rechannel their expressions of selfless generosity along the more traditionally feminine pathway of emotional generosity.

The work I do with men often focuses on helping them

develop these emotional skills. I call it "developing emotional intelligence." Much of it has to do with learning how to feel and express emotions and how to be sensitive and responsive to other people's feelings. Men who do develop these skills invariably report that their lives become richer and deeper as a result. But change isn't easy. It's difficult and scary—all the more so when the change men are being asked to make requires going against a lifetime of gender-role socialization which has instilled in them, among other things, a terror of the shame attached to failing to live up to the good-provider norm.

That's where a lot of men get stuck. Even when they understand that they're fighting a losing battle against forces beyond their control, their fear of failing to meet this criterion makes it impossible to admit defeat. Instead, men often try to convince themselves that they are what they're not. They construct a fictitious image of themselves as the good provider, then cling to that false image by ignoring, rejecting, or squashing anything that threatens it. This is what the architect mentioned earlier was doing by insisting to his wife that they couldn't afford to buy a new house when, as he admitted himself, they really could afford it now that she was earning a large salary. But to buy the house on her salary would mean surrendering his image of himself as the family's chief financial provider, which he wasn't willing to do.

The other thing men often do when they find themselves falling short in their efforts to live up to this ideal is to redouble their efforts—usually by plunging themselves deeper into work. It's as if, so long as a man keeps working harder, he can tell himself, "Well, okay, so maybe I haven't reached the goal yet, but at least nobody can say I'm not trying." That's what people do when they feel blocked in their efforts to do something they feel they have to do. They go to extremes—in this case, self-sacrificial extremes that can often lead to workaholism. We'll talk more about workaholism in the next chapter. The point I want to make here is that men aren't the only ones who suffer when they get caught up in these extremes of self-sacrifice. Nor is this behavior as selflessly noble and virtuous as many men think. It has a flip side, which is anything but selfless.

MEN WHO SACRIFICE ALSO INDULGE

We've already discussed how the "normative developmental traumas" of being pushed away by mothers and denied nurturance by fathers give rise, in adulthood, to unconscious dependency, defensive autonomy, and destructive entitlement—the unconscious belief that it's okay to put our interests before anyone else's because, after all, we're owed. The key word here is *unconscious.* A man doesn't decide to be insensitive to other people. Most of the time he doesn't even realize that's what he's doing. He's just going along on automatic pilot, doing what feels right to him with little or no awareness of how his behavior affects others. That's another unfortunate consequence of not having been trained to sense other people's emotions. It makes a man even less aware than he otherwise might be of how his behavior affects those closest to him. And the more he's caught up in self-sacrifice, the more clouded his vision becomes.

I think, for example, of a man I once counseled who worked long hours as head of his own construction company and who invariably had a temper tantrum if he came home to find his wife chatting with a friend. "I'm tired when I get home," he said angrily. "I want some peace and quiet. I don't think that's asking too much. And then I find her sitting there, gabbing with someone. It really pisses me off. I tell her, 'Look, you wanna see your friends? Go to their house. Go to a restaurant. Just don't bring 'em here.' " Now, if this man's wife were in the habit of having friends over many times a week, his anger could seem justified. But that wasn't the case. His wife, who also worked, seldom had friends over more than twice a month, and he wanted to forbid even that—which is unreasonable, of course, but which seemed perfectly reasonable to him.

That's what happens when self-sacrifice interacts with destructive entitlement. The former aggravates the latter. The more a man sacrifices, the more entitled he feels to indulge himself and the more he expects or demands indulgences from other people. Sacrifice, indulge. Sacrifice, indulge. That's what I call it—the sacrifice-indulge cycle.

Some men caught up in this cycle will work a fourteen-hour day, then come home and behave like spoiled, overgrown babies—sometimes violent overgrown babies: "Where's my beer? Where's my supper? Tell the kids to shut off that damn TV. I told you never to let the dog into the house. What do I have to do? Pound it into you?" Other men feel entitled to have extramarital affairs. Defensive autonomy comes into play here. As Harvard psychiatrist Stephen J. Bergman writes in a 1991 paper, "The fantasy is that by achieving a man will win love." And yet, although men say they want love, writes Bergman, "I don't think that this whole process is *able* to feel as good to us men, in the same sense of *what feels good to women.*" The reason: Love is rooted in intimacy—and an unconscious sense of defensive autonomy makes many men uncomfortable with intimacy. A man may tell himself it's love he's after, but, in fact, what many men really want—and feel entitled to having—as a reward for achieving or sacrificing isn't love but the gratification of nonrelational sex. Other men turn for gratification to alcohol or drugs. Or they may seek their reward in the accumulation of material objects—the best stereo system, the most expensive car, the most ostentatious Rolex watch.

The cycle can play itself out in all kinds of ways—sometimes to the detriment of the man caught up in it, almost always to the detriment of his relationship with his partner. The man doesn't see that, of course. He's too busy sacrificing and indulging, sacrificing and indulging. A number of couples have come into counseling with me because of this very problem—usually at the woman's initiation and often only after she'd basically threatened to leave if her partner didn't agree to see someone who could "talk some sense into him." But you can't just tell a man to stop indulging, because he can't stop indulging until he stops sacrificing. And he can't stop sacrificing until he frees himself of the fear and shame that drive his self-sacrifice. That's what a man has to get at. Once he rids himself of the underlying fear and shame, the sacrificing and indulging often correct themselves.

This was the case with Jeffrey.

He Wants It, He Deserves It, So He Buys It—Is There a Problem?

"Nice cabinet," Jeffrey said, eying a carved wood cabinet in the corner of my office as he and his wife, Karen, settled in for our first session. He studied the cabinet a moment longer. "You know, that'd really look great in my den." A pause. "I don't suppose you'd be interested in selling it."

"Jeffrey!" his wife hissed, angry and embarrassed. "You see? That's what I mean!"

"What? All I said was I like his cabinet."

"No, that's not all you said. You asked if you could buy it. You'd do it, too. You'd just go right ahead and buy it. For our den, Jeffrey. Not for your den—for our den." She turned to me. "That's what he does," she said, still angry. "He wants something? He just goes out and buys it—without even telling me."

"Yeah," Jeffrey muttered half under his breath. "And I'll bet he can see why, too."

"Jeffrey, I've told you—"

"Okay, let's slow it down," I said. "Clearly, this seems to be a problem for the two of you."

"Not for me it isn't," Jeffrey grumbled.

"That's the problem!" said Karen, exasperated.

"Okay, we'll get to that," I said. "But I think it would help if you both take a moment to collect yourselves."

A tall, dark-haired, classically good-looking man, Jeffrey settled back in his chair somewhat sulkily. In the chair next to his, his tall, dark-haired, equally attractive wife folded her hands in her lap and took a few deep breaths. "That's better," I said. "Okay, I'd like to start by having each of you tell me a little about yourself. Karen, let's start with you."

As both took their turn answering my standard get-acquainted questions, I began assembling a portrait of two intelligent, articulate, accomplished individuals who loved and respected each other and cared enough about their relationship to seek professional help for a problem that was putting their marriage under increasing strain. Karen, thirty-nine, was the director of a small but prestigious fine-arts museum, a position I later learned earned her a slightly higher income than her forty-two-year-old husband earned as number-two person for the state branch of a human rights organization and adjunct professor of law at a highly respected law school—work he described as extremely demanding but also extremely fulfilling. Married seven years, the parents of a five-year-old son named Luke and now expecting another child, Jeffrey and Karen were financially comfortable: so much so that Karen had lately begun urging Jeffrey to cut back on the amount of unpaid, volunteer legal counseling he did in order to spend more time with his family—a request he had thus far refused. Karen didn't like it that Jeffrey's multiple professional commitments kept him away from home so much of the time. But that wasn't what had brought them to my office. The problem for which Karen had insisted they seek help was what she described as her husband's self-indulgent spending.

"It's just getting worse and worse," said Karen. "First it was the pool table. He decided we needed a pool table, so he just went out and bought it. I didn't know about it until it was delivered. Then he decided we needed a screened-in sun porch. Same thing. I didn't know anything about it until the workers arrived. And then, last week, he came home driving a Porsche! That's when I insisted we see someone. I mean, a Porsche! He just went out and bought a Porsche without even telling me!"

"A used Porsche," Jeffrey said testily. "And I didn't tell you because I knew how you'd react. I've told you that. I don't tell you because you always react the same way."

I asked him to explain what he meant.

"Well, like with the pool table," he said. "I happen to enjoy playing pool. It relaxes me. I work my ass off, so I think I'm entitled to a few pleasures. I don't think that's asking a lot. But whenever I decide to treat myself to something, she has a fit."

"I have a fit because you never consult me," Karen said angrily.

"I don't consult you, as you put it, because I know you'll only have a fit."

Again, I had to ask them to slow down. "How long have you two been having these arguments?" I asked.

Karen sighed. "I'd say about three years. He's always had a habit of buying things for himself on impulse, but it used to be smaller things. The pool table was the first big thing. That was just after I was made head of the museum, and that was a little more than three years ago." She glanced at her brooding husband, who avoided her gaze. "It's just getting to be too much," she said. "Every time it happens, we end up having a really ugly fight. And for him to do it again, now, with the baby coming . . ."

Jeffrey shook his head wearily. "You just don't get it, do you?" he said to his wife. "You just can't see my side of it at all."

"No," Karen said sadly. "I don't. I've tried to, but I can't. I just don't understand how you can keep doing something that you know hurts me so much."

I suspected Karen might be wrong on this point. It was quite possible that she was mistakenly assuming her husband was as capable as she of emotional empathy and therefore had to understand how much his behavior hurt her, when the probability was he didn't. They both knew his behavior made her angry. She'd made that clear enough during our session. Her mistake, however, was in believing he understood that the reason she became angry was because his behavior hurt her—a connection emotionally skilled women make automatically but emotionally unskilled men often do not. I made a note to raise this point during our next session—and would have done so had not a last-minute cancellation by their baby-sitter prevented Karen from attending. A fortuitous glitch, actually. I'd also noticed during our first session that Jeffrey had seemed extremely reluctant to speak about his father. He'd offered terse answers to my direct questions—his dad was alive, still married to his mom, he and his dad didn't talk much—but had volunteered nothing more. I suspected that something about his relationship with his father was helping to drive his sacrifice-indulge cycle and had hoped to delicately probe this issue during our next session. So when he called to inform me of the baby-sitting screw-up, I suggested he come in for an individual session. It'd give us a chance to go over a few things, I said.

"Like what?" he asked guardedly.

"Like your relationship with your father. That seems like a charged subject for you."

The session proved pivotal. The main subject of the session having been targeted, Jeffrey arrived fully prepared to lay out the reason for his reticence about his father—the reason being that his family had suffered tremendously as a result of his father's inability to meet the good-provider ideal. His dad had been an entrepreneur, and not an astute one. "He was always betting the family savings on these fly-by-night business ventures that inevitably went bust," said Jeffrey. "He was always running himself into debt, then making us pull up stakes and move to evade his creditors." When Jeffrey was seventeen the creditors had finally caught up with his dad, forcing him to sell off everything the family owned to pay off some of his debts and avoid legal prosecution. The family was also forced to move in with Jeffrey's maternal grandparents while both his parents worked low-paying jobs to satisfy the rest of the debts. His father had straightened up after that. But though he'd never again gotten into financial hot water, neither had he ever achieved any kind of financial or professional success. Still a gambler at heart, he'd spent the rest of his working life leap-frogging from job to job, always believing the next one was the one that would finally "lead to something big." Nothing ever did. Meanwhile, to provide the family with a modicum of financial stability, Jeffrey's mother had stuck it out at the department store where she'd started as a sales clerk, eventually working her way up to assistant manager. She'd been the reliable parent, Jeffrey said. He'd never understood why his mother had stayed with his dad. But she had.

"I see now why you're so angry at your father," I said. "It's understandable that you would be."

"That's just it," he said, looking perplexed. "I'm not angry at him. I used to be, God knows. But now?" He shook his head. "No, not so much anymore. He's an old man now. And he can't help who he is. In his own fucked-up way he was doing the best he could. I can see that now. So I've pretty much forgiven him. And yet . . ." His words trailed off.

"And yet what?"

"I don't know. It's like . . . Well, for example, they're coming for their yearly visit in a few months, and we'll be having our annual fund-raiser while they're here—big, fancy affair. And I've been trying to decide whether to skip it or take them along. Karen says we should take them. She says they'd love it. And she's right. But . . ." Again his words trailed off.

"What's your reservation?"

"I don't know. It's like I'm not sure I want him mixing with the people in my professional and social circle. I'm just not comfortable with the idea of my friends and colleagues meeting him. There's something about it that kind of gives me the creeps."

"Do you have any ideas why?"

He thought, shook his head. "No," he said. "You got any?"

"Well, maybe you're afraid he'll say or do something to embarrass you."

"No, he's pretty polished in social situations. He's quite a charmer, actually. People usually love him."

"Well, maybe you don't like the idea of him basking in your reflected glory. Maybe you're concerned that people will treat him with more respect than you feel he deserves just because he's your dad—that they'll assume that, since he is your dad, he must be a lot like you. Maybe you're worried they'll buy into the old adage about an acorn never falling far from the tree."

As I spoke, Jeffrey's expression turned grave. He sat in silence for a long moment. Then he grunted. "Close," he said. "But no cigar."

"No?"

He shook his head, lips curling downward. "Just the opposite. It's not people thinking he's like me I'm afraid of. It's their thinking I'm like him."

We were getting warm. "Why would you worry that people would think you're like your father?" I asked.

"Because it's true," he said. "I am like him. In a lot of ways, I'm just like him." He frowned. "That's what scares me."

I'd suspected as much. That's where many men's secret fear and shame comes from—a deep anxiety about how much they do or don't resemble their fathers.

I had a hunch that Jeffrey's fears of being just like his father were exaggerated, but that wasn't for me to say. My task, now that he had flushed his fears out of hiding, was to help him examine them closely in order to determine for himself how much was substance and how much was shadow.

We spent the rest of the session doing just that. "In what ways specifically do you think you resemble your father?" I asked.

He looked down, frowned. "Well, I've taken some pretty big gambles myself," he said finally.

"For example?"

"Well, like when I quit the corporate law firm I used to work for back in Oregon to come east to work for human rights. That was a big, solid, well-respected firm, and the top mucky-mucks had made it clear they thought I had a bright future with them. The problem was I was bored to death with the kind of law I was practicing. I'd always had a passionate interest in human rights. So when I got the offer to come here, I grabbed it. That was just after Luke was born. Karen wasn't working then, so we were living on my salary, and taking the job meant taking a pretty substantial pay cut, not to mention having to move clear across country—with no promises of any kind. For all I knew I could have been out of work in six months. Everything worked out—better than I expected, actually. But it was a pretty big gamble." A pause. "And there have been others."

"Such as?"

"Like at the law school where I teach. There've been times when I've really hung my ass out on a limb over different things. Like a couple years ago we had a problem with one of the other professors harassing the female students—pressuring them for sex. One woman finally made a stink about it, and once she spoke out a lot of other women came forward to say he'd pulled the same number on them. There was no question that he was guilty. But the school wanted to hush it up. When I found out, I just flew into a rage. I went to the dean and said, 'Look, either he goes or I go. And if I go, you can be damn sure everyone will know why.' " He shook his head. "It's a wonder the dean didn't fire me on the spot."

"But he didn't."

"No."

"What happened?"

"They got rid of the guy. But it could easily have been my ass instead of his." He frowned. "I do that sometimes. If something makes me angry enough, I'll take this real hard-line stance. I'll just gamble everything . . ." A beat. "Just like my dad."

Jeffrey had named one way in which he thought he resembled his father. "But you said you were like him in many ways," I said. "Can you name any others?"

He thought for a moment. "Not right off the bat," he said. "I think there are others, but I can't put my finger on them right now. That's the main one, I guess."

"I'm wondering if you'd be willing to try an exercise that might help you get a clearer fix on how much you and your dad do and don't resemble each other."

"What kind of exercise?" he asked guardedly.

"A simple one. You might find it interesting." Some time before our next session, I said, he might want to sit down with pen and paper and try to compile a written character-trait inventory on himself and his dad. "Just take a piece of paper and divide it into four squares by drawing a double line down the middle and a single line across," I said. "The left side of the paper is you, the right side is your dad. The top two boxes are for positive qualities, the bottom two are for negative ones." He was to do himself first, I said. "Start with your positive qualities. List as many as you can think of—no censoring and no second guessing. Just write down whatever comes to mind. When you've run out of positives, do your negatives. Same process." When he'd finished doing himself, he was to cover up his side of the paper, so as not to be influenced by what he'd written about himself, and do his dad—again, first positives, then negatives. "When you're done, read over what you've written to see what similarities and what differences you can spot. If any other positive or negative traits come to mind later—either for yourself or for your dad—just add them to the list. I'd also like you to bring the list in with you next week so we can go over it."

As I'd anticipated, Jeffrey did find the exercise interesting—as did Karen. When they entered my office the following week, it was the first subject she raised. "Will you please tell me what you put him up to?" she asked, smiling at her husband. "All week he kept going, 'Oh, that's another one.' And then he'd write something down on this piece of paper.

I kept asking what he was doing, but he wouldn't tell me."

Jeffrey smiled sheepishly. "I didn't know if I was supposed to talk about it," he said.

"Would you like to?" I asked.

"Yeah, I would." He turned to Karen. "That is, if you don't mind listening."

Karen looked surprised and a little hurt. "Mind listening?" she asked. "My goodness, why do you think we're here? You're my husband, remember? I love you. I want to know what's going on with you."

"I'm glad to hear you say that," I said to Karen, "because that's exactly what I was about to ask of you. Last week, when you weren't here, Jeffrey and I began exploring his relationship with his father—specifically, the ways in which he thinks he resembles his dad. The notes you saw him taking were part of an exercise I asked him to do to help him get a clearer fix on that. I'd like to stay with that for a while. For the next few sessions I'd like to concentrate on exploring Jeffrey's feelings about himself in relationship to his father. Your role will be to support Jeffrey in his explorations and offer feedback that might help him put some of his concerns into clearer perspective. Then, later on, I'll be asking him to do the same for you as we explore some of your issues." I looked from Karen to Jeffrey. "Are you both comfortable with that?"

Husband and wife exchanged gently questioning looks.

"I am," said Karen.

"Yeah," said Jeffrey. "Me, too."

"Good. Okay, Jeffrey, why don't we go over what you came up with. Anything interesting?"

He let out a half-laugh. "Yeah," he said, pulling a much folded sheet of paper out of his jacket pocket. "A lot, actually."

As he unfolded the sheet of paper and took a moment to peruse it, I briefly explained to Karen what I'd asked Jeffrey to do.

"Well?" I asked him.

"What I said last week about being a lot like my dad," he

said. "Well, it's true. I am. But maybe not quite as much as I thought. I mean, I sort of am, and I'm sort of not. That's one thing I found myself rethinking." A pause. "The other is that maybe some of the ways in which I am like him aren't so bad." He shook his head and chuckled. "That one really surprised me."

"For example?"

"Well, for example, what I said about my dad being very smooth in social situations. It's true. He is. And so am I. I don't normally admit to that, but I've got a lot of that in me, too. I can be a real charmer when I want to. I'm pretty good at getting people to come around to my point of view."

Karen laughed. "You can say that again," she said, smiling.

Jeffrey chuckled. "Yeah, well. It comes in handy in my work. But, like I said last week, I can be a real hard-ass, too, sometimes. I've also got a temper—which my dad doesn't have. He was always more timid—too timid, in fact. I think that's one of the reasons he was always getting ripped off." He frowned. "It was really painful to watch sometimes—the way he'd let people walk all over him."

"So that's one similarity and one difference," I said. "Anything else?"

He nodded. "Yeah. Actually, this is the biggest one. It's funny I didn't see it until now."

"What's that?"

"Well, what I said during our first session about working my ass off. When I sat down to list my positive qualities, that was the first one that came to mind—that I'm hard-working. Which I am. That I've always known." A pause. "But you know what? So was my dad. None of his grand dreams and schemes ever panned out. But he never stopped working toward them." He shook his head, a look of sad wonder on his face. "I'd never seen that before."

"That's sounds like a pretty important discovery," I said.

"Yeah, it is. I couldn't believe I'd overlooked that. And then I thought, 'Well, that's probably because he was always falling on his face.' That sounds harsh, but it's true. So I got to thinking about why that is—why I've managed to achieve a certain amount of success and all he ever did was dig himself into these holes."

"And what did you come up with?"

"Well, I think one difference is that I'm a lot shrewder than he is—not as much of a dreamer, you could say. I have dreams about what I want to accomplish, but I don't naively entrust my fate to other people the way he did. And I don't go off half-cocked the way he did, either. Or not as much. I take chances, but not before I've got a pretty good idea of the risks involved. And I usually make sure I've got a fall-back plan in case something goes wrong."

I asked him to elucidate, using as his examples the two "big gambles" he'd talked about during our last session.

For example, he said, before moving his family across country to accept the job with his current employer, he'd made a reconnaissance trip east to interview with other law firms in the area—two of which had indicated they'd be pleased to have him if the job he was taking didn't work out.

"So you had other job possibilities lined up," I said. "You didn't mention that last week."

"I'd forgotten about it," he said, looking embarrassed. "I guess I just haven't thought about it in a while. It didn't come back to me until I did this exercise."

As for his confrontation with the dean of the law school—well, he'd been pretty sure the dean wouldn't risk firing him and having him go public with the sex-harassment scandal. "But even if he had, it would have been okay," he said, "because there's this other school that's been wooing me for a long time, and that kind of publicity would only have made me a more valuable commodity to them. And I was also thinking it might be nice not to teach for a while, so I could finish this book I'm writing."

"You're also writing a book? You didn't mention that, either."

He shrugged. "Yeah, well . . ."

"So it seems that, contrary to what you said last week,

you're really not at all the same kind of reckless gambler your dad was."

He looked down. "No. I guess not."

"In fact, it sounds like you think things through pretty carefully before making a move."

He nodded. "Yeah, I guess."

I turned to Karen, who'd been listening to her husband with a look of soft surprise and tenderness on her face. "Karen, what are your reactions to what you've been hearing?"

"I don't know quite what to say," she said softly, turning from Jeffrey to me. "I've always known there was tension between Jeffrey and his father." She turned back to Jeffrey. "But I never knew you thought you were like your father. Why didn't you tell me?"

Jeffrey shrugged. "I don't know," he said. "I don't think I realized it myself until Ron and I got to talking last week. I mean, I did but I didn't, if that makes any sense."

Karen's expression became all the more tender. "Well, I'm glad we're talking about it now," she said. "Because it's not true. You're not at all like your father. I could have told you that. In fact, I did tell you that."

Jeffrey frowned. "You did?"

"You don't remember?" Karen turned to me. "I told you that my father abandoned my mother and sisters and me when I was fourteen, didn't I?"

"Yes, you did," I said.

"Well, as I'm sure you can understand, that made me very frightened of marriage." She turned back to her husband. "Remember, sweetheart? I told you when we were dating that I could never marry a man I didn't feel I could trust. That's one of the reasons I did marry you! Because I do trust you! I told you that when we got engaged." Her eyes shimmered with tears. "Honey, you're not at all like your father. I wouldn't have married you if you were. Why, you're the most solid, reliable, trustworthy man I've ever known."

Jeffrey sat staring at the sheet of paper he held in his hands.

"You didn't see this difference between you and your father before?" I asked.

He shook his head no.

"And how do you feel now that you do see it?"

He shrugged. "Kind of embarrassed—like I should have seen it earlier."

"Anything else?"

"A little confused, maybe. It's sort of unsettling to have to rethink your image of yourself."

"Anything else?"

A long silence. "Kind of relieved, I guess." A pause. "But something else, too. It feels like a kind of sadness or something."

"Do you know what about?"

He thought, frowned, shook his head. "No. I just feel kind of sad."

I had a hunch where the sadness was coming from and took it as a good sign that Jeffrey was able to feel it—even if he couldn't yet pinpoint its source. "Would you be willing to try another exercise that might help you identify what's causing the sadness?" I asked.

"What this time?"

"I'd like you to write a letter to your dad telling him how you feel about him and about yourself."

He chuckled. "You've gotta be joking."

"I don't want you to mail it. I just want you to write it." We all have thoughts and feelings about our fathers and how their parenting affected us that we would never actually share with them—some of which we consider so unacceptable that we conceal them even from ourselves. The point of the exercise was for Jeffrey to explore these thoughts and feelings as honestly as he could in the form of a letter to his dad. I've assigned this same exercise to other men, and they usually find it pretty powerful. If I'm trying to help a man move past anger toward acceptance of his father, I'll ask him to write the letter, put it away for a day, write the letter his dad might write in response, read both letters, then go back and revise his original letter to his dad. In Jeffrey's case, we were trying to figure out how his feelings about his father were coloring his feelings about himself, so I dispensed with the second letter. "I'd like you to just write the letter to your dad, put it aside for a day or two, then reread it and revise it," I said.

He thought for a moment. "Okay," he said. "I'm not sure what'll come out of it. But I'll give it a shot."

A lot came out of it. But it didn't come without pain.

Having agreed to do the exercise, Jeffrey found the actual doing of it much more difficult than he'd imagined it would be. The thought of writing the letter made him feel so anxious and edgy that he kept putting it off, which only made his anxiety worse. "It got to the point where I was having trouble sleeping," he said during our next session. "All because of that damn letter." He'd finally forced himself to begin writing it only two nights before. "Now I know why I kept putting it off."

"Why's that?"

"Because it meant having to confront some things I'd been doing a pretty good job of not seeing until now."

"Things having to do with your feelings about your father?"

He shook his head. "Not really. Well, sort of." The letter had started as a letter to his dad, he said. "I started writing about how hard it had been as a kid, always covering up for him, always pretending to friends that he was as good a dad as theirs were, that my family was as good as theirs were . . ." A pause. "That I was as good as they were . . ." He shook his head. "And always knowing it was a lie. Always worrying that they were going to find out the truth—which, eventually, they always did." A long silence. "So, anyway, that's how I started. And then, I'm not sure how it happened, but the next thing I knew, instead of writing to my dad, I was writing to myself. It was like this other part of me kind of took over and started writing all this stuff I didn't even know was there. It was like, 'Yeah, and look at you. You're still doing it. You're still doing the same damn thing.' " He fell silent again.

"Still doing what?" I asked.

He glanced up at me, vulnerability in his eyes. "Still trying to prove I'm good enough," he said softly. "Still trying to prove I'm . . . man enough." He shook his head. "That's why I'm always busting my ass. I say it's because I love my work—and I do. But there's more to it than that. It's like some kind of fear—like I'm afraid that if I let up even for a second, everyone's going to find out I'm a fraud. It's like I'm still trying to cover up for the fact that I'm not good enough." A pause. "That *I* don't think I'm good enough. That's where the sadness was coming from. It was sadness for myself. For my own lack of pride." He shook his head. "It was like suddenly realizing that I've been living in this prison all these years." A pause. "All these years," he said again sadly. "And the only person who's been keeping me there is me."

"Sounds like that was a pretty painful realization," I said.

He nodded. "Yeah. When I saw that . . . Well, I just broke down and cried." He glanced at Karen, who sat gazing tenderly at her husband. "I don't know what I would've done if Karen hadn't been there," he said. "She was just the best. She really helped me get through it. We must have been up half the night, just talking things out." A pause. "I'll tell you something else I realized. I never thought it bothered me that Karen makes slightly more money than I do. But the more we talked, the more I realized it does—I think because it plays into my fears of being like my dad and having to depend on Karen's income the way we depended on my mother's when I was a kid. It's silly, I know. I can see that now. But I didn't realize that before, either—that I did resent Karen for making more than I do." He shook his head. "I didn't finish the letter. But I don't think I need to now."

"Why's that?"

"I don't know. I just feel like some weight's been lifted off me. It's hard to explain, but as soon as I saw how ashamed I'd been feeling, for no reason . . ." A beat of silence. "For *no reason* . . ." He smiled sadly. "It was like, as soon as I saw that, I didn't feel so ashamed anymore."

Once We Get Past Sacrificing, Other Bad Habits Tend to Fall Away, Too

That was the turning point for Jeffrey. He and Karen continued in therapy for another five months, but it was after this third session, as Jeffrey gradually began easing up on the shame-induced pressures he'd been inflicting on himself, that the tensions between husband and wife also began to ease. For the next few sessions I continued to work with Jeffrey to help him get in touch with and mourn the normative developmental traumas that had been helping to drive his sacrifice-indulge cycle by fueling his unconscious sense of destructive entitlement. Then, with his sense of destructive entitlement eased to the point where he was more capable of empathy toward his wife, I switched the focus to Karen, helping her see how the traumas she'd suffered in childhood had given rise to similarly destructive attitudes and behaviors that were also contributing to their marital difficulties—among them, a tendency to fly into a rage when she felt her needs or feelings were being ignored.

Together, Jeffrey and Karen worked hard to understand their respective responsibilities for the problems they'd been having and to replace these destructive attitudes and behaviors with more constructive ones. Their hard work paid off. Two months into counseling, Jeffrey decided of his own accord to cut back his volunteer legal counseling from eight to two evenings a month and to take the following semester off from teaching. "It's just too much," he said. "Especially now, with the new baby coming. I pretty much missed Luke's babyhood, and I don't want that to happen again. And, anyway, I have to clear some time for Lamaze classes. I can't believe I was too busy for that last time around."

Now that he'd begun realizing, as he put it, that "you can feel like a man without killing yourself," Jeffrey also found himself feeling less desire to indulge in expensive treats. As his sense of destructive entitlement diminished and his sensitivity to his wife's needs increased, he found he was also more inclined to consider and even solicit her feelings before giving in to his self-indulgent impulses when they did arise—something that became easier for him to do as Karen, in turn, became more skilled at checking her impulse to fly into a rage when he did suggest a purchase and learned to hear him out calmly and ask for a day to consider the suggestion before giving her reply. He still slipped occasionally, as did she. Every now and then he'd come home with some new something—a new pool cue, a new car phone—and get huffy when she questioned him about it. And, every now and then, she'd lose her cool and become angry over some perfectly innocuous purchase. But by the time they finished therapy, these slips had become fewer and farther between. Jeffrey had become much more conscious and considerate of Karen's feelings, and Karen, in turn, had learned to respect Jeffrey's right to indulge himself in an occasional modest treat.

Not surprisingly, Jeffrey's feelings toward his father also began to warm. "I'd always thought I'd forgiven him for what he put the family through," he said during one session. "And I had—in my head. But I guess I didn't really feel it deep down, the way I do now. I'll tell you something else. Listening to Karen talk about what it was like for her after her dad abandoned her family made me realize another thing I've never given my dad credit for. I've always given my mom credit for sticking with him. But I've never given him credit for sticking with us. There must have been plenty of times when it would have been easier for him to run off and leave us. But no matter how bad things got, he never did."

And as Jeffrey's feelings for his father began to warm, so did their relationship. Well before his parents' visit, he found that, when he called home and his dad answered the phone, instead of immediately asking, "Is Mom there?" as he'd always done previously, he was now more inclined to talk to his dad for a while—about sports, current events, Luke's latest accomplishments, the family's excitement about the coming baby. By the time his parents' visit did roll around, he and Karen had also decided to take his mom and dad along to the fund-raiser.

"Karen was right," he said, smiling, when I asked later how the evening had gone. "They loved it. They really had a great time. And the funny thing is, so did I. I actually enjoyed having them there—my dad as much as my mom." His father had been every bit the charmer Jeffrey had expected he'd be. "He was a big hit," he said. "He was really in his element. And that actually made me feel good. I never thought I'd get such a kick out of seeing him have a good time."

Jeffrey had even gone out of his way to introduce his dad to the mayor. "Good to meet you," the mayor had said, shaking his father's hand. "You must be proud of your son."

His father had turned to Jeffrey, admiration shining in his eyes. "I am," he'd said. "Prouder than he knows. I remember when he was a boy, I used to tell his mother, 'You watch. This one's not like me. He's going places.' "

Overcome by emotion, Jeffrey had been momentarily speechless.

"Oh, come," the mayor had said. "You're being too modest, I'm sure."

His father had smiled charmingly. "No, sir. I'm not."

"Yes you are, Dad," Jeffrey had said, surprising his father and himself. "I mean, come on. Who taught me to dream big dreams? Who taught me to keep working to make them come true? And where do you think I get my incredible personality and good looks?" His father had looked astonished. "No, sir," he'd added. "You don't get off that easy. You know what they say about fathers and sons—'The acorn never falls far from the tree.' "

During our last session Jeffrey recalled something else he'd never given his father credit for—the amount of time and attention he'd given his children when they were young. Unlike many fathers of his generation, Jeffrey's father had not been so caught up in defining himself exclusively through his work that he let family life go by the boards. To the contrary, he seemed to take more pride and satisfaction in his family than he did in his work. "In a lot of ways, he was really there for us," said Jeffrey. "More than I've been there for my family." Having finally exorcised the secret shame and fear that had fueled his sacrificing and indulging, Jeffrey had begun to see how much he'd been missing out on by sacrificing family life to work and had started taking steps to correct this imbalance.

Our work together came to an end just as Jeffrey was embarking on this journey, so I don't know the details of how he fared. I know from my work with other clients, however, that men who do attempt to correct this imbalance usually discover that it's both an unexpectedly challenging and a richly rewarding undertaking. In the next chapter we'll examine how men come to be so lopsidedly over-invested in work, the positives and negatives of that over-investment, why it's now crucial that men recognize and correct this common male proclivity, and the obstacles and rewards they can expect to encounter when they do attempt to balance work and family life.

CHAPTER SEVEN

Men and Work: Life after the Death of the "Good Provider" Ideal

RAISED TO WORK

Imagine you're at a party with your wife or girlfriend—a cocktail party or wedding reception where she knows a number of the other guests present and you don't. She introduces you to another couple—a work colleague of hers and the colleague's husband. We'll call him Bill. After a few minutes of conversation, during which the two women talk office politics while you and Bill listen politely, they spot a mutual acquaintance they haven't seen in a while and excuse themselves to go say a quick hello—leaving you and Bill to make conversation with each other.

I often begin my talks on "Men and Work" by asking men to imagine themselves in this situation. "Now, we're going to play a sentence-completion game," I tell them. "When I pause, I'd like you to say whatever comes to mind. Okay. So you're standing with this man you've just met. There's a moment of awkward silence. Then you turn to him and say, 'So, Bill, . . .' " And there I pause, waiting for their response—and for the laughter that follows when they hear themselves respond in near-perfect unison: "What do you do?"

Two women meeting for the first time are now likely to ask each other this question, too. But when women ask it, it doesn't carry the same weight. Confident of their status as women and more interested in relating than in competing, when women ask this question, they're usually simply being friendly and inquisitive in a nonthreatening and non-threatened way. Men are often doing something else. As discussed in the last chapter, few men ever feel completely confident of their manhood—a status they achieve through testing and retain by continuing to pass these manhood tests. To be a man, in other words, a male has to "do." And men's natural mode isn't to try to connect but to compete. So when men ask each other, "What do you do?" the question is often more fraught. They may feign casualness. But what they're often really asking is, "Are you more of a man than I am? Are you a better provider than I am?" Fulfilling the good-provider role has always been a core masculine requirement; it's extremely important to a man's sense of self-worth. That's why this question tends to carry more weight when a man asks it of a man—because that's how men take each other's measure. You want to know who a man is? Ask him what he does. So far as men are concerned, that is who they are. In the final years of the twentieth century, however, many men are finding they can no longer depend on work for their masculine validation—which puts them in a difficult quandary: Where do they turn for their sense of self-worth now that this linchpin of identity has come loose?

The First Lesson We Learned as Boys: We Were Put on This Planet to Work

How did men come to identify so completely with their work? No mystery, there—not when you consider how men were socialized. As psychologist Robert S. Pasick writes in *Men in Therapy: The Challenge of Change*, men's upbringing is essentially a long period of preparation for entering "the real world"—the world of work. Males, he writes, were "raised to work." That's the aim of much of the gender-role socialization we've discussed. This training was about drilling us in the skills that men traditionally have had to draw upon in order to be able to work and provide for their families. It was about teaching us to be self-reliant, uncomplaining, aggressive, cool-headed, pragmatic, logical, resourceful, action-oriented, goal-oriented, good at problem-solving, good at strategizing, and good at giving every endeavor our all.

These skills—all still valuable in many ways—served men and their dependents especially well back in the days when men were solely responsible for doing the providing and when doing that providing was physically punishing, frequently dangerous work. Society has changed a lot since then, but the masculine code hasn't. Men are still very much committed to fulfilling the traditional male-norm requirement of being the good provider—in part because so much of their sense of masculine purpose depends upon it, in part because it's one of the few ways they traditionally have been allowed to demonstrate their love, and in part because that's what they do best. That's when a man feels most in his element—when he's working. He's much less confident of his skills as a family man, because he never really learned how to "do" relationships and family life. So rather than try to do something he's not good at and risk making a fool of himself, he devotes himself to his work. That he is good at. In fact, it's often the only thing he's good at. Take that away from him, and he's lost.

How lost? To get men pondering this question, I often ask them to envision another scenario. "Imagine that you've suddenly come into a lot of money," I'll say. "Enough for you and your family to live on quite comfortably without your ever having to work another day in your life. Think seriously, now. And then a show of hands, please. How many of you think you'd quit working?" The response this question received during a recent workshop was fairly typical. Of the fifty men present, twelve raised their hands. "Twelve hands," I said. "That's a little over twenty percent. That's almost exactly what a sociologist named Robert S. Weiss found when he and a colleague asked men this same question. Now, another question. Of those of you who would keep working, how many would keep working because you genuinely love your job?" Fifteen hands went up. "Fifteen out of thirty-eight," I said. "That's almost half. That's surprising."

"Surprisingly low?" one man asked.

"No. Surprisingly high." When Weiss and his colleague asked the men in their study why they'd keep working, only three percent said it was because they enjoyed their work. The majority said they'd keep working because they needed something to do.

What Weiss found, in other words, is that many men feel that if they didn't work they wouldn't know what to do with themselves. Or, to put it another way, because men feel they have to be "doing" in order to prove their manhood and because they often don't know how to do much of anything else, many men feel they must work in order to feel like men. As Weiss writes in his 1990 book, *Staying the Course: The Emotional and Social Lives of Men Who Do Well at Work*, "Quite apart from income, satisfactory work provides men with a sense of worth and of place that together provide a foundation for their . . . lives."

Work provides other rewards as well, of course. As Weiss writes, "The gratifications of jobs well done and of solid achievement are many and real." Unfortunately, these gratifications and rewards often blind men to the unhealthy aspects of over-investing in work, which are also many and real.

Consider, first of all, that when Weiss talks about the sense of "worth and place" men derive from work, he's talking about the sense of worth and place they derive from doing satisfactory work—in other words, work they feel counts for something and that makes them feel they count for something. In a perfect world, all men would be doing that kind of work. But in the real world huge numbers of men don't. Many men work in jobs that do more to diminish than to enhance their sense of manhood, while others can't find any work at all—because they don't have the right education or training, or because of discrimination, or because the jobs simply aren't there.

Consider also that the rewards men derive from doing satisfactory work don't come without strings. As Weiss writes, "Because the rewards of devotion to work can be substantial and the penalties of sloughing it off severe, work can be, in Lewis Coser's phrase, a greedy institution. . . . The attractions of doing well and the fears of doing badly may . . . lead men to want to do as much as they possibly can." Combine the attractions and fears that compel men to work as much as they can with the lack of relationship skills that make them uncomfortable doing anything else, and add the emotional numbness that prevents them from recognizing when they're working too much and too hard, and what you come up with is workaholism and undiagnosed work-related stress disorders that take a toll not only on men's health but on the health of their relationships as well.

None of this is news. These stresses have always made up the underside of men's traditional over-investment in work—so much so that until recently men never thought to question them. To the contrary, men accepted them stoically and took pride in their ability to bear up under them. That's what being the good provider was all about. Men's reward for making these sacrifices was the satisfying sense of pride and purpose they derived from fulfilling this traditional male role. As long as their sacrifices earned them that reward they had no reason to grumble about making them. But they do have reason now. Now, men's sacrifices no longer earn them this reward—because they aren't the sole providers anymore.

What the Dinosaurs Went through after That Meteor Hit the Earth—That's What Men Are Going through Now

In workshops I often ask men another series of questions that help to drive home this point. "Another quick survey," I'll say. "This one for men aged thirty-five to forty-nine. First, how many Baby-Boomer men here grew up in two-parent households and are currently married or living with a female partner?" The responses of the men attending the workshop mentioned above were again fairly typical. Forty of the fifty participants raised their hands. "Okay, same men," I said. "How many grew up in households in which the mother worked outside the home?" Eight hands. "Eight. That's twenty percent. Okay. Again—same men. How many are married to or living with a woman who doesn't work outside the home?" Four hands went up. "Four. That's ten percent." As usual, the survey turned up evidence of a recent flip-flopping of long-standing norms. Here was a group of men who had grown up in households in which twenty percent of mothers did work outside the home and eighty percent didn't. Now, about forty years later, these same men were living in households in which ten percent of the wives or partners didn't work outside the home and ninety percent did.

This is anecdotal evidence of one of the most sudden and profound societal shifts ever to occur. And this evidence is consistent with national norms. Statistics compiled by the U.S. Census Bureau indicate that between 1950 and 1990 the percentage of mothers of children under age six who worked outside the home rose from 12 percent to 60 percent. That's an astounding five-hundred percent increase in forty years. What it boils down to is that the traditional family model of "male as breadwinner/female as homemaker" has become obsolete, and men now find themselves struggling to adapt to a cataclysmic change in social climate. Trained to derive their core sense of identity from being the good provider, they now find that role is no longer theirs to fulfill.

This is a tremendous loss for men, who rightfully took great pride in demonstrating their generosity of spirit by dedicating themselves to fulfilling this honorable role. Men feel the resulting loss of masculine pride. Some have tried to compensate for this loss by working harder—by sacrificing even more of themselves to their work in order to earn more money, power, and status. But no amount of money, power, or status can satisfy the hunger men are really trying to satisfy—which is the hunger to feel the same sense of indispensability to their loved ones that work provided when they were the sole providers.

That's not to say men should abandon their deeply ingrained work ethic. All human beings need to feel productive. But men do have to examine their beliefs about what kind of rewards work can provide. Like it or not, they can no longer expect work to serve as their fundamental reason for existing, because it isn't anymore.

So what is?

That's the question men are wrestling with right now. If they can no longer measure their worth according to their ability to provide for their families, how do they measure it? If their partners no longer need them to put bread on the table and a roof over their heads, what do they need them for?

What many men fear is that they're becoming superfluous, that their wives and partners don't really need them anymore. It certainly seems their mates don't respect them as much anymore—not as much as their mothers respected their fathers, at any rate. They never saw their moms pressuring their dads to pitch in more around the house the way their mates are pressuring them—not even those of their mothers who worked outside the home. But there are reasons for that. One is that even when their mothers did work, they usually worked at low-paying jobs, which meant that, for all intents and purposes, the father was still the primary provider. The other is that back then the traditional family model was still the norm couples tried to emulate. So even if a woman did work, it was a matter of pride to both husband and wife that she still do all the homemaking and child-rearing, because both husband and wife still considered this her primary role. Now that's changed. Today working women are the norm rather than the exception. And their incomes are more likely to approach, match, or even exceed men's, which puts them on more of a par with men when it comes to providing for their families. This, in turn, has contributed to the demise of the traditional family model and the rise of the new family model of husband and wife as equal partners in all aspects of family life—including homemaking and child-rearing.

Men aren't sure they like this new model. Many aren't ready to surrender the role of good provider—because they haven't yet found another role on which to base their sense of self-worth. Nor do they respond well to the pressure their partners are now putting on them to take on more household and child-care duties. It's as if, now that women are earning their own incomes, the only thing they need men for is to make their lives easier by taking on more of this women's work they're too busy to do themselves.

That's what many men think. But they're wrong. True, women are now pressuring men to take on these responsibilities in part because that's what they need men to do. Yes, they're saying they'd be happier if men became more involved with their families. But they're also saying men would be happier, too.

What Our Partners Know That We Don't: There's More to Life Than Just Working

It used to be that males and females lived equally unbalanced lives. Males were allowed to experience the gratifications of working, achieving, and providing for their families; females, the gratifications of homemaking, child-rearing, and relationship-nurturing. So far as men were concerned, they had the better deal. And it seemed clear that women thought so, too. Indeed, back in the early days of the feminist movement, it looked as if women might decide that the rewards of working and achieving so vastly outweighed the rewards of homemaking and child-rearing that they could live quite happily without the latter.

But they didn't. Having fought to secure the right to choose between family and career, the vast majority of women in a position to choose are choosing instead to combine career and family. Not an easy task, as our partners are the first to tell us. So why do they do it? Because, having now experienced both the gratifications of working and the gratifications of homemaking and child-rearing, they realize that to have one without the other is to experience only half the joy and richness of life.

That's what women are trying to tell men. They're saying that if men are feeling superfluous now that the era of male as breadwinner has passed, it's because they're still investing too much of their masculine stock in their ability to fulfill this role and not enough in the equally gratifying work of homemaking, child-rearing, and relationship-nurturing. But men are skeptical—and wary. Having had little direct experience with the rewards of domesticity, they have no way of knowing whether they'll find these rewards as richly satisfying as women do. What if they don't? Or what if it turns out they're just not very good at this kind of work? Men have a deep need to be good at things, which makes them reluctant to try their hand at anything they don't think they'll be good at.

These fears are understandable—and also baseless. In my twenty years of professional practice I've helped a number of men make this transition, and every one has found the rewards to be well worth the effort. I'm not saying it's an easy transition to make. It entails a lot of learning, and a lot of unlearning of deeply entrenched attitudes and behaviors. What I am saying is that every man I know who has made this shift has come out ahead. Without exception these men report that their lives have become more satisfying and meaningful than they were back when they considered work their only real reason for being alive. Indeed, the only regret I've ever heard these men express is that they didn't make the shift sooner.

LIFE AFTER THE DEATH OF THE "GOOD PROVIDER" IDEAL

A story told by one workshop participant helps illustrate the depth and power of men's belief that a male's worth and identity come through work. "Our son just turned three a few weeks ago," this man said, "so we had this birthday party for him. At one point all the kids were sitting around the table, eating cake and ice cream, and my brother and I were standing there watching them and talking about my son—about what he was going to be when he grows up. My brother said, 'Well, if he keeps growing at the rate he's growing, he might have a future in basketball.' And I said, 'Yeah, but he's crazy about airplanes. I wouldn't be surprised if he becomes a pilot.' You know, the kid's only three, and we're already talking about what kind of work he's going to do—which didn't strike me as at all odd at the time. But I was just trying to remember if I've ever had that kind of conversation about my six-year-old daughter. And I don't think I have. I'm very aware of her interests and talents—she's very musically inclined, for example. But when I talk about her, it's more along the lines of, 'She really loves music,' not 'Maybe she'll be a pianist.' I didn't see that before, and it kind of bothers me, because I want to encourage her in her career, too. I don't want to just do that with my son. And yet that's what I was doing. I guess old values die hard."

Indeed they do. And the centrality of work to men's lives is one of the most deeply entrenched of these values. In his 1993 book, *The History of American Manhood,* social historian E. Anthony Rotundo points out, for example, that back in the nineteenth century it was a very clear if unwritten rule that a man couldn't marry until he had established himself in a career—that it was by establishing himself in a line of work that he established both his manhood and his position in his community and proved himself ready to marry, father children, and join the fraternity of men. Things are looser now. But the traditional belief that work is the foundation of a man's personal and social identity is still very much alive. If a man works, then he and society feel he has earned the privilege of entering into these other adult social contracts. If he doesn't work, then he hasn't earned that privilege. He may marry and father children anyway, but he will neither be granted nor feel he deserves to be granted the respect afforded to real men—men who work. That's why, despite our best intentions to the contrary, men still worry about what our sons will be when they grow up more than we do about our daughters' future careers. Because, although we're living in a time of disorientingly rapid change in traditional values, we're still very much the product of those values. And they tell us that, for males, work is the bottom line. As Weiss writes, "Work may not be the most important part of life—family counts much more—but work is fundamental to the rest. It is fundamental to maintaining your place in your home and fundamental to having enough self-respect so you feel comfortable with your neighbors. Plus, it is truly absorbing."

When I read this quote in workshops, men invariably latch onto the word *absorbing.* As another workshop participant said about his work, "It's demanding, sure. But I also really enjoy it. Some of my happiest moments are when I'm so absorbed in a project that I lose track of everything else."

That's one of many satisfactions work provides. Others include the sense of accomplishment that comes from meeting difficult challenges and the recognition that flows from doing a job well. "And there's the satisfaction of knowing you created something," said another workshop participant. "I own my own business. And I take a lot of pride in the fact that I built it myself. I started with nothing. And now, twenty years later, I'm doing . . . Well, let's just say I'm doing pretty well. And that's a good feeling. I really get off on that." Other men talk about the pleasure they take in the competitive nature of their work. As one man said about his work as a computer-software designer, "You really have to stay sharp to keep up with all the changes. It really keeps you on your toes." Others talk about the satisfaction of doing work that contributes to the common good. "I like knowing that what I do really matters," said a firefighter. "When you pull someone out of a burning building—that's as basic as it gets."

Work: The Grand Passion That Often Takes Over Men's Lives

It's no wonder, then, that men invest themselves so deeply in work. Given all the satisfactions and rewards it provides it's perfectly possible, writes Weiss, "for men genuinely to find work more enlivening than anything else." But he also warns that if a man focuses on work to the exclusion of everything else his work will eventually lose meaning. "Work is important for men's lives partly because it provides a foundation for everything else," he writes. "But if there is nothing else, then work is a foundation still waiting for a structure. If immersion in work were to prevent men from functioning as husbands, fathers, and participants in the wider community, that would be irony indeed."

For all its satisfactions, in other words, immersion in work also has its dangers. One is the danger of slipping into workaholism, which may or may not be a widespread problem among men. It depends on how we define the term. If we define it, as Weiss does, as a state of pathological addiction that "so alters men's physiological states that unless they have a work fix they experience withdrawal," then most men probably would agree with Weiss that the term gets flung around too loosely and that the majority of men who are labeled workaholics aren't really workaholics. They're just hard-working men who put a lot into and get a lot out of their jobs.

But Pasick offers another definition. Elaborating on other researchers' definition of a workaholic as someone "who has a compulsive need to work, because it provides a tangible reinforcement of self-worth not found elsewhere," he describes workaholics as people who "prefer working to anything else" and who are "restless and unhappy" when they're not working because they don't know "what else to do with themselves." They also "have difficulty sustaining family relationships," in part because of "lack of time" spent at home nurturing these relationships and in part because even when they are home, they're so preoccupied with work that they're "emotionally unavailable" to their loved ones. More, they're so dependent on work to bolster their self-esteem that their "mood on any given day" depends on how well or how poorly work is going. And, finally, although they experience a transitory increase in self-pride and lessening of chronic work-related anxiety when they lose themselves in work, they eventually become "disappointed" with work. They believe that "working will increase happiness," but they eventually discover that "it does not."

Are men workaholics? If we use Pasick's definition of workaholism it seems that, yes, most men are.

This isn't to say that men are at fault. As one young Hispanic man said, "What choice do we have? Take me. I'm a financial analyst. If you want to move up in the bank I work for, you have to go through their officer-training program. I'm about halfway through, and it's a bitch. Do I work ridiculous hours? Yes, I do. Am I available enough to my wife and son? No, I'm not. I know that, and I don't like it anymore than my wife does. But, like I tell her, I don't make the rules. I just play by them."

He raises an important point. It's hard not to develop workaholic habits given the way most jobs are presently structured. The unfortunate fact is that we do live in a work culture that still largely adheres to the traditionally masculine ethic of demanding that workers sacrifice everything to their jobs if they want to advance. There's some evidence that this is beginning to change now that men are starting to tire of the rat race— and especially now that women have entered the work force and begun pressuring employers to adopt policies that make it easier for workers to balance work and family. Flexible work hours, part-time work, and job sharing are becoming somewhat more prevalent, for example. And some employers are beginning to pay more attention to their employees' child-care needs and to offer more generous family-leave benefits. But these more enlightened policies won't become the norm until men join women in pressing employers to adopt them. There's some evidence that this is starting to happen. In addition to pressuring for and making use of paternity leave and child-care benefits and services, for example, increasing numbers of men are also stepping off the job-relocation treadmill out of unwillingness to uproot their families—which has forced a number of companies to re-examine these relocation practices. But men are still more the passive beneficiaries of these policy changes than active agents in bringing them about. So far it's still mainly women who are doing that work. This is partly because they still do most of the balancing of family and career and thus have more invested than men do in bringing about these changes. But it's also partly because, being relative newcomers to the world of work, they see more clearly than men do how unhealthy the traditionally masculine work culture is—for women and men.

Men, in contrast, are so accustomed to this culture that they have difficulty seeing how unhealthy it is. In *Men in Therapy*, Pasick offers a sampling of the kinds of quagmires a man's blind devotion to work can lead him into when it gives rise to problems that can't be resolved except by surrendering some of that blind devotion—which many men find difficult to do. He cites, for example:

- The man who realizes he has a drinking problem but is reluctant to stop drinking for fear his career will suffer if he can't drink with clients.

- The man who doesn't attend the family-therapy sessions deemed necessary to help his troubled teenage son because he can't spare the time off from his work as a high-ranking executive.

- The man whose hatred for his job is spilling over into and poisoning his family life but who can't bring himself to quit the job because it offers a decent salary, good benefits, and job security.

- The man who can't say no to a lucrative job offer that requires moving to another city, even though he knows it will probably spell the end of his relationship with the woman he considers his ideal mate.

One recent workshop participant told of having made this last mistake when he was offered the job that brought him to the East Coast. "I'm from Ohio originally," he said. "The woman I was involved with is still there—married now."

"She wouldn't come east with you?" I asked.

"She couldn't. Her husband had died two years before we met, and her kids were still dealing with that. So there was no way she was going to introduce more upheaval into their lives. She begged me not to take the job. But it just sounded too good to pass up—like one of those once-in-a-lifetime opportunities."

"And was it?"

"Yeah, it was definitely the right career move. But if I had it to do over?" He shook his head. "I wouldn't do it. Because it cost me that relationship. And she was a once-in-a-lifetime opportunity, too. I didn't see that then because I was too focused on my career. But I see it now. It was one of the biggest mistakes of my life."

We Men Like to Believe Our Work Doesn't Get to Us—But Believing It Doesn't Make It True

The results of my study indicate that men are now beginning to think more carefully when asked to choose between relationships and career. So change is happening. But it's happening slowly—not only because men have been trained to put work before all else, but because they've also been trained to blind themselves to the price they pay for doing it. Men are so thoroughly trained to numb themselves to their emotions and ignore signs of physical distress that they don't even know when the demands of work are pushing them up to or past the limits of their endurance.

A particularly telling example of the toll this training can take on men comes from a story published in the December 12, 1993, issue of the *New York Times* about Apple's push to release a hand-held computer called the Newton, which debuted in the summer of 1993. It was supposed to be out in the spring of 1992, but it wasn't anywhere near ready. The designers had to push to get it out when they did, and apparently they had to push too hard. The article states that the "pressure to finish, exhilarating at first, eventually overwhelmed some of the young designers. After 18-hour days, some engineers went home and cried. Some quit. One had a breakdown [attacked his roommate] and ended up in jail. One took a pistol and killed himself."

Obviously, this is an extreme example of the kind of intense and prolonged stress a job can put a man under and what can happen when he doesn't realize or can't admit that it's getting to be too much and doesn't take steps to alleviate it—as some of these designers did do. When work-related stress is less extreme, its consequences are also less severe. But they're still there, even when men aren't conscious of them— which they're usually not. Weiss reports, for example, that "wives say that their husbands systematically underestimate how often they are tense or irritable as a result of their work."

That's one of the milder symptoms of work-related stress. As Weiss writes, "The immediate consequences of stress are preoccupation, irritability, tension, and difficulties sleeping. The longer-term consequences include depression, burnout, and somatic disorders"—in other words, physical problems such as ulcers, headaches, and chronic back pain, to name a few. Studies have found a relationship between work-related stress and quite a number of physical ailments. And they've also found a link between heart disease and Type A behavior —a combination of traits that include chronic activity, a compulsive need to do more than one thing at a time, chronic impatience over even minor delays, chronic hostility, explosive temper, intense competitiveness, and an intense drive to achieve.

The bottom line is that men ignore these and other signs that they're too consumed in and by their work at their own peril. And yet that's exactly what men usually do. Instead of paying attention to these symptoms, men ignore them and try to bull through. But a man can't reduce stress by ignoring it. The only effective way to alleviate stress is by confronting it— by feeling it, naming it, tracking it to its source, and correcting the situation that's creating it before it destroys physical and emotional health. This may sound like a difficult process, but it actually isn't. I've helped many men learn how to do this, and most catch on fairly quickly. Once they master this skill and begin seeing how much of their health and happiness they've been sacrificing to work, they almost automatically start taking steps to create more balance in their lives.

It's worth noting that the Apple designers who suffered the worst stress-related outcomes during the push to release the Newton seem to have been those who were so much the prisoner of traditional masculine training that they didn't know or couldn't admit they were being pushed past their breaking point. But not all these designers suffered so horribly. One, Steven Capps, who went through a similar push while helping to develop the Macintosh computer, is described as having discovered that he "still had an amazing capacity for work. He converted his house into an office and worked there with two other . . . engineers, often around the clock." The article doesn't specify whether Capps has a wife or children—or, if so, how they were affected by his work habits. The point here, however, is that we all have different tolerance levels for stress and pressure. It's all about knowing and respecting our own limits.

Some of the other designers who didn't possess Capps's capacity for work came through intact by doing just that. They realized and admitted they were being pushed beyond their limits and had enough sense and courage to say, "Enough." One, Michael Tchao, is described as having realized he was "at the breaking point" when he found himself coming home at midnight and crying after sixteen hours of nonstop meetings. Tchao is quoted as saying, "I remember there was this point where I said to myself, 'I'm not going to feel guilty, I just can't do it' "—whereupon he immediately scaled back his work hours. Another, Jerome Coonen, is described as having decided to quit after the birth of his second child convinced him that "being a full-time father would be just as rewarding as being a double-time Newton developer." Coonen is quoted as saying, "I looked at a baby being born and then at where this project . . . and . . . my career . . . was headed and the whole thing seemed absurd." He quit the job in favor of free-lance consulting and spending more time with his two sons.

Measuring Our Worth by the Work We Do Leaves Too Many Men Feeling Worthless

After reading Coonen's quotes aloud during one recent workshop, I glanced up to see one man frowning and invited him

to share his thoughts. "I was just thinking, 'Well, that's great,' "
he said. "Here's this guy with a job a lot of men would kill for
who can afford to quit and go out on his own. Well, good for
him, you know? But what if you don't have that kind of choice?
You wanna know what I do? I'm a security guard at a printing
plant. Real glamorous, right? But try finding something better
when you don't have a college degree. I'd love to find a better
job. Not so much one that pays better, but something more . . .
Well, something I could feel better about saying I do. But if
you don't have that degree, forget it. The door gets slammed
in your face."

He wasn't the only participant who felt dissatisfied with his
job. Another young man who'd been job-hunting since grad-
uating from college six months before felt no better about the
work he was doing to make ends meet. "Four years of college,
and I'm driving a cab," he said. "That doesn't do a hell of a
lot for your self-esteem, either." Other men voiced worries
about job security in today's tight job market. Another man
recalled the shock of being let go when the company he'd
worked for was bought out. "My wife still had her job, fortunately," he said. "And they gave me a decent severance pack-
age, so we weren't too worried about money. But it was a tense
time until I found another job. In a way, it was kind of nice
being home for a while. Our kids were in elementary school
then, and it gave me more time with them. But it's hard to
relax into that when you're worrying about finding another
job. After I found my job—that's when I was able to enjoy it.
I had this two-week stretch before I started, and that was a
great time. The kids and I would do things like cook surprise
dinners for my wife. We do that on Saturdays, now. We call it
our 'Saturday Surprise'—and surprise is the word, all right.
But I don't think that would have happened if I hadn't had
that stretch where I wasn't worried about finding a job. That's
the worst. The worry just really wears you down."

It's not the worst, of course. The worst is being able to find
no work at all. A minister talked about the severity of this
problem in his inner-city community. "Our community has

the highest unemployment rate in the metropolitan area," he said. "And it isn't just because the economy is bad right now. Our community has always had an appallingly high unemployment rate, even when the economy was booming. It goes deeper than that, I'm afraid. It has to do with lack of equal educational opportunities, with under-funded and over-crowded schools, with families being forced to live in a culture of poverty, and with the overt and covert prejudice and discrimination that are unfortunately still all too prevalent in our society." As director of his church's counseling programs he witnessed every day what becomes of men who are consistently denied the opportunity to do legitimate work. "Try convincing men who've turned to substance abuse as an escape from self-hatred that there's any reason for them not to drown themselves in alcohol or drugs," he said. "Try persuading young drug dealers and gang members that there's some other way to prove their manhood than by turning to violence and crime."

But it isn't only unemployed or under-employed men who suffer as a result of men's traditional reliance on work for masculine validation. Now that men are no longer the sole financial providers, many well-employed men are finding that when this role is taken away from them, their work suddenly seems less meaningful. As one man said, "I'm vice president of a sports-equipment manufacturing company. Good title, good salary, all the perks. But what do I do really? I push papers. I take meetings. I mean, so what? Sometimes I think, 'Is this what I was put on this earth to do?' It's a pretty depressing thought."

The Challenge of Change: Where Do We Find the Meaning We've Lost?

When providing was still the man's role, there was no such thing as meaningless work. The fact that it enabled men to fulfill this role gave it meaning. Now that it no longer serves that purpose, many men are asking what purpose it does serve. More to the point, they're asking what purpose they serve.

In a certain sense, this loss of the good-provider role is really an opportunity in disguise—because it forces men to start thinking more seriously about what kind of work they want to be doing just when the world needs men to do that thinking. Do they want to continue making career choices based solely on what a job offers in terms of money and status? Or would they rather be doing work that perhaps promises less in the way of personal gain but offers the satisfaction of knowing they're engaged in some worthy endeavor? There are all kinds of ways to make work more satisfying. A man might decide to make a job switch—say, from working for a company concerned only with its own bottom line to working for one that's trying to do something he believes in. Or he might decide to cut back on the late nights at the office and devote some of that time to volunteer work. Or he might decide to work for change at his place of employment by pressing for the inauguration of more enlightened programs and policies. That's one of the good things to come out of the loss of the good-provider role. Back when men were solely responsible for providing for their families, they couldn't afford to worry about whether their work contributed to the greater good or not. Now they can.

But if men concentrate only on trying to make their work more meaningful, they're still depending on work to provide them with their core sense of self-worth—which it can't. Men have to realize that no job is going to satisfy the hunger they're really looking to satisfy—which is the hunger to feel the same sense of indispensability to their families that men felt back when they were the breadwinners.

Basically men need to consider doing what their wives and partners are encouraging them to do—ease up on their over-investment in their jobs and invest more of themselves in the work of homemaking, child-rearing, and relationship-nurturing. Men tend to think women are urging them to take on these responsibilities just to make women's lives easier. And that's one of women's concerns, certainly. But it's not the only one. Women are also encouraging men to become more involved with their families because they know, as men don't, that it will also make men's lives more meaningful and fulfilling.

One workshop participant who had recently married and become a stepfather spoke of experiencing this difference in his own life. "I work for a company that publishes industry newsletters," he said. "I'm in charge of putting out six newsletters a week. I could work twenty-four hours a day, and it still wouldn't be enough. Which is pretty much what I was doing before I got married. All I did was work—because I didn't really have anything else in my life except work. Now I do. My wife has two boys by her first marriage. Their father moved back to England five years ago—that's where he's from. He keeps in touch, but not much. So it's really the four of us now. We all know we're a stepfamily. But we don't feel like a stepfamily. We feel like a family." He smiled. "And it's changed my whole life. I still work hard, but I don't kill myself anymore. Now I do what I can within reasonable work hours or I'll stay late or work weekends on occasion. But I don't do it as a regular practice anymore. Because I can't—or because I don't want to, I should say. I want to go home to my family. I want to be with them." He smiled. "And they want to be with me." A pause. "And you know what? I find that I'm actually enjoying work more now that I'm not working twenty-four hours a day. It's like I have more energy, and it's made me more efficient. I think I have a better attitude, too. I don't sweat the small stuff anymore, which I can see now that I used to do. It's like my whole life has become . . . more balanced."

We Like the *Idea* of Becoming Involved Family Men—But Making It Happen Takes *Work*

The recent plethora of films and television and print ads that promote the new ideal of the caring, involved family man attests to the fact that some sort of shift is happening in our culture. The people who produce these films and ads wouldn't be promoting this new ideal if someone weren't responding to it. And it's clear from the way men talk in workshops about being touched by these films and ads that it isn't only women who are responding to this new ideal. On a fantasy level, at least, men are responding to it, too. The fact that men are now beginning to refuse job transfers and to make more use of paternity leave and flexible work schedules indicates that they're also beginning to allow family considerations to influence their work lives. But there's evidence that men still aren't coming through in the ways their partners need them to and in the ways that would ultimately prove most rewarding—that is, by really getting in there and taking on their share of the responsibilities of day-to-day family life.

I'm not referring only to housework, though that's certainly a big part of it. I'm referring to everything that goes into running a household, raising children, tending to relationships with relatives and friends, and nurturing an intimate bond with one's partner. I prefer to call this work "family work" because it entails so much more than just cooking, cleaning, and doing laundry—which is what men think of when they think of doing housework. Men are doing more than they used to do, but various studies indicate that, on average, they're still doing only about one-third of all there is to do. And they're still not doing it voluntarily. A recent study found, for example, that although men are doing more childcare work than they used to, they still depend on their wives to assign them tasks rather than just getting in there and doing these tasks themselves.

It's true that some men are constrained from doing more around the house by the grueling demands of their jobs. But for most men, that's not the case. They could find the time to take on more household responsibilities if they wanted to. But they don't want to. Some feel they work hard enough at work and should be able to relax when they get home. Others can't shake the belief that this family work is women's work. Others feel they already do plenty around the house. As one man said, "Who takes care of the car? Who's down in the basement when the boiler goes out? Who does the taxes?"

Men do still shoulder most of the responsibility for these traditionally masculine jobs. But when one compares the amount of time and energy these tasks consume to the amount consumed by family work, it becomes obvious that men get off light. The boiler doesn't go out every month, after all. Nor do taxes have to be done every week. But cooking, cleaning, shopping, and all the other work that goes into raising children and running a household is never-ending.

More important, what men don't realize is that it's by performing these traditionally feminine tasks that they become truly integrated and indispensable members of their families. That's what family life is all about. It's not only about providing for their families' material needs. It's about being there on a daily basis to provide for their never-ending, ever-changing, day-to-day physical and emotional needs as well. The only way for a man to become more involved with his family is by taking on these duties. And yet even men who understand this will still balk at doing it—often out of unrecognized resentment toward their partners, who aren't as available to them as they'd like now that women are also working. On an unconscious level most men are quite dependent on their partners for nurturing, soothing, and emotional sustenance. And when their partners aren't there to give it to them, they get anxious and cranky. An unconscious sense of destructive entitlement can also cause men to believe that their partners are supposed to minister to them—i.e., that they shouldn't have to do any family work because they're entitled to be waited on.

Men also often hold back from doing more around the house for fear that their efforts will be criticized by their partners. "I think the whole competency thing has a lot to do with it, too," said one man. "I can cook and clean and all that. But I'm not nearly as good at it as my wife is, and that makes me kind of reluctant to do stuff—because nothing I do meets her standards. Like, I'll make the bed in the morning while she's in the shower, and when she gets out, she'll fix it over again because the pillows aren't right or something, which annoys the hell out of me. After a while, you figure, 'Why bother?' " Another told of how his wife will ask him to chop vegetables for dinner, "and, then, instead of just letting me do it, she'll hover around watching, and I can just feel her getting tense. And then she'll take the knife out of my hand and say, 'No, not like that. Like this.' Like there's only one right way to chop vegetables."

This is a common complaint among men—one that has to do with the issue of control. Much as women genuinely want men to pitch in more on one level, they sometimes have difficulty actually relinquishing family-work duties to men because on a deeper level, they feel conflicted about going against the early life training that taught them the performance of these duties is their job. Even when they do relinquish some of these duties, they may still feel a need to dictate exactly how these jobs are to be done, which conflicts with a man's need to prove his competence and independence by doing them how and when he chooses—and which often leads, in turn, to arguments over whose way is right and who's in charge. As another man said, "I get real prickly when my wife asks me to do something and then tries to show me how to do it. It feels like she's trying to give me orders. And I don't like taking orders. I'm used to giving them."

He was speaking, of course, of giving orders at work. But home isn't the workplace. It's an entirely different world in which many men feel lost. As one man said, "At least work has some kind of logic to it. You've got a project. You map it out. You attack it step by step. It's all pretty concrete. And at least you know what the rewards are. You do an acceptable job, you get paid a salary. You do an especially good job, you get a raise or a promotion. At home . . ." He grimaced. "I don't know. It's all so intangible. One day your kids are angels, and you think, 'This is what it's all about.' And the next day they're hellions, and you want to give 'em up for adoption. And how do you know if you're doing a good job or not? Are you supposed to tell yourself, 'Well, my wife hasn't divorced me yet, and my kids haven't turned to a life of crime, so I guess I must be doing okay'?"

This is a serious problem for men. Males are trained all their lives in the art of competing and achieving. This training prepares them to function well in the world of work, which operates much like a structured, competitive game. But it leaves them ill-prepared to function in the world of intimate relationships and family life, which doesn't operate by the same rules. It seems to men, in fact, that it doesn't operate by any rules at all. At home, unlike in games or at work, there are no rigid rules and procedures—because there can't be. Family life is by its nature ever fluid, ever unpredictable, and ever changing. Nor does there exist any clear-cut way for men to rate how they're doing as husbands and fathers, as they're so accustomed to being able to rate their performance at work. As one man said, "It's not like your kids come up to you and say, 'By the way, Dad, we just wanted to say you're doing a great job.' "

Ever Visit a Country Where No One Speaks Your Language? That's What Family Life Is Like to Men

At work a man is supposed to give orders. He's supposed to be bossy and argumentative. He's supposed to be logical, rational, aggressive, competitive, emotionally unexpressive, and insensitive to his own and other people's feelings. But that's definitely not the case at home. At home the very traits and skills that serve men so well at work do nothing but cause problems.

Take men's deeply entrenched competitiveness. At work that's how a man achieves and excels—by competing and going for the win. But family life isn't about competing and winning. It's about nurturing, cooperating, and understanding. And yet, having been trained all his life to compete, a man has a hard time not being competitive at home. Instead of approaching arguments and disagreements with his partner and children as opportunities to explore and work through differences in order to achieve more closeness and mutual understanding, he approaches them as win–lose contests that he's determined to win.

Or take men's over-reliance on logic and reason and their distaste for anything that smacks of the emotional, which is what family relationships are all about. In order to foster close family relationships a man must be able to feel and express his emotions and to sense and respond to other people's feelings. Lacking these skills, many men fall back on trying to manage conflict with logic and reason—which can work if the conflict is a logistical one, but which usually doesn't work if the conflict is emotional, as most conflicts are. In fact, the more a man tries to solve heated emotional conflicts with cold logic, the more he usually succeeds only in making the conflict worse.

Or take men's sense of "defensive autonomy," which gives rise to the belief that a man must always "stand alone." At work this belief serves men well. It's what makes them so self-reliant. But family life isn't about standing alone. It's about intimacy. And in that world a man's defensive autonomy often creates problems, causing him to unconsciously reject intimacy by throwing up walls or pulling away when his partner comes too close.

So it's not easy for men, this family stuff, because their

training is so antithetical to it. The result is that when men do try to achieve a healthier balance between work and family life, the first thing that often happens is that instead of immediately beginning to feel better about themselves, they begin feeling worse—because they begin to realize how little they know about how the world of family life functions and how to function within it.

That doesn't mean a man shouldn't attempt this transition, however. It simply means that he needs to be forewarned about some of the problems he's likely to encounter so that he and his partner will be better able to recognize and deal with them—and so he doesn't become so frustrated by them that he gives up and retreats back into work before he has tasted the rewards that deeper involvement with his family has to offer. Because—make no mistake—the rewards are worth the effort.

One workshop participant spoke, for example, of how much he felt he had gained from spending two years at home caring for his kids. A lawyer who had just resumed part-time office hours since his youngest started kindergarten and who planned to resume full-time hours when his wife finished medical school, he told a story that held the other men enthralled.

From Workaholic to Family Man: One Man's Journey of Discovery

Rick and his wife, Julie, had met and fallen in love during their senior year in college. They'd married the following year, after which Julie had gone to work to support Rick until he finished law school, with the understanding that once he got a job they'd live on his income while she went to medical school. "That was the plan," Rick said, smiling. "But it didn't work out that way." Instead, just as he was settling into his first job with a prominent law firm, Julie discovered she was pregnant. "We're what I call quasi-Catholic," said Rick. "Not so Catholic that we don't use birth control, which is why the pregnancy surprised us—she'd been using her diaphragm. But we're Catholic enough not to believe in abortion. And it wasn't that we didn't want a family. We just hadn't planned on starting one so soon." Together they had agreed that Julie's medical training would wait until the child—a girl—started kindergarten. In the meantime Julie would quit her job and stay home to care for their daughter while Rick concentrated on his career—which took off like a rocket, with him strapped to it. "I was definitely doing the fast-track career climb," he said. "But it didn't come without a price. I was working seventy, eighty hours a week, minimum—and it never occurred to me that there was anything wrong with that. That's the scary part. If events hadn't intervened, I might have gone right on that way, being this non-person to my family, without ever realizing what I was missing."

The event that intervened was Julie's discovery, just as she was again gearing up for medical school, that she was once again pregnant. "The one time, the *one time*, we didn't use birth control," Rick said. After much discussion he and Julie had agreed that this time she'd stay home with the baby for the first three years, during which time Rick would begin cutting back on his work hours and start helping out more at home. At the end of three years he'd switch to part-time office hours and they'd hire a part-time baby-sitter so that he and the baby-sitter would be handling all the housework and child care and Julie could start studying for her M.D.

"You agreed to that?" a workshop participant asked, startled.

Rick nodded. "Yeah."

"Why?"

"For a couple of reasons. One was that I could see it wasn't fair to ask Julie to make all the career sacrifices. Or maybe I should say she made me see that. And the other was that I really didn't like a lot of the work I was doing. Most of the cases I got assigned had to do with defending corporate clients against harassment and discrimination suits, which left a bad taste in my mouth. So I kind of welcomed an excuse to cut back on my work hours. I wasn't crazy about the idea of pulling more weight around the house because I'd never had to do that before. But I figured if it's a choice between doing housework and doing work that violates my ethics, I'd rather do housework. As for eventually cutting back to part-time, I was hoping Julie would change her mind about that and decide to wait until our second child was in kindergarten before starting medical school. So I figured I'd take it one step at a time."

The first step was to talk to his boss about cutting back on his work hours. The consultation didn't go smoothly. "Which was just as well," he said, "because it gave me the shove I needed to find another job." He'd found it with his present employer—a consulting firm that specializes in helping companies review and amend their corporate policies with an eye toward boosting morale and productivity by better serving the needs of their workers. "The pay wasn't as high," he said, "but the hours were more reasonable. And it was a much better match in terms of my own interests. I even told them there was a chance I'd have to cut back to part-time for a few years somewhere down the road. And they said they'd be able to work around that. So that was good."

The next step was to begin getting his feet wet on the home front, as he put it, by taking over responsibility for getting his daughter up, dressed, and fed in the morning. "Fortunately I still had only one kid," he said, smiling. "But it was still hard at first. I was accustomed to doing things at my pace, and the first thing I learned is that you can't expect a four-year-old to come up to your speed. You have to slow down to hers, which was a rough adjustment at first. But, you know, a lot of wonderful stuff happens when you spend that kind of time with your kid. Like, my daughter and I got into this ritual where I'd wake her up, and then I'd sit with her before she got out of bed while she told me her dreams." He shook his head. "It hadn't even occurred to me that she had dreams—that's how out of touch I was. And not only does she have them, but they're really fascinating—much more imaginative than the dreams I remember having as a kid." He smiled. "So we'd talk about her dreams. And then we'd do the bathroom routine, and all the while, she'd be chattering away about whatever came into her mind. And she'd be asking me questions like 'What makes water hot?' and 'Why does it get dark at night?' And then we'd pick out what she wanted to wear that day." He chuckled. "I discovered that my daughter has definite tastes in clothes. She likes sweaters but she doesn't like blouses. She'll wear yellow, but she won't wear green because green is 'yukky.' " He smiled. "It was like I was really starting to get to know her for the first time."

With some initial coaching from his wife he also began polishing up his homemaking skills. "The housework I could live without," he said. "But I discovered I actually enjoy cooking." Gradually, as his wife's due date approached, he began taking over more responsibility for the daily running of the household until by the time their second child—a boy—was born, husband and wife both felt confident that there wasn't much of any kind of family work he couldn't do in a pinch. "And that was good," he said, "because there's no way Julie could have handled it all without . . . Well, I don't even want to think about the toll it would have taken on her. I mean, the midnight feedings alone are enough to wipe you out."

"You did midnight feedings?" another man asked.

Rick smiled. "Yep."

"Your wife didn't breast-feed?"

"She did for the first four months. But then she came down with bronchitis and had to take antibiotics, so she couldn't. So after that we took turns." He shook his head, his expression a mixture of sadness and amazement. "I never did that with my daughter," he said. "And I really regret that now, because there's something about holding your baby and feeding your baby and having him look up at you with his big, beautiful eyes. It's just . . . Well, it's just an incredible thing. And then when he smiles at you!" He put a hand to his chest and fell back in his seat, as if his heart had been pierced by an arrow.

Much happier in his new job, Rick also found himself enjoying his work more. But he felt no desire to go back to his former fast-track ways. "There was plenty of opportunity to do that," he said. "But it didn't appeal to me anymore, because I could see how much it would mean having to give up." Indeed, as the time approached for him to cut back to part-time hours—Julie was determined not to postpone her medical training any longer—he'd found himself looking forward to the change. "Not that I expected it to be a picnic," he said. "By then I'd been through enough of the crappy times when the baby wouldn't stop crying and my daughter was being a brat to have a pretty good idea of what to expect. But, you know, it comes with the territory. And I guess I liked the territory enough that I didn't mind spending more time there for a while."

He liked it so much, in fact, that after a few months of working mornings in the office, he went back to his employer and worked out an arrangement that allowed him to work from home. "There were still times when I'd have to go in for a half a day or a day. But it didn't happen all that often. It was more a case of my asking the baby-sitter to come in every once in a while when I needed a break—because you do need a break sometimes, or you go nuts."

He also made a point of "keeping his hand in" during his two years at home by staying active in a couple of professional organizations. "That was an experience," he said, chuckling. "I'd go to these professional meetings, and there'd be all these hot-shot lawyer types I used to work with, and they'd say hello, but it was obvious they weren't comfortable talking to me. It was always, 'How ya doin'! Good to see you! Yeah, well, uh, catch you later.' " He chuckled again. "The conversations were usually pretty brief. And, every once in a while I'd catch one of them looking at me like, 'Poor guy. Guess he just couldn't cut it. Well, better him than me.' I understood where they were coming from, though. I'd probably have reacted the same way if I were in their shoes. But I don't want to be in their shoes—that's the thing. It's kind of ironic, actually.

There they are, feeling sorry for me—and, meanwhile, there I am, feeling sorry for them. I mean, their careers are going well, they're making good money. And yet you can see in their eyes that they're not happy. It's like they can never enjoy what they've got because they're always worrying about who's got more and who's gaining on them. So, no matter what they've achieved, it's never enough."

"Are you talking about married guys or single guys?" another man asked.

"I'm talking about married guys," said Rick. "Guys with kids, too. That's the sad part. They're so busy scrambling for success that they don't even realize what they're sacrificing. I know—because I used to be one of these guys. And now that life just seems so . . . so empty to me. Don't get me wrong. I wouldn't want to be a house husband forever. But I'm glad I've had the experience, is what I'm saying—because it really opened me up to a world that I didn't know existed. I mean, I knew it existed, but I never really appreciated it. I never put it on a par with working because I didn't think it was all that interesting or challenging—which it is. In some ways it's even more challenging, because it's all about being patient and understanding and sensitive and all those other things we're not so good at. It brings you up against your limitations real fast. And that's not a pleasant experience, let me tell you. But that's how you learn, I guess. That's how I learned, anyway."

"You're fortunate," I said. "A lot of men get stuck when they start coming up against these limitations. But it sounds like you managed the transition pretty well."

"Well, I give Julie the credit for that," said Rick. "She was pretty patient. So I got lucky there. And it's not like we didn't have our share of fights. We did—some real whoppers, too. But it's worth the effort. It really is. And not just because I feel closer to my kids now. It's made a difference in my marriage, too. Before, it was like Julie and I were living in two different worlds. And now it's like we're more of a unit, more like real partners. Instead of cutting our life together down the middle and her taking the family half and me taking the work half, which is what we were doing before, we've made it into this joint project we're working on together. And that puts everything in a different perspective. Because once you do that, work isn't the only thing you're living for anymore. It's still an important part of your life. But it isn't your entire life, because there's this whole other part that—" He smiled. "I was about to say there's this whole other part that matters just as much," he said. "But that's not true. It doesn't matter just as much. It matters more. A lot more." He shrugged. "That's the bottom line for me now. I mean, I still take pride in my work. But Julie and I both feel that ultimately our family is our most important creation. And that's a good feeling. It makes me feel more grounded. It just feels good to have that straight in my head and to know I'm putting my best efforts where they matter the most."

As Rick spoke, I couldn't help think he was probably benefiting more than he knew from the changes he'd made in his life—that the good feeling he talked about experiencing probably extended beyond enhanced psychological well-being to enhanced physical health as well. That's another strong argument for balancing work and family life. Not only does deeper involvement with family reduce a man's risk of falling prey to workaholism and other work-related stress disorders, but it also mitigates against the sense of emotional isolation so common among men that takes its own toll on physical health.

In the next chapter we'll take a closer look at the ways in which loyalty to the traditional masculine code puts men's health in jeopardy and discuss how men can avoid these health hazards.

CHAPTER EIGHT

Men's Health: The Code That Kills

THE SOBERING STATISTICS

We don't hear the term *weaker sex* used much anymore, but we still know which sex it refers to—or which one we think it refers to. Compare the sexes in terms of average height, weight, muscle mass, and physical strength, and there's no question that females are inferior. But what happens when we set aside these pro-masculine standards of measurement and look instead at male versus female survival statistics—i.e., who lives and who dies? Which sex emerges as the weaker sex then? Consider:

- Although approximately 125 male fetuses are conceived for every 100 female fetuses, only approximately 106 live boy babies are born for every 100 girls.

- Approximately 33 percent more boy babies than girl babies die during the first year of life.

- The death rate among males aged fifteen to twenty-four is almost twice as high as it is among females.

- Average male life span is seven years shorter than average female life span—currently, 72.0 years for males compared to 78.9 years for females.

- As a generation ages, the ratio of males to females steadily declines until, by the time that generation reaches old age, there are only about half as many men alive as women.

What to make of these statistics? We want to keep in mind first that they apply specifically to the United States. As psychologist Bonnie R. Strickland notes in a 1988 article on sex-related differences in health and illness, with the tragic exception of AIDS, most of the infectious diseases that were once largely responsible for limiting male and female American life span to approximately forty-six and forty-eight years respectively have now been brought under control. As she also notes, women have easier lives in the United States than they do in many poor and developing countries, where female infants are considered undesirable and women's health needs are ignored.

But the fact that females have it easier in our society doesn't mean they have it easy. Strickland reminds us, for example, that females in our society are more likely than males to have a history of childhood sexual assault; that women are harassed, raped, and battered by men, not vice-versa; that women in our society still don't enjoy the same economic benefits as men; and that women's health concerns are still underserved by the predominantly male medical and power establishments.

So how is it that women still manage to outlive men? Because Nature designed it that way?

The sex differential in number of fetuses conceived versus live babies born and in deaths during first year of life would seem to indicate that females hold what Strickland calls "some biological advantage over males." In her study she cites another researcher's theory that "the extra genetic material furnished by the [female's] second X chromosome . . . reduces the possibility of sex-linked abnormalities and could . . . play other unknown beneficial functions." In their seminal study, "Why Do Women Live Longer Than Men?" researchers Ingrid Waldron and Susan Johnston note, for example, that females are more resistant than males to infectious diseases, in part because "the X chromosome carries . . . genes for the production of immunoglobulin M [one of the immune system's infection-fighting antibodies] which result in higher serum levels of immunoglobulin M in females." They also note that estrogen and progesterone (the female sex hormones) boost the female immune system's ability to attack and destroy foreign bacteria and cells, whereas testosterone (the male sex hormone) does not. Estrogen also provides pre-menopausal women with some protection against heart disease by stimulating production of high-density lipoprotein (HDL)—the "good" cholesterol—whereas testosterone predisposes men toward heart disease by stimulating production of low-density lipoprotein (LDL)—the "bad" cholesterol.

What Nature gives with one hand, however, she takes away with the other. The same hormones that offer women some protection against heart disease, for example, have also been implicated as a causative agent in cancer of the breast and reproductive organs. And once women pass menopause and their estrogen levels decline, they not only lose their protection against heart disease but are also predisposed toward potentially crippling osteoporosis (loss of bone mass). Indeed, across all ages, Strickland writes, "women generally have higher prevalence than males of chronic diseases. . . ." Females, in other words, are more likely than males to get sick. Males, on the other hand, are more likely than females to die.

But not because Nature planned it that way. She didn't stack the deck against males. Culture and conditioning does that. If men want to pin the blame somewhere, they should pin it on their gender-role training and on the traditional masculine code to which they've been trained to pay undying allegiance. Or maybe we should call that dying allegiance.

Because that's what this code requires of males. It requires that they sacrifice their health and sometimes their lives in order to prove themselves men.

Caution: Traditional Masculinity Is Bad for Your Health

Let's take a look at heart disease, which is this country's number-one killer of both women and men. Every year, heart disease—the cause of approximately one-third of all deaths—takes the lives of almost twice as many males as females. Why twice as many males? Findings from the well-known Framingham, Massachusetts Heart Study—an ongoing forty-six-year study of some 5,000 people designed to identify the risk factors for heart disease—indicate that, in general, the risk of a woman developing heart disease is about half that of her male age-cohort. The study has also found, however, that women whose husbands develop heart disease are twice as likely to develop the disease as are women whose husbands remain healthy—that these women cancel out their "biological advantage," in other words, by engaging with their husbands in unhealthy behaviors such as smoking, not exercising, and eating high-fat foods.

So what we're really talking about is behavior. The main reason more men than women develop heart disease is because men are more likely than women to engage in the various behaviors that have been identified as bad for the heart.

Take smoking. Although it's now on the decline among men, the percentage of men who smoke still exceeds that of women in all age categories. It's well established that smoking increases the risk of heart disease—not to mention lung cancer and emphysema. And yet men still smoke, not only because smoking is physically addictive, but also because, on a subtle yet powerful psychological level, there's something appealing to men about knowing they're flirting with death. That's what a man's supposed to be, after all. He's supposed to be daring, fearless, heedless of danger.

Same goes for indulging in an unhealthy diet of burgers, fries, steaks, and all those other "he-man" foods that contribute to heart disease. Worrying about their deleterious effect on health—that's about as wimpy to many men's way of thinking as running to the doctor each time they experience a little shortness of breath or a twinge of pain in their chest. And that's assuming men are aware of these symptoms, which many men aren't. Having been trained all their lives to numb themselves to pain and physical discomfort, many men aren't aware of these symptoms at all. As for exercise—working out with weights to build muscle and strength or engaging in aggressive, competitive, or strenuous sports has manly appeal. But making time for the kinds of regular moderate exercise like walking that have been shown to be equally if not more beneficial to health? Forget it. Men would rather put their time and energy into something more challenging, goal-oriented, and productive—such as work.

As for the connection between heart disease and the various Type A behavioral traits that seem to serve men so well in their professional lives, if it's a choice between having a healthy heart and doing well at work, many men will choose the latter—because doing well at work is how they define themselves as men. As already discussed, men's traditional over-investment in work can also lead to dangerous levels of unrecognized and unmanaged stress, which elevates the risk of heart disease even more. Focusing on work to the exclusion of all else in a futile attempt to extract from it an enduring sense of self-worth it can no longer provide can also leave men feeling cynical and hostile. And as Dean Ornish, M.D., reports in his 1990 book, *Dr. Dean Ornish's Program for Reversing Heart Disease*, recent studies have identified "self-involvement, hostility, and cynicism" as the three components of Type A behavior "most toxic to the heart"—all of which Ornish believes are exacerbated by that other condition more common among men than among women: emotional numbness, or alexithymia. As Ornish writes (italics his), "In my work with heart patients, I have noticed that people who have silent ischemia [symptomless heart disease] often have a significant dissociation between their . . . thoughts and feelings. If you ask them what they are *feeling*, they will tell you what they are *thinking*. . . . In other words, their feelings are often walled off—not only from other people but even from themselves. . . ."

That's one of the biggest advantages women have over men when it comes to avoiding heart disease and other illnesses— a host of advantages, actually. And these advantages aren't biological. They're cultural. Females are allowed to experience and express emotions and are also allowed to seek out closeness with other human beings. Males, on the other hand, learn from birth onward to be emotionally and physically insensate, to stand alone, and to need no one—all central tenets of the masculine belief system that leave men isolated from themselves and others and prey to a variety of ills. As Ornish writes (italics his), ". . . *anything that promotes a sense of isolation leads to chronic stress and, often, to illnesses like heart disease. Conversely, anything that leads to real intimacy and feelings of connection can be healing.* . . ."

When's the Last Time *You* Saw a Doctor?

Let's move on to cancer, which is the second leading cause of death in this country. Although the causes of most cancers are still unknown, we know that smoking causes lung cancer in both men and women. We also know that the percentage of male smokers still exceeds the percentage of female smokers and that lung cancer kills approximately six times as many men as women. (Emphysema, the other major smoking-related disease, kills approximately five times as many men as women.) Nor is cigarette smoke the only carcinogen men are more likely than women to breathe into their lungs. There are others to which men are also more frequently exposed due to the fact that more men than women work in traditionally masculine trades where they're exposed to asbestos and other cancer-causing dusts and fumes—and to the fact that, having been taught to scoff at risks, men are less likely than women to take recommended precautionary measures to protect their health, such as wearing protective face masks.

Non-gender-specific cancers of the digestive organs and other organs are also about fifty percent more common among males than among females—a sex differential that researchers suspect may be due in part to physiological differences between the sexes, but only in part. Here again the differential seems more likely to be due to nonphysiological gender differences in dietary and smoking habits, exposure to carcinogens, and emotional and physical self-awareness. Various studies suggest, for example, that chronic, unrelieved stress can hamper immune-system functioning, which can in turn leave an individual more susceptible to cancer. But it's pretty difficult for a person to do something about stress if he doesn't even know he's experiencing it—which many men don't.

Nor do many men heed the early warning signs of physical illness. Instead, they do the kind of thing I once did, back in my marathon-running days, when, while jogging through a wooded area, I ran through a pile of leaves, stepped on a fallen tree branch, heard a crack, and kept running—ignoring the pain in my foot until it finally became unbearable. An X ray revealed I'd kept running on a broken metatarsal bone. As Abraham Morgantaler, M.D., author of *The Male Body*, was quoted as saying in a recent *Newsweek* article on prostate cancer, "Men grow up learning it's unmanly to make too much out of any health problems"—particularly those having to do with their private parts. As Hank Porterfield, chairman of a support organization for men with prostate cancer, put it bluntly in the same article, "Anything associated with sexual organs or the natural processes of elimination, men tend to be squeamish talking about."

Whether it's a problem "down there" or anywhere else in our bodies, our training is not to feel, think, or talk about it. The result, as Waldron and Johnston write, is that men "generally underestimate their illness more than women do. . . ." There seems to be "no sex difference in the readiness to see a doctor once symptoms are perceived . . . [but] women . . . perceive more symptoms and apparently as a consequence visit doctors more often. . . ." Women also "make more use of preventive services than men do." In all these ways, they write, "women appear to take better care of their health, and this may contribute to their lower mortality."

The only one of the "big four" causes of death that takes the lives of more women than men: cerebrovascular disease, or stroke. The reason: Stroke is an age-related disease. To put it plainly, most men don't live long enough to die of stroke. The traditional masculine code sees to that.

Danger: Traditional Masculinity Can Flat-Out Kill

Consider the statistics on accidents—the fourth leading cause of death in this country, which also take the lives of far more males than females. Studies indicate that death rates from car accidents alone are almost three times higher for males—a differential that can be attributed in part to the fact that men do more driving than women do, particularly when conditions are hazardous, and in much larger part to the gender-role training that teaches men it's manly to flirt with death. That's why men pay higher car-insurance premiums than women do. Insurance companies know from their statistics that males—especially young ones—are more likely than females to speed, to forget or refuse to use seat belts, and to take other unnecessary driving risks. Waldron and Johnston note, for example, that observational studies of drivers at intersections found that "15 percent of the male drivers entered the intersection when the light was yellow or red, compared to only 10 percent of female drivers," and that "47 percent of the males and only 20 percent of the females failed to signal the turn."

Combine these statistics on death by car accident with the statistics on death by other accidental causes, and what we come up with is that males are somewhere between three and four times more likely to die in accidents. Waldron and Johnston estimate that approximately half this excess is caused by work-related accidents and that another third is due to "accidental drownings and accidents caused by firearms, which are five times as common among males."

And this estimate doesn't even include homicides, which are another major cause of fatalities among males—especially young inner-city males—and which can be traced, again, to traditional male gender-role training. Males learn that aggression and violence are not only acceptable but that they should take pride in aggression and violence because that's how they prove themselves men. Males are taught to be tough, daring, fearless, assertive, to respond to threats with anger, and never to back down from challenges—all of which conspire to propel males into life-threateningly violent situations and prevent them from retreating or fleeing once they're in them. The results of my study indicate that men are now beginning to stop and think more carefully before acting in accordance with some of these traditional masculine dictates. But this shift is happening slowly. A large-scale 1989 study conducted by the National Institute of Mental Health (NIMH) found that anti-social personality disorders were much more common among men than among women and that behavioral problems were much more common among boys than among girls. When anxious, frustrated, threatened, or dared, in other words, an unfortunately large percentage of males are still reacting in accordance with traditional masculine dictates that require they act out aggressively rather than risk the shame attached to admitting fear or vulnerability. The unfortunate truth is that many men—young and old—would still sooner die than risk being judged unmanly. And they often do. Particularly while under the influence of alcohol or drugs.

The Siren Song of Substance Abuse

In their study, Waldron and Johnston note, for example, that half of all fatal car accidents involve drunken drivers and that men are "particularly likely to be heavy drinkers." That's not to say that women don't also have problems with substance abuse. But there's no question that male problem drinkers outnumber female problem drinkers—four to one, according to the NIMH study, which also found that men are far more likely than women to abuse drugs. It's worth noting that this wasn't always the case. As Waldron and Johnston write, "At the turn of the century, when opiates were widely available from legal sources and relatively safe to use, two-thirds of addicts were women. Now, when opiates are illegal and generally associated with a dangerous life-style, [the vast majority] of the addicts are men. . . ."

Even in drinking and drug-use patterns, in other words, traditional gender-role training will out. Males, again, are supposed to take risks. They're supposed to flaunt danger. They're supposed to challenge authority and be bad. Waldron and Johnston also note that cross-cultural comparisons of alcohol consumption indicate that "heavy use of alcohol is correlated with greater socialization pressures to achieve and with lower tolerance of dependent behavior." They offer no theory, however, as to why pressures to achieve and be independent should cause men to drink. A significant factor, I think, is that the more men sacrifice themselves to their work in order to achieve, the more they also feel entitled to reward themselves for these sacrifices. And one readily available reward in which they very often choose to indulge is alcohol—for two reasons. One is that drinking is an extremely effective way of numbing themselves to job-related stresses and anxieties. The other is that drinking is also a way to retreat from or fend off their partners' bids for closeness while also numbing their own craving for closeness, which they've been taught they shouldn't feel.

What it comes down to is that males are taught they shouldn't feel much of anything. Hence, when forbidden feelings do rise up, they often seek to numb these feelings through the use of alcohol or drugs, which too often have the converse effect of loosening the lid they keep on these feelings and allowing them to rise to the surface and spill out in the form of anger, rage, or violence—sometimes directed against others, sometimes directed against themselves. This brings us to another major cause of death in this country, which is suicide.

Suicide: Men Don't Attempt It— They Do It

Women attempt suicide more often than men do. But men are twice as likely to actually kill themselves—a death-rate differential that can be traced, again, to differences in gender-role training. An unsuccessful suicide attempt is often a desperate cry for help, and women are allowed to do that. They're allowed to say, directly or indirectly, "I'm hurting. I'm frightened. I'm desperate. I need help." Men aren't. The traditional masculine code leaves a man no alternative when these forbidden feelings rise up except to try to escape them—which men often do through impulsive and irreversible means. Again, particularly while under the influence of alcohol or drugs.

Just how deadly the disinhibiting influence of intoxicants can be to men was horribly demonstrated in December 1993, when Jeff Alm, a defensive tackle with the Houston Oilers football team, crashed his car into a guardrail on a highway exit ramp at around two-thirty in the morning while driving with his best friend, Sean Lynch—both of whom had been drinking. According to news reports, Lynch, who apparently hadn't been wearing his seat belt, was thrown out of the car, over the guardrail and down onto a service road some twenty feet below. He died instantly. Alm wasn't injured, but what apparently happened is that when he realized his friend was dead, he became so distraught that he went for the shotgun he was carrying in his car and shot himself in the head.

When men hear a story like this, they are often tempted to dismiss it as just one of those freak occurrences, or to distance themselves from it by focusing their twenty-twenty hindsight on everything the men involved "did wrong"—in this case, getting into a car together after they'd been drinking, not wearing seat belts, and having a gun too readily available. Men who do this, however, are engaging in a certain amount of blaming the victim as a way of buttressing their own sense of invincibility and convincing themselves that such a thing could never happen to them. That's the trap. The more invested a man is in seeing himself as invincible, the more likely he is to take foolish chances with his health and his life. Maybe not these particular chances. But he shouldn't be too quick to congratulate himself. Before he does that, he needs to take a look at some of the other traditionally masculine attitudes and behaviors that have been found to be risk factors for suicide and ask himself how good he is at recognizing and avoiding those.

In a 1983 analysis of a number of studies, sociologists Ronald C. Kessler and James A. McRae found that the gender gap in suicide attempts was narrowing due to a drop in suicide attempts by women and an increase in attempts by men. In a 1981 analysis of five national mental-health surveys, these same researchers found that the incidence of symptoms of psychological distress rose three times more rapidly among men than among women between 1957 and 1976—the same period during which the tectonic plates of gender relations began to shift.

It seems, in other words, that women's psychological health

has been improving over the past few decades while men's psychological health has deteriorated. Why should that be? I would suggest that it's because women have come a long way in breaking free of certain limiting aspects of their traditional gender-role training while men have continued to cling to certain bedrock beliefs about masculinity that are becoming increasingly hazardous to their physical and mental health. Since the social upheavals of the sixties and seventies, women have achieved more flexibility and balance in their lives—whereas men have not yet achieved the same flexibility and balance in theirs.

Consider, for example, that, as Waldron and Johnston note, "suicide rates of men are more strongly correlated with unemployment rates than the suicide rates of women." Why the correlation? One reason, clearly, is that working and being the good provider has traditionally been the core masculine role and responsibility, which makes being out of work so devastating to men that it can be enough to drive them to suicide. Now that women are working, however, some of the responsibility for providing for their families is being lifted off men's shoulders, and they're being encouraged to achieve a healthier balance between work and family life. This could have the beneficial effect of reducing the distress men experience when they're unemployed—if they were willing to make that shift. But many men aren't. Instead, many are struggling to hang on to the good-provider role by investing even more of themselves in their work—which not only leaves them all the more vulnerable to distress if they lose their jobs, but which also leaves them all the more prey to severe work-related stress.

Consider also that whereas marital status seems to have no significant influence on a female's risk of dying prematurely as a result of illness, accident, or suicide, being unmarried or divorced significantly increases the risk of premature death among men. Why? The basic reason is that women traditionally do so much more care-giving than receiving in marriage that losing or living without the care received from a mate often amounts to no significant loss at all. Divorced women sometimes say in all seriousness, in fact, that having a husband to take care of is a lot like having an extra child to take care of and that, in this sense, single life is easier. That's definitely not the case for men. Unlike women, men are quite dependent on the care they receive from their partners. And by care I don't just mean having someone around to do the cooking, cleaning, and laundry. Men enjoy being taken care of in these ways. But they're perfectly capable of doing these things for themselves. What most can't do is sense, name, express, interpret, and manage their own emotions. Most men depend on their partners to manage their emotions for them, just as they depend on their partners to provide them with the warmth and affection they can't admit they crave.

Deprive a man of that kind of care-taking, and his physical and mental health suffers. Unlike women, who invest a great deal of energy in maintaining a network of close relationships, a man who loses a mate may also find himself with no other close relationships to fall back on, or may be reluctant to turn for comfort to the people who do care about him. Isolated with his grief and pain, he resorts to the traditionally masculine way of handling these forbidden feelings, which is to try to distract himself from them or numb himself to them—by burying himself in his work, for example, or by drowning himself in drink. Instead of experiencing, expressing, and seeking help for these feelings, he tries to wall them out—an effort that requires such a prodigious expenditure of physical and psychological energy that it may begin interfering with his ability to function day to day. Without even realizing it's happening he may become less careful about watching what he's doing while handling dangerous tools or start driving through stop signs and red lights without even seeing them. And, meanwhile, he may let his diet go to hell and forget about exercising because, after all, what difference does it make? And then maybe one night, after having a few too many, he falls asleep with a lighted cigarette in his hand, or he examines his life through an alcoholic haze, decides he's got nothing to live for, and goes to the cabinet and pulls out a gun.

THE ROOT CAUSE OF OUR ILLS

One begins to see, then, why females outlive males. As psychologist James Harrison wrote in his 1978 analysis of the factors contributing to men's shorter life expectancy, "the male role may be hazardous to your health." After examining the contributions made by physiology and by gender-role training, Harrison concluded that the contributions made by the former are vastly outweighed by the contributions made by the latter. He pointed in particular to what he considered the five most health-hazardous components of men's traditional gender-role training:

1. Their socialization to engage in high-risk and health-jeopardizing work and leisure activities.

2. Their reluctance to seek medical attention during the early stages of a physical problem.

3. Their inability to feel and express vulnerable emotions.

4. Their socialization to be aggressive and to transform vulnerable emotions into anger.

5. Their over-indulgence in alcohol and drugs, often as a way of coping with stress.

We don't have to look very hard to find the common thread here. All of these components of men's gender-role training require that men numb themselves—to their emotions, to physical sensation, and to their desire for closeness and intimacy. They require that men cut themselves off from others and from themselves.

Much of the work I do with men focuses on helping them overcome this numbness. And men can overcome it, if they want to. That's the critical factor. The exercises I teach are effective with men who want to overcome this condition and who are ready to work through the feelings that start to surface when they do. But some men aren't ready to do that. They think they are. But once the feelings start surfacing they realize they're not.

The Man Who Wanted to Be a Car

A former client, George, was one such man. A fifty-three-year-old, hard-driving, self-made millionaire and bachelor, George came to see me after collapsing one day in his office and being rushed to a hospital emergency room, where a complete medical examination revealed no problem other than physical exhaustion. It turned out that he'd taken a red-eye back from the West Coast the night before, come straight from the airport to the office, worked all morning, then tried to run a sales meeting in the afternoon. That's when he collapsed. Now, you'd think a person would realize he was exhausted before he became so exhausted that he collapsed. But this man didn't. That's how out of touch he was with himself.

He knew it, too. During our first session, he mentioned that his hobby was race-car driving and that one of the things he thought made him good at it was that he was very much in sync with his car. He said he could always tell what was going on under the hood from the way the car handled and how the engine sounded. Then he laughed and said, "I think I'm more in sync with my car than I am with myself. Maybe what I need is a set of dials and gauges I can look at that'll tell me if I'm overheating or running out of gas."

I told George that I couldn't offer him dials and gauges but that I could teach him how to tune into himself the way he tuned into his car, if he was interested in learning. He said he was, so I explained what keeping an emotional response log was all about and urged him to begin keeping one that same day, which he did. George did well during the first phase of this process, when all he had to do was note symptoms of physical discomfort and the situations in which they occurred.

But when we began trying to identify the emotions responsible for triggering these symptoms he became uncomfortable.

He'd been aware even before he started keeping his log that he often got into foul tempers, but he had no idea what caused them. All he knew was that once they took hold, he became a real pain in the ass to be around. So we focused on that for starters. When we looked at the situations in which he succumbed to foul temper, we found that the core circumstance was always the same: Someone he'd been counting on for something had failed to come through. Once we had that figured out, we began working on identifying the unacknowledged and unexpressed emotions that triggered these fits of foul temper—which were, of course, hurt, sadness, disappointment, anxiety, and fear. That's when he started getting uncomfortable. To admit that he felt these feelings when others failed him meant admitting that, like all human beings, he needed other people. And that didn't fit with his image of himself as a self-reliant, autonomous man. I give George credit for coming that far. It's not easy for a man who believes he shouldn't have certain needs to admit that, in fact, he does have them. Admitting this truth to himself is hard enough. Admitting it to someone else is even harder.

That's when George quit therapy. In the last of our five sessions we began exploring how else he might handle these feelings other than by transmuting them into anger. When he was unable to come up with an alternative himself, I asked if he'd considered simply talking to the person who'd failed him—perhaps saying something like, "You know, I was counting on you, and I'm disappointed that you let me down." Perhaps the other person didn't realize how much George was depending on him or her. Or perhaps this person hadn't meant to disappoint him but extenuating circumstances had made it impossible to do otherwise. Or maybe the person was simply being irresponsible, in which case he would at least have a chance to apologize. George didn't like hearing this. The idea of expressing his disappointment—of admitting to another person that he needed him—was too frightening to him. He didn't say that, but I could tell from the way he fidgeted in his chair and avoided my gaze that this option was out. So I backed off. "Just a suggestion," I said. "Think it over. Maybe next week we'll come up with others."

Two days before our next session George had his secretary call and tell me that he wouldn't be able to keep our appointment. A bad sign: He'd had scheduling conflicts twice before, and both times he had called me himself. "He said to tell you he'll call in a few days to reschedule," said his secretary. He never did.

Living in Fear of Being Human Makes for a Miserable Life

It's possible that after mulling things over, George decided to try out this other way of handling his feelings. He'd progressed far enough to at least understand why he got into foul tempers and to realize that another option was available. That's more insight than many men possess. Many have little awareness of how imprisoned they are by gender-role training. Nor do they realize how adversely their health is affected by living in a constant state of guardedness against admitting or revealing human feelings and needs.

Men don't have to reach the extremes of going thirty hours without sleep or flying into regular fits of foul temper in order for their health to be negatively affected. The stress of simply living in a constant state of guardedness is enough to do damage. In his ongoing investigations of Masculine Gender Role Stress (MGRS), psychologist Richard Eisler has found that the more rigidly a man adheres to traditional masculine ideology (as measured by his self-scoring of how stressful he'd find forty hypothetical situations such as "telling your mate you love her" or "having your children see you cry"), the more pronounced his body's stress response (as measured by elevated heart beat and blood pressure) when his masculinity is challenged. Eisler found that it makes no difference whether the challenge is physical (e.g., putting a hand in ice water) or psychological (e.g., being challenged by a female researcher about professional performance). The higher a man's estimate of how stressful he'd find the hypothetical situations, the more his heart rate and blood pressure increase when presented with either challenge. The reason, Eisler proposes, is that the more rigidly a man adheres to traditional masculine ideology, the more he perceives these challenges as threats, which triggers his body to kick into fight-or-flight response.

Take the example of putting a hand in ice water. That's a physically uncomfortable experience no matter what a man's ideology. But the man less wedded to the traditional code is more able to experience and acknowledge that discomfort—to say to himself and perhaps to others, "Yep, this is uncomfortable, all right." He's less threatened by it, so his body registers less stress. The traditional man is more likely to think, "I shouldn't be feeling this. I can't let this get to me." He fights that discomfort because he does experience it as a threat.

The same goes for psychological discomfort. What we're really talking about is fear—men's fear of being judged or judging themselves as unmanly. The more fearful a man is of failing to live up to his own rigid beliefs about what a man's supposed to be, the harder he has to work at defending his masculine self-image and the more threatened he's going to feel when he thinks his masculinity is being challenged. In his work, Eisler has found that the situations that trigger Masculine Gender Role Stress are those that violate the traditional masculine prohibitions against: (1) physical inadequacy; (2) emotional expressiveness; (3) subordination to women; (4) failure to be rational and logical; and (5) sexual or work-related failure. That makes for fear, defensiveness, anxiety, and stress in an all-encompassing range of life situations.

A CURE FOR OUR ILLS

The results of my study indicate that men have begun reconsidering the wisdom of trying to live in accordance with this code. And it's obviously in their interests to do so. Uncomfortable as it can be for men to acknowledge and reveal feelings and needs, studies indicate that the results can be both physically and psychologically healing.

In a recent series of studies investigating the effects of writing about personal experiences, psychologist James Pennebaker found that, during the actual writing process, students who wrote about pleasant events and emotions experienced soothing physical sensations—as measured by decreased galvanic skin response—whereas those who wrote about unpleasant events and emotions experienced physical discomfort. To put it another way, he found that writing about positive experiences and emotions can trigger a physically pleasant warm glow, whereas writing about negative experiences and emotions can hurt—in the short term. He also found, however, that whereas students who wrote about pleasant events experienced more immediate physical benefits, those who endured the discomfort of writing about unpleasant events and emotions experienced more improvement in health in the long term—as measured by enhanced immune-system functioning at the end of the study and fewer visits to doctors during the next six months. He found, in other words, that admitting and working through feelings of hurt, rejection, abandonment, and all the other feelings men don't acknowledge having can be beneficial to health. Put simply, he found that breaking through the wall men build between themselves and their feelings and reconnecting with forbidden emotions can be healing. Healing, as Ornish writes, "in the real sense of the word"—meaning "to bring together, to make whole."

That's the first step in overcoming emotional numbness and reducing isolation. The second step is for men to open themselves to more closeness and connectedness with other people. And by that I don't mean just spending time in the company of other people. It's perfectly possible for a man to be with people and still feel alone if he's always guarding against revealing his true thoughts and feelings, which many men do so automatically they don't even realize they're doing it—not only with their partners but also with their male friends. We'll discuss male friendships in more detail in Chapter Ten. The point I want to make here is that male friendships are characterized by a number of wonderful traits, but intimate sharing tends not to be one of them. As a rule, male friends prefer to engage in pleasurable activities rather than intimate talk. But intimate talk is what real closeness is all about. It's about revealing enough of ourselves to other people to feel truly known by them. It's about knowing the comfort and security of feeling accepted and loved for who we really are. And, of course, it's not only about feeling accepted and loved by others. It's also about accepting and loving them in return. It's about being sensitive and responsive to their feelings and needs just as we want them to be sensitive and responsive to ours.

Men aren't all that good at this kind of relationship nurturing and intimate sharing because, unlike women, they were never encouraged to develop these skills. But they can learn them, and it's clearly in their interest to learn them—particularly where family relationships are concerned.

In one 1991 study, psychologists Rosalind C. Barnett and Nancy C. Marshall found that a man's satisfaction with the role he played as a father was a significant predictor of his physical well-being. The more satisfied he was with the role he played, the more likely he was to enjoy good physical health. In another 1991 study, Barnett, Marshall, and psychologist Joseph Pleck found that a man's satisfaction with his fathering role was also a significant predictor of his psychological well-being—as was his satisfaction with the role he played as a husband. What these and other findings tell us is that a man's physical and mental well-being is significantly affected by the quality of his family relationships, which is significantly affected in turn by his capacity for intimacy: his ability to experience and express his feelings and needs and to be sensitive and responsive to other people's feelings and needs, to be known and loved for who he really is and to know and love others for who they really are—strengths, weaknesses, and all.

Traditional Masculinity or Good Health—The Choice Is Yours

What all these findings boil down to is that the more men wall themselves off from themselves and others, the more their health suffers. The more connected they are to themselves and others, the more likely they are to enjoy good physical and mental health.

It's one thing for men to understand this truth intellectually, however, and quite another for them to act on that understanding. That's where men often run into trouble. Even when they genuinely want to overcome their own physical and emotional numbness, they often have difficulty actually doing it. Even when they know where their difficulties lie, they may still have trouble overcoming these obstacles. It takes hard work. But I've yet to meet a man who's done this hard work who doesn't feel that the rewards that come of doing it are more than worth all the effort involved.

In Chapter Ten we'll take a closer look at some of the common obstacles that prevent men from drawing closer to friends and loved ones, some of which operate on extremely subtle levels and do particular damage to a man's relationship with his partner—which is, of course, the most important relationship of all. Before we turn our attention to those obstacles, however, we need to take a good look at how poorly men and women are both served by one of the most deeply ingrained and most intimacy-destroying sets of attitudes instilled in men as a result of their traditional gender-role training.

That is, men's attitudes toward sex.

CHAPTER NINE

Men and Sex

UNCONNECTED LUST:
RECONSTRUCTING THE
MALE SEXUAL CODE

Working out at my gym one day recently, I overheard two men talking about President Clinton. Not about his health-care plan, or the Whitewater investigation, or his handling of Haiti, but about his past and present-day sex life.

"So he had affairs," one man said to the other. "*No* kidding? I mean, come on. The guy was governor of Arkansas. Someone in that position? I'd fool around, too. And I'll tell you something. Now that he's president?" A low chuckle. "I say he should be able to sleep with whoever he wants. I mean, hell, what's the point of being president if you can't have affairs?"

His companion laughed—one of those tight, unenthusiastic laughs one produces to signal discomfort, in a comradely way, with a subject one would rather not pursue.

The first man looked puzzled and disappointed—as if he'd

been hoping his remark would stimulate some juicy male banter. But he got the message and, embarrassed and annoyed by the other man's lack of response, let the subject drop.

There was a time, not that long ago, when the majority of men would have seen nothing wrong with engaging in this kind of male banter. But those days are gone. With sensational events such as the Clarence Thomas hearings, William Kennedy Smith's date-rape trial, Mike Tyson's rape conviction, the Joey Buttafuoco/Amy Fisher affair, the Tailhook scandal, and the O. J. Simpson trial now occupying the news, traditional male sexual attitudes have come under intense scrutiny.

Too intense scrunity to many men's way of thinking. In my workshops men often grumble about feeling as though the entire male sex has suddenly been put on trial. "You know what?" a man will say. "I'm tired of having to go around walking on eggshells, watching every move I make, every word that comes out of my mouth. I mean, sure, there are guys out there doing terrible things to women. But since when does that make us all bad guys? You can't just lump all men together like that. Guys who do that kind of stuff—they've got problems. Most men don't have anything in common with them."

True—and not true. The vast majority of men are indeed decent, honorable, good-hearted men who would never think of engaging in the kind of male sexual misconduct that has been making the headlines lately. They may have ogled women's breasts now and then. Or they may have called a woman Honey or Babe. Or they may have joked to their mate that her butt was getting a little big. That kind of thing. But that's different.

That's where they're wrong. I'm not saying that men who've engaged in these behaviors are capable of more serious forms of sexual misconduct. What I am saying is that all these behaviors are related. They're all part of the same syndrome, and, to one degree or another, most men suffer from it. I've taken to calling this syndrome unconnected lust. Lust, of course, is the desire to satisfy purely physical sexual urges. Unconnected, as I use it, means separated from our other human desires and separated from a relationship with a person—un-influenced by sufficient awareness of how our emotions, needs, and fears drive our sexual behavior, and unmoderated by sufficient sensitivity to women's needs and how our behavior affects them.

Male Versus Female Sexual Styles

It's now being recognized that when it comes to what "turns us on," men and women are different. For example, hard-core pornography tends to appeal more to men whereas erotica and romance tend to appeal more to women. Men, for the most part, respond to straightforwardly sexual materials whereas women usually prefer a heavy dollop of story line and some sense of relationship between sexual partners.

That's a bit of an oversimplification and isn't meant to imply that there's no crossover between male and female sexual tastes. Men and women both like their sex hot and lusty. Men and women both find sex especially exciting when a relationship is new. And as Erica Jong informed the world in her 1973 novel, *Fear of Flying*, like men, women also fantasize about and sometimes engage in the brief, anonymous sexual encounter, which Jong dubbed the "zipless fuck." That's what the sexual revolution of the sixties and seventies was all about. It was about women breaking free of the good-girl conditioning that required they tamp down their lustfulness and claiming the same right to sexual pleasure that men have always enjoyed.

That's one of the plusses of men's traditional sexual style. Men have always been allowed much more freedom to own their sexuality. They feel perfectly entitled to their sexual desires, and they're generally much less conflicted and inhibited than women are about satisfying these desires. Indeed, that's a trait many women say they both envy and appreciate in men. Recently, for example, three colleagues and I invited some of the men and women attending an American Psychological Association convention to participate in what we call an intergender dialogue workshop. As part of the workshop the men and women were asked to name the strengths each feels the other brings to relationships. A number of the women said they appreciated men's franker enjoyment of and greater willingness to initiate sex—men's "sexual friskiness," they called it. They said men's friskiness makes them feel friskier, too.

That's one facet of traditional male sexuality that can work to the benefit of both partners in a relationship. But it doesn't always. It depends on whether a man indulges that friskiness within the relationship or outside it. In a 1993 analysis of gender differences in sexuality, researchers Mary Beth Oliver and Janet Shibley Hyde found that males "had considerably more permissive attitudes" toward casual sex than did females. Women, much more than men, in other words, view sex not only as a way of satisfying physical urges but also as a mode of intimate sharing and communication. To women sex is about closeness whereas to men sex is about sex.

So what's wrong with that? In his 1992 book, *The New Male Sexuality*, psychologist Bernie Zilbergeld writes that men have "taken a lot of heat in recent years" over their attitudes about sex. "We are told that we are obsessed with sex, especially sex without love and commitment, that we push too hard for it and in inappropriate ways. . . . Such attitudes, we are told, are immature and maybe downright sick." Zilbergeld argues that these criticisms are "wrongheaded and destructive." Males "can't help having their attitudes, which are probably due at least as much to physiology as to learning," he writes. "Sex, after all, is life-affirming, and there's no point in feeling bad about that."

Having stated his position, Zilbergeld goes on to list fourteen common characteristics of "men's style of sex." Among them, he lists:

- **Sex is very important to men.** Males "spend more time thinking, dreaming, and fantasizing about sex than females. . . . Many of them are willing to pay for sex and some will even use force to get it, neither of which is common among women."

- **For men, sex has intrinsic value.** Like women, men "prefer sex in a loving relationship. But men also . . . view sex as a good thing in and of itself, regardless of whether it's part of a loving relationship or if the participants have any other feelings for each other."

- **Men sexualize all sorts of situations and behaviors.** "Because sex is so important to men, they tend to see sex and sexual invitations everywhere, often much to the surprise or even shock of the recipients of their attentions."

- **Men tend to get aroused by aspects of female anatomy that they see.** Men are more visually oriented than women are, which may explain why men "generally prefer young, physically attractive women. . . . Women seem more flexible with respect to age and physical characteristics."

- **Men tend to view sexual arousal as a runaway train; once in motion, it should not be stopped or deflected until it reaches its destination.** Some "nasty scenes occur" when men feel led on by women who want to stop that train before it reaches its destination or who "haven't wanted to have sex at all."

- **Men are goal-oriented in sex.** Women like lots of touching. Men, on the other hand, "often view touching as . . . a means to an end, and go for the genitals and orgasm as quickly as possible." Women can enjoy sex without orgasm. "But many men can't . . . largely, I think, because they . . . don't enjoy sex much except for orgasm."

- **Men don't necessarily want to be emotionally or physically close after sex.** For some men "the problem is that they aren't sure what to do. . . . Others are uncomfortable with so much closeness. For others, it's more the case that since sex was all that was wanted, now that it's over there's no point in hanging around."

- **Men are interested in a variety of sexual partners for the sake of variety.** Even men who are happily married to gorgeous, sexy women will patronize prostitutes and/or have affairs, not because "something is lacking at home," but simply because they hunger for variety.

- **Men don't like to admit to sexual problems, especially their own.** Women are able to admit to sexual shortcomings and "look for ways of making things better." But men can't. "Since so much rides on a man's being good . . . in sex, it's very difficult for men to hear they have a problem in this area."

Zilbergeld sees nothing wrong with these characteristics of men's sexual style. Like the female sexual style, the male sexual style is "really OK," he writes. After all, "everyone is doing what comes naturally, whether naturally be defined as what's built in or what's been learned over the years."

True, men are doing what comes naturally. That's the problem. These sexual beliefs and behaviors are so deeply ingrained that they seem inborn and therefore not to be tampered with. But such thinking is fallacious. What Zilbergeld calls "men's style of sex" and what I call "unconnected lust" is no more inborn than is the language a person speaks. Like the capacity for language, the human sex drive is born into us. But like the specific language a person speaks, men's sexual style is learned. It's a product of early life experiences and the training males receive from parents, peers, and the culture at large.

A SHORT HISTORY OF MALE SEXUAL SOCIALIZATION

Let's dispense, first of all, with the belief shared by many men and women that males have a stronger biological sex drive than do females. As psychologist Robert Allan Silverberg notes in his 1990 book, *Psychotherapy for Men: Transcending the Masculine Mystique*, there's "no definitive evidence" to support this "fairly widespread notion." If we examine the evidence that's offered, what we find is that it's circumstantial—that the reason we think males have a stronger sex drive is because males behave as if they have a stronger sex drive. Zilbergeld notes, for example, that "males start to masturbate earlier and they do it more often [than females]"—a fact that Oliver and Hyde's study confirms. But is this evidence that males have a stronger biological sex drive? Not necessarily. As Silverberg and other researchers note, this gender disparity is just as likely to stem from the fact that males have an external penis that makes itself the all-the-more fascinating focus of a young male's attention by becoming erect and that is also easily accessible to stimulation. As for men's greater willingness to initiate sex—to attribute that gender difference solely to differences in biological sex drive is the equivalent of saying that the only reason men are more aggressive than women is because testosterone makes them that way. It completely ignores the powerful influence of differences in male and female gender-role socialization.

Sex: Why Men Need to Keep It Impersonal

One result of male gender-role socialization is a discomfort with closeness that prompts males to separate sex from emotion. This discomfort dates back even further than their discovery of the pleasures of masturbation—all the way back to infancy, when males first learn to equate being male with being separate from their mothers and first begin burying their unfulfilled dependency needs. As we've already discussed, these needs often surface in adult men as unconscious dependency on their partners, which conflicts with their unconscious sense of defensive autonomy. A man hungers for closeness, but when his partner comes close he retreats or pushes her away, because he experiences closeness as a threat to his male identity. As psychologists Liam Hudson and Bernadine Jacot write in their 1991 book, *The Way Men Think: Intellect, Intimacy and the Erotic Imagination*, ". . . the adult heterosexual male *must* view the intimately personal—and, more specifically, the intimately sexual—ambivalently. On the one hand it is a chance magically to recover a primitively symbiotic comfort. On the other, it represents a return to a state of defenselessness. Either the male holds himself back from intimate experience, treating the people he desires as objects; or he abandons himself to it, thereby exposing himself to anxiety, even psychic annihilation. In the first mode, he is less than wholly human: a copulatory gadget. In the second . . . he is exposed to intolerable extremities of psychic pleasure and psychic pain. In the first case, he retains his sense of agency, . . . seeking intense but containable discharges of pleasure. In the second, he will experience a collapse of agency, and the need, thereafter, to effect repairs; to gather himself back together as a being who has boundaries to maintain and a life of threats to endure."

Agency means ability to take action and accomplish goals. That's another aspect of male gender-role training that contributes to men's problems with unconnected lust. From earliest childhood males are taught that men are supposed to be assertive, action-oriented, good at getting what they want. What they aren't taught is to be sensitive to other people's feelings and needs. By the time an infant male becomes a young child his capacity for this kind of emotional empathy has in fact been thoroughly squelched—as has his ability to feel and express his own emotions. These lessons then get driven home by the similar messages he later receives from his peers, teachers, and society.

Sex: The Only Access to Intimacy Men Are Allowed

The emotions most forbidden to males fall into one of two categories. The first is vulnerable emotions such as anxiety, fear, sadness, and humiliation, which young males learn to transform into aggression and anger. The second is caring emotions such as warmth and affection, for which young males are permitted no outlet at all. Not by other males, that is. Mothers tend to be fairly accepting of their sons' expression of caring emotions. But a boy quickly learns that being physically affectionate or engaging in traditionally feminine pretend-nurturing kinds of play with a teddy bear or a doll is frowned upon by his father. And heaven forbid a boy should let his male friends catch him behaving in a caring, considerate, or affectionate manner, because there's nothing but hell to pay if they do. Then it's either, "What are you, some kind of queer?" or, "Aww, look at the mama's boy," or, if he's even so much as friendly or polite to a girl, "Are you in looovvve?" It doesn't take more than a couple such incidents for a boy to learn the rules: Hugging, kissing, touching, holding hands, trading confidences, sharing feelings, showing compassion, expressing affection—that's girls' stuff or "queer" stuff. Throughout childhood and especially as they pass through adolescence, when they become consumed with proving their masculinity, boys hold themselves and one another to the standard of needing and caring for no one, of standing and acting alone.

Deprived of any outlet for expressing caring feelings, the young male drives these forbidden emotions underground. There they lie dormant, along with his unfulfilled dependency needs, until he reaches his early to mid-twenties, when he has matured enough to become involved in his first committed relationship and to feel a little less uncomfortable with these feelings and needs. A little less. He's still not self-aware or self-accepting enough to be truly comfortable with these needs and feelings. Nor is he verbally facile enough to freely express them in words the way women can more easily do. He can manage the occasional "I love you"—which some men blurt out during a moment of passion, not realizing that what they really mean is, "I love being able to feel close for once." But that's about it. He does have somewhat more of an inkling that these feelings and needs are there, however, and does have somewhat more of an urge to express and satisfy them. So he seeks to satisfy this urge through the only means available to him, which is sex.

That's another reason sex is so much more important to men than to women. Women are allowed to satisfy their needs for touch, tenderness, connectedness, and affection more directly—through verbal assurances that they're loved, for example, or through affectionate, nonsexual hugging, kissing, and cuddling, or through emotional sharing with women friends. Men aren't permitted to have these needs, much less to fulfill them. Even when simple touch, tenderness, connectedness, and affection are what they want, they often don't know it. What they think they hunger for—because it's the only thing they're allowed to hunger for—is sex.

This gender difference can be a source of deep frustration and pain to both partners in a relationship. I think, for example, of one couple I counseled who hadn't had sex in three months. Their story was a familiar one. He saw the deterioration of their sex life as their main problem. She saw it as a symptom of their main problem, which to her was a lack of emotional closeness and connectedness. She wanted more open and intimate verbal communication. He didn't. Whenever she tried to share feelings with him or to get him to share feelings with her, he closed down. "We never talk," she said. "All we do is exchange information." "I don't know what she wants from me," he said. "I don't have anything to say." Stalemate. To her, sex was an expression of closeness and connectedness. She didn't feel close to him; therefore, she wasn't comfortable having sex. To him, sex was a route to closeness and connectedness—his only route. What did talking have to do with having sex?

Because a man's fear of closeness runs so deep, he would feel an impulse to fend off intimacy even if all other aspects of his gender-role training mitigated against it. But they don't. They encourage it.

The Sexual Gospel According to Henry Miller, Hugh Hefner, and 2 Live Crew

We've already established that males are taught from earliest childhood to be independent, emotionally unexpressive, and goal-oriented. As mentioned earlier, young males become particularly concerned with living up to these standards as they pass through adolescence. Put the two together, and what we come up with is that most young males' first sexual experiences have little to do with the expression of caring emotion and everything to do with satisfying physical lust and, more important, with proving their manhood by "scoring."

During their first, formative sexual experiences, in other words, young males become practiced at seeing and using females as sexual objects. And it's during this same period, of course, that impressionable young males are most attuned and susceptible to the cultural messages they receive concerning what kind of female does or doesn't make for an appropriate sexual object. Zilbergeld writes, for example, of often watching "a group of . . . boys at a bookstore looking at *Playboy* or *Penthouse*"—a scene he considers "charming." There's "something truly wonderful about it, a lot of what I'd call good energy," he writes. "I rarely sensed any disparagement of women. The same was true in my high school days when we boys passed around novels with explicit sexual descriptions.

Desire, curiosity, and great enthusiasm, but really no ugly feelings toward girls or women."

I'm not so sure I agree. But be that as it may, there remains the question of what young males learn to want in a woman when they look at these magazines. The women pictured are never average-looking or merely sort of pretty, after all. They're invariably gorgeous, lush-bodied young females depicted in sexually provocative poses. The message to young males is clear. The female deserving of attention, writes Silverberg, "possesses, in the male mind, a body flawlessly built and sexually insatiable; given the extent to which magazines such as *Playboy, Penthouse,* and *Cosmopolitan* along with television and movies portray women with apparently 'perfect' faces and bodies, it is understandable . . . why men are so concerned with women's physical attributes and so often dissatisfied or uninterested with real-life women 'in the flesh.' "

As for the sexually explicit novels to which many men turned in their youth, as Zilbergeld writes, "to learn everything we could about the doing of sex"—Silverberg notes that what males learned from these novels is: (1) A "real man" has a huge, rock-hard penis, which he works with "expert, total, inexhaustible maneuverability"; (2) women want sex all the time and want to be "forcefully taken" by men, despite "any protestations to the contrary"; and (3) women "require little foreplay or interpersonal communication" prior to sex.

Today, of course, young males don't have to turn to magazines or books to absorb these messages. All they have to do is flip on MTV or listen to certain rap lyrics. Now we have adolescent boys in both inner-city and affluent suburban neighborhoods thinking it's cool to call females "bitches" and "whores."

A single mother of a fifteen-year-old boy told me that she recently overheard her son and a friend calling a female classmate a bitch and immediately gave both boys hell for it, warning her son that if she heard that word come out of his mouth again, he'd be grounded for a week and that the punishment would escalate with each succeeding offense. "He knows I mean it," she said. "And I'm pretty sure he'll never let me hear him use that word again. But that's not the same as his understanding he shouldn't use it at all. I'm not sure he understands that, and I don't know how to make him understand that." She sighed. "It's at times like this that I wish he had a father. Because that's where he really needs to hear that this kind of language is unacceptable. I don't think it has as much impact when he hears it from a woman. He needs to hear it from a man."

She'd put her finger on another aspect of traditional male upbringing that complicates men's problems with unconnected lust. All boys look primarily to their fathers to teach them how to be a man: what a man does and doesn't do, what he does and doesn't say, what is and isn't the right way to treat a woman. Is it okay for a man to admit mistakes, inadequacies, and worries, or must he always be a pillar of self-confidence and strength? Is it okay for him to express emotions, get misty-eyed or cry, or are anger and stoicism his basic on-off switch? Is it okay for him to be sensitive and responsive to other people's feelings, or is it everyone else's job to accommodate and defer to him? Is it okay to be physically affectionate with a female just to be affectionate, or must all physical contact lead to sex?

A boy learns the answers to these questions from many sources. He takes in the messages conveyed through television, movies, books, magazines, and music. He observes how other adult males behave and heeds the rules of acceptable masculine conduct within his same-sex peer group. But those are all secondary sources of information to which he'll give more or less credence depending on whether the information he gathers corresponds with or contradicts what he's learning from his father.

But what if a boy has no father? Or what if his father isn't around because of divorce? Or what if his father is a traditionally distant, demanding, difficult dad who's so locked into what he considers his primary roles as chief breadwinner and family disciplinarian that he simply isn't physically or emotionally available to his son? Where is the young male then?

Lost is where he is—with no trusted, respected, male role model to help him sort through and evaluate what he's learning about manhood from other sources. And there's little chance of a boy being able to do this on his own. Emotional numbness has already blocked his ability to listen to his own feelings about what kind of man he wants to be. And gender-role training combined with peer pressure insure that he doesn't dare risk violating the exaggerated standards of masculinity that rule most adolescent peer groups. Nor is he likely to risk expressing doubts about them and the other messages he's absorbing about manhood from popular culture to even his closest male friend. Adolescent females confess doubts, worries, and insecurities to each other. Adolescent males don't. They use each other as mirrors in which to practice and polish their masculine act. With no way to distinguish fictional manhood ideals from the reality of manhood, a young male with no father to guide him is likely to take fiction as reality and shape his sexual beliefs and behaviors accordingly.

The more perfect a product a male is of this kind of traditional gender-role training, the more predisposed he'll be in adulthood to limiting sex to unconnected lust. In a 1993 paper on men's fixations with women's bodies, psychologist Gary R. Brooks, of the Veterans' Administration Medical Center in Temple, Texas, describes something similar to this syndrome and lists various ways it can manifest in a man. Telltale signs include:

- His preferred sexual outlet is masturbating while looking at pictures of naked women.

- His masturbatory fantasies are always of naked women and never of himself with a woman he loves sharing a sensual, intimate moment.

- He can't enjoy sexual intercourse or maintain an erection without fantasizing about naked or semi-naked women.

- He can't stay away from topless bars.

- He can't stop watching bikini beauty contests and can't make himself look away during sexually provocative TV commercials.

- He derives enormous sexual pleasure from persuading his parter to "dress up" (as a French maid, hooker or dominatrix) or to "perform" (as a stripper or topless dancer).

- He can't imagine having sexual relations with a woman whose body has aged.

- He would urge his female partner to consider painful, expensive, and dangerous plastic surgery to "save" their relationship.

- He can't have a meaningful conversation in a public place with a woman he loves without repeatedly breaking eye contact to stare at the breasts or rears of women passing by.

To the degree a man's lust is unconnected, he's likely to try to satisfy it through means that alienate or insult his partner—which reduces his chances of satisfying it and increases his sexual frustration. In the more extreme cases, Hudson and Jacot write, "The male, separated from his source of primitive comfort, an agent, his imagination fueled, will also be susceptible in ways that the female is not to elaborations and displacements of sexual appetite. He is more likely than the female to displace his desire for a person onto part of that person or onto an object; and he is more likely to act out such desires in literal terms, rather than simply fantasizing about them. In as much as a man finds his chosen form of sexual endeavor cutting him off progressively from primitive comfort, he is likely, too, to infuse his behavior with misogynous resentment or hatred. He may resort inappropriately to violence or become promiscuous. He may also become a pervert."

What that means in lay language is that men who fear closeness and view it as a threat to their sense of self tend to be susceptible to transferring, or displacing, their lust onto a part of a woman's body (such as her breasts or feet), or onto an object (such as a woman's panties or shoes), or onto a child's body as a way of protecting themselves from the anxiety about closeness that normal sexual activity provokes. And having been trained all their lives to be "agentic" and go after what they want, they don't just entertain these desires in fantasy— they act on them. But, of course, the more unconnected their lust, the less likely they are to find a partner who's willing to satisfy their desires—which means they must either pay or force someone to satisfy them.

Certainly, most men's problems with unconnected lust aren't this severe. But many men suffer from this syndrome to at least a mild degree, and some take it a lot further. At the mild end, some men are able to express tenderness during sex but only during sex, while others have to fantasize about other women in order to be able to make love to their partners. Further along the continuum, some men are chronic oglers of women's body parts, and others are compulsive womanizers. At the far end, some men sexually harass and verbally abuse women, while others are gripped by perversions and fetishes, and still others commit rape, sexual violence, and child molestation.

Most men's problems with unconnected lust fall into the mild to moderate range, edging up to and sometimes including compulsive womanizing but stopping short of the more severely dysfunctional behaviors. In a certain respect, then, men are right to resent being lumped in with the likes of Mike Tyson and Joey Buttafuoco. But what they don't recognize is that their own more mildly disconnected sexual behaviors also do harm.

Destructive Entitlement: Self-Pity Leads to Self-Indulgence

What some men don't see is that their sense of entitlement to engage in these behaviors is destructive. That's what it's called: "destructive entitlement." And it's there inside most men, all tied in with their conflicting yearning for and fear of closeness and their unconscious dependency needs. All three date back to infancy and early childhood, when males are prematurely forced out of their infantile state of oneness with their mothers and deprived of compensatory nurturing from their fathers. As discussed earlier, the psychological term for these early life experiences is normative developmental traumas—"normative" meaning they're considered such a normal part of male upbringing that they're not even recognized as traumas. But if they're not acknowledged they can't be mourned. And if they're not mourned a man doesn't recover from them. He carries the hurt inside, which can give rise to an unconscious sense of "destructive entitlement"—a belief that he's entitled to always put his own desires first and take more than he gives to make up for the hurts he suffered in infancy and childhood.

And because most men unconsciously look to their partners to minister to their needs, it's usually their partners who bear the brunt of men's sense of destructive entitlement. Some men feel entitled to demand that their partners accommodate their sexual desires without ever returning the favor. Others feel entitled to poke fun at their partners' body parts, just for laughs, even though this kind of joking hurts their mates. Others feel entitled to ogle other women in the presence of their wives.

Combine destructive entitlement and unconnected lust with men's drive to sacrifice themselves to their work, and the result can be a particular form of the "sacrifice-indulge" cycle in which men feel entitled to reward themselves for sacrificing by indulging in different forms of nonrelational sex, such as one-night stands or extramarital affairs. Social attitudes reinforce this cycle. The idea that beautiful women are sexual prizes to which powerful men have right of unlimited access is beginning to give way now, but it's still fairly widespread. In workshops and counseling sessions I still hear many men expressing views similar to the one expressed by the man I overheard in the gym, who thought any man who becomes president has earned the right to sleep with any woman he wants.

In a recent "Doonesbury" comic strip that poked fun at the Tailhook scandal, cartoonist Garry Trudeau artfully lampooned this deeply entrenched male mindset. The setting is a Naval convention. A high-ranking Navy official is standing behind a podium, concluding his address to a room full of men.

> **Official**: Before you gents head off for the party, any other questions? Yes, officer in the front.
> **Lieutenant**: Sir, I'm a naval aviator. Every day I put my can on the line flying high-performance fighters for my country. I'm the elite of the elite. After a hard day at Mach 2, aren't I entitled to some action on the ground?
> **Official**: No, lieutenant, you are not so entitled.
> **Lieutenant**: Mach 2 gets me nothing?
> **Official**: Let me be clear. Mach 2 and fifty cents gets you coffee.

One can understand the lieutenant's and other men's confusion. Here they are, suddenly being told it's no longer acceptable to view women as sexual prizes even as our culture continues to portray women in precisely this way—not just in magazines such as *Playboy* and *Penthouse*, but also in films, on television, in print advertisements and TV commercials, and in a number of women's magazines.

RECONNECTING LUST:
A RETURN TO INTIMACY

The results of my study indicate that men are beginning to move away from this traditional "male as stud, female as sex-object" sexual ethic toward a more intimate, egalitarian, less goal-oriented philosophy about sex. The men in my study still felt that it's important for a man to be "good in bed," and they didn't buy the idea that "a man doesn't need to have an erection in order to enjoy sex." But when they were presented with a host of other traditionally masculine beliefs about sex, their response was essentially: "Not that old saw." They disagreed, for example, with the traditional beliefs that "a man should always be ready for sex," that "a man should always take the initiative," that "touching is simply the first step toward sex," that "hugging and kissing should always lead to intercourse," and that a man "shouldn't bother with sex unless he can achieve an orgasm." They also disagreed that a man "shouldn't have to worry about birth control." Finally, these men repudiated the notion that it doesn't matter who a man's sex partner is so long as she's willing, agreeing instead that a man "should love his sex partner."

I think this study is picking up on the beginnings of a movement on the part of men to reconnect lust with emotional intimacy. I take these findings to mean men are beginning to realize that while satiating unconnected lust can be gratifying, its gratifications are transitory and shallow compared to the richer, more enduring rewards of gratifying lust within the context of an intimate relationship. I think men are beginning to realize how much they've been missing out on by holding themselves back from experiencing these rewards.

And what have men been missing out on? First and foremost: the joys of emotional intimacy—of being able to share deeply with and feel deeply connected to and deeply cared for by another person. Many men deprive themselves of this deeply comforting experience. They also deprive themselves of the deep sense of satisfaction and indispensability that comes of being able to provide that comfort to another human being. When sex becomes a form of intimate communication between two people who feel truly known and cherished by each other, it becomes a different thing entirely. It becomes a safe haven where both partners feel relaxed and free enough to open themselves to intimacy and pleasure—to play, experiment, take chances, and explore.

As a man draws closer to his partner, he often also begins to realize that this woman he thinks he knows so well is in fact full of mysteries and surprises, and that he, too, has needs, desires, and sensitivities he never knew were there—or did know were there but never before dared reveal. That's both the most frightening and the most liberating aspect of emotional and sexual intimacy. One reason a man avoids intimacy is because he's afraid that if he lets his partner in too close she'll see him for the flawed, imperfect human being he feels he is and won't desire or love him anymore. But what a man almost invariably discovers when he does let his partner in close is that she already knows him much better than he thinks she does—better than he knows himself, often—and that it's the real human being he is that she loves and desires, not the false image he's trying to protect. What he discovers, in other words, is that he doesn't have to pretend anymore.

When a man overcomes his fear of closeness enough for these things to start happening, he begins to realize what he's been missing out on by holding back from intimacy. But it takes work to overcome this fear. And it does mean giving up some of the more superficial, intimacy-destroying pleasures in which he feels entitled to indulge.

The Man Who Couldn't Stop Ogling

A former client named Peter is a good case in point. A forty-five-year-old history professor, husband and father of two, Peter thought of himself as a liberal, enlightened man. And in many ways he was. His problem, which he didn't see as a problem even when his wife, Kate, a forty-three-year-old English professor, became so fed up with it that she insisted they see a counselor: He was addicted to ogling young women's breasts.

He didn't deny that he did it. His stance was that he couldn't help it—that he had no control over himself. To use Zilbergeld's phrase, he was just "doing what comes naturally" and felt wronged when Kate became angry and "punished" him later by refusing to have sex. Note that it hadn't seemed to occur to him that his behavior might make his wife feel rejected. Many men don't understand how much damage they do to a woman's self-esteem by indulging in this kind of behavior, which not only makes her feel insulted and momentarily unattractive but also reinforces her belief that no matter how hard she works to look good, she can never look good enough—because the only way a woman can look good is by looking like an eighteen-year-old *Playboy* Bunny or fashion model. What woman isn't going to refuse sex when that happens? What woman feels like getting sexually intimate when she's just been made to feel unattractive?

You'd think a man would understand that. But Peter didn't. Nor would it have done any good simply to tell him, "This is what you're doing to your wife." He'd have understood intellectually, but he wouldn't have understood emotionally. My task was to bring Peter to the point where he was capable of actually feeling Kate's pain—which meant first helping him identify and overcome the obstacles preventing him from feeling emotional empathy with his wife. So I suggested he and I meet privately for a while to explore why he had such difficulty controlling these impulses.

During our first private session it emerged that, like many

men of his generation, Peter had been raised in a traditional "male as breadwinner/female as homemaker" household. His father, who'd worked for a railroad, had been a demanding, emotionally distant man who'd disapproved of Peter's lack of mechanical aptitude and preference for books over sports. His mother had doted on him in private but had kept silent when his father ridiculed him for being "a mama's boy" and "a sissy."

It seemed clear that Peter was carrying a lot of unrecognized anger and grief over the hurts he'd suffered in childhood. The first order of business, therefore, was to go back over these early life experiences and guide Peter to the point where he could finally allow himself to experience, express, and release these feelings. This work took eight sessions—the last a highly emotional one.

That was the first breakthrough. Once he reconnected with these feelings, it was as if a light that had been switched off inside him in childhood was switched back on—the light of what I call emotional intelligence. Once that light was back on, he began reconnecting with all kinds of feelings and seeing all kinds of things about himself that he'd never seen before: his conflicting desire for and fear of closeness for one thing; his previously unacknowledged emotional dependency on his wife for another. He also began to see that for all his complaints about feeling wronged when Kate "punished" him for ogling women's breasts by refusing to have sex, this was actually one of the reasons he did it. Ogling, he began to realize, was his way of distancing from her and punishing her for his dependency on her, which he felt ashamed of.

It also came to light that he'd actually learned this behavior from his father, who'd encouraged his fixation by passing his own men's magazines along to him and by doing things such as nudging him when a buxom female walked by and saying, "Hey, Pete, get a load of those"—seeming, if anything, to enjoy the hurt and embarrassment this caused Peter's mom.

His recollection of the pain he'd felt for his mother at these times provided another crucial opening. In the midst of reconnecting with these feelings he had a sudden flash of insight. "My God," he said. "That's what I've been doing to Kate." He held my gaze for a moment, then turned and stared out the window. "I used to hate it when my dad did that to my mom," he said. "I used to think, 'How can he be so cruel? To her of all people?' " A pause. "And, here I am, doing the same thing." A long silence followed. When he looked back at me, his eyes were wet. He looked down, frowned. "Jesus," he said softly.

Heart opened and vision cleansed, Peter experienced a profound upwelling of love for his wife and sadness over the pain he'd been causing her. "You should see her, up every morning, doing her exercises, nothing but salads for dinner," he said. "I'm always telling her, 'What kind of craziness is this? What're you trying to do? Starve yourself?' " He frowned. "But then I go and . . ." His frown deepened. "I guess actions speak louder than words."

"Yes, they do," I said. "So what do you want to do about that?"

"I guess that's pretty obvious. I have to work on changing my behavior." He frowned. "I love Kate. I don't want to hurt her if I can help it." A pause. "I'm not sure I *can* help it. Something tells me it's not going to be easy. But I want to try."

Peter was right. It isn't easy for men to change this kind of behavior—no easier than it is for an alcoholic to kick alcohol or for a drug-abuser to kick drugs. That's what we were working with—a kind of addiction. We began by discussing the hard fact that the urge to indulge in this behavior would probably always be there and that, no matter how long he abstained, he shouldn't kid himself that he could afford to indulge even once. The only way to stop this behavior was by saying "No" to the urge each time it arose. This would require vigilance and self-discipline, I said. But if he stuck with it for the first few months, he'd find the vigilance and self-discipline becoming habitual. And once he'd stuck with it long enough to start reaping the rewards of that self-discipline, his motivation would become even stronger and would help him through those moments when he was tempted to cheat.

"You mean when I see how much happier Kate is," he said.

"That's one reward, yes," I said. "And there are others."

"Like what?"

"I could try to describe them," I said. "But describing them won't do them justice. You have to experience them to appreciate them. And you'll know them when you do."

This sounded good to Peter. He couldn't really know what these rewards were, however, until he began experiencing them directly—which was going to take time. Until then, the only thing he had to draw upon to sustain him in his efforts to stop this behavior was his new awareness of the pain it caused his wife and his genuine desire to avoid putting her through more of that pain. To his credit, that was enough to keep him going through the two months it took for these rewards to start kicking in. Once that happened and he understood not only what he was working to avoid but, more important, what he was working to achieve, his resolve became fierce.

The turning point came at a retirement party for the head of Peter's department. Returning from the bar with a glass of wine for Kate, whom he'd left chatting with a colleague, he was waylaid by a junior member of his department eager to introduce him to his attractive, extremely buxom, young wife. Alarm bells ringing in his head, Peter shook her hand and, keeping his eyes on her face, told her what a pleasure it was to meet her. "Listen, while I've got you," his young colleague said. "About the meeting tomorrow . . . ." Unable to make a getaway and desperate to focus his attention somewhere safe, Peter jockeyed around from a position facing the young man and his wife to a safer position on the man's left side, where he could chat while gazing across the room at . . . Kate.

"At first I latched on to her more out of fear of letting my eyes wander than anything else," he said during our next session. "But, then . . . I don't know how to explain it. The more I watched her, the more I got drawn into her. It was like I began seeing her in a way I'd never seen her before. She was engrossed in conversation, so she didn't see me watching. And I just stood there, watching her talk and laugh, and I thought, 'My God, what an attractive woman.' Here I am, watching my own wife, and I'm thinking, 'I want to get to know this woman.' "

A few moments later he watched Kate scan the room in search of him—and saw a shadow of pain cross her face when she found him and noticed the man and woman with whom he was standing. The moment their eyes met, he smiled. She smiled back uncertainly. He lifted the glass of wine he'd been bringing her, shrugged "I got stuck," then winked and lifted his chin in invitation. She raised her eyebrows quizzically. He smiled and lifted his chin again. By the time she reached him, she was smiling, too.

"Hi," he said warmly.

"Hi to you," she said just as warmly.

"I've been watching you," he said.

"Have you," said Kate.

"Yes, I have. Has anyone told you you're a beautiful woman?"

Kate smiled. "Not this evening."

"Well you are. Listen, think you'd like to go home and spend some time getting to know each other a little better?"

"Right now?"

"Whenever you're ready. Me, I just realized I've been waiting twenty years."

In an instant Kate's expression went from playful to astonished to tender to wary. "Is that a joke?" she asked guardedly.

"No. It's not a joke."

"You mean that?" she asked softly, searching her husband's face.

"I mean that."

For a moment husband and wife stood silently gazing into each other's eyes. Then Kate smiled a slow, inviting smile. "I'll get my purse," she said.

They talked little on their way home, as they made their

way into bed, and during their lovemaking. Afterward, Peter talked a lot—about how hard he was working to change his behavior, how sorry he was for having hurt her, how grateful he was that she'd stuck by him, and how frightened he was that he might "slip" and hurt her again.

"You worry about that?" Kate asked tenderly.

"Yeah, I do," he said, his voice thick. "I love you. And I don't want to lose you."

"That's the first time you've ever said that," she said even more tenderly.

"I know. I've been wanting to say it for a while now. But . . . Well, I guess I was scared."

"How do you feel now that you've said it?"

"Scared," he said, laughing. "How about you? How do you feel?"

Kate was silent for a moment. "Do you know," she said, "that's the first time you've ever asked me that."

"It is?"

"Yes, it is."

He sighed. "Twenty years, and I've never asked my wife how she feels." A silence. "Jesus." Another silence. "But I'm asking now."

"Yes, you are."

"So . . . How *do* you feel?"

She touched his cheek. "I feel like I'm starting to get to know you," she said softly. And then, sliding her body close, "And I want to know more."

We Have to Get Past Gender Stereotypes to Realize We're All Human Beings

This is the kind of comfort men miss out on by limiting sex to unconnected lust. What they stand to gain by overcoming this syndrome is the best of what life has to offer—the profound pleasures and satisfactions of a deeply intimate sexual and emotional relationship with another human being. And it's not just their sexual relationships that improve when they discard outmoded sexual beliefs and behaviors. Once men break free of the traditional sexual code, they invariably find that their relationships with women improve overall—that they become more capable of sustaining and enjoying more satisfying relationships with all the women in their life.

That's the goal we goal-oriented men really want to work toward. And that's the value we want to instill in our sons. We want to teach them, even as we're learning it, that although males and females are different in some essential and wonderful ways, the similarities between the sexes are greater and more important than the differences. Like women, men need and deserve closeness and connectedness, and like men, women need and deserve to be treated with consideration and respect. We all want to feel understood, accepted, cared for, and respected. Male and female, we're all human beings.

The more we hold that thought in mind and treat ourselves and one another accordingly, the more meaningful and satisfying all our relationships will be. And as our relationships go, so go our lives. Because that's what life's all about.

It's about relationships.

CHAPTER TEN

Men and Relationships: Coming in Out of the Cold

Money. Sex. Power. Fame. Sure, these things are gratifying. But they can't take the place of relationships. They're no substitute for the satisfactions of closeness and connectedness with other human beings.

It's the great tragedy of men's lives that they were trained to feel ashamed of their need for closeness. And it's the great irony of men's lives that having been trained to avoid intimacy, they now find themselves living in a time when emotional isolation and inexpressiveness have fallen out of favor and they're being pressured to become skilled at fostering the very closeness they were taught to shun.

This is the essence of the crisis in which American men now find themselves. But men's crisis is also their opportunity—to do for themselves what women have already done: to throw off the shackles of gender-role training that prohibit them from experiencing the full range of life's pleasures and blend the rewards of working and achieving with the contentment of close relationships with other human beings.

That's the opportunity men are being offered: the opportunity to change their lives for the better—not by relinquishing any of their still valuable traditionally masculine traits, but by adding the skills that I call emotional intelligence to their repertoire of strengths. That's what men need to do in this time of changing gender roles and shifting gender relations. They need to develop the various emotional skills that will enable them to change their lives for the better by enabling them to function more effectively in that "other world" men are only now beginning to enter—the world of relationships and family life.

In the last nine chapters we've identified these skills and discussed how men can develop them. In this final chapter we'll look at how men can use these skills to improve the quality of their relationships with their children, parents, friends, and mates.

MEN AS FATHERS

When the traditional family model of "male as breadwinner/ female as homemaker" was the norm, fathers and mothers played distinct roles. Now that mothers have mastered the skills required to function in both the traditionally masculine world of work and the traditionally feminine world of family life, fathers are being called upon to do the same. Like Bruce, who took over the morning shift with his sons, and Rick, who spent two years as a full-time father, men are now doing more of the day-to-day homemaking, child-rearing, and relationship-nurturing work that was once considered Mom's job. And as any man who has made this transition from traditional dad to involved family man can attest, it's not easy. Rewarding, yes. Easy, no—especially now that parents and children must contend with the modern-day dangers of violent crime, drug abuse, sexual assault, and sexually transmitted disease, and now that the prevalence of divorce and remarriage has spawned a plethora of contemporary family models that make family life and relationships all the more complicated.

Becoming the kind of father a man's family now needs him to be is a huge challenge. The best way for men to meet that challenge is by putting some effort into developing the skills that I call emotional intelligence—emotional self-awareness, emotional expressiveness, and emotional empathy. The more emotionally intelligent a man is, the more in touch he is with his sense of defensive autonomy, unconscious dependency, and destructive entitlement. This gives him a much better chance of overcoming these deep-seated sources of his resistance to becoming more involved with his family and taking on more family duties. The more he's worked free of the traditional masculine belief that a man must sacrifice himself to his job, the more available he'll be to his wife and children. The more he sheds the notion that cooking, cleaning, and diaper-changing are "women's work," the more willingly he'll take on this work without fear of being judged or judging himself unmanly.

The emotionally intelligent man also becomes more aware of all the ways in which males and females are both damaged by traditional gender-role training. And the more aware he is, the more likely he is to think carefully before imposing these gender rules on his own children. He'll be able to catch himself before automatically admonishing his son that "big boys don't cry." He'll make a conscious effort not to withhold hugs and kisses from a son or discourage his bids for physical affection. When he sees his son playing with a teddy bear or doll —one of the key ways children practice and develop nurturing skills—he'll check his impulse to grab it away. Instead of teaching his son that "winning is everything," he'll teach him that effort counts more than outcome and that the true measure of a man is how gracefully he handles defeat.

Instead of encouraging fearfulness and timidity in his daughter by being overly protective and restrictive with her, the emotionally intelligent father will work hard to allow her the same freedom to experiment and explore that he'd allow a son. He'll resist the impulse to rush to her aid when she encounters frustrations and setbacks and encourage her instead to figure out how to rescue herself. He'll praise her for her intelligence, talents, and strengths, not just for being polite and pretty. And he'll encourage her self-sufficiency by teaching her the same range of traditionally masculine skills—such as how to throw a baseball and change a tire—that he'd teach a boy.

The more a man is capable of experiencing and expressing his own feelings, the more his children will learn from his example that it's okay for men to do that, and the more they'll come to know and love him for the real human being he is. They'll also be spared the terrifying explosions of temper characteristic of emotionally out-of-touch men whose feelings build up until they finally spill out as rage. The more sensitive and responsive a man is to his children's feelings, the better he'll be able to understand, empathize, and communicate with them, and the more they'll confide in him and trust his guidance when the time comes to discuss such sensitive subjects as smoking, drinking, drugs, and sex. The more emotionally intelligent the man, in other words, the better his children's chances of developing into capable, responsible, resourceful adults—and the better their chance of enjoying the kind of close, affectionate relationship with him that many men yearned to have with their own dads.

I think of one client, for example, who didn't understand the source of his eight-year-old daughter's antagonism toward him until he made the connection between her behavior and his own boyhood juvenile delinquency—which he'd only recently come to understand had been an angry cry to his emotionally absent father to "Pay some attention to me!" His daughter's behavior, he realized, had become a problem only after he'd been put in charge of a special project at work that required he spend most of his evenings and weekends at the office. Once he made that connection, he was able to get past his anger at his daughter and concentrate on soothing the hurt and satisfying the hunger he now understood her behavior expressed. The first thing he did was delegate more project responsibilities to other members of his team in order to spend more time with her. Within two weeks of his making this change, his daughter's antagonism toward him subsided, and she was once again the happy, loving child she'd been before. "That's all she needed," he said. "All she needed was more attention from her father. She just wanted the same thing I always wanted but never got."

MEN AS SONS

"The father wound," Harvard psychologist Sam Osherson calls the mix of grief, anger, and longing so many men feel toward their dads—a painful mix of emotions that poet Robert Bly deserves much credit for encouraging men to acknowledge and explore by speaking so openly about his own struggle to resolve his feelings toward his alcoholic father.

The key word is *resolve.* We've taken a close look at how these painful feelings, when left unresolved, can do untold damage not only to a man's relationship with his dad but to his relationships with his loved ones as well. It was Eric's unresolved feeling of inadequacy in relation to his dad, for example, that fueled his need to humilate his wife. And it was Jeffrey's unconscious fear of following in his father's financially irresponsible footsteps that drove him to extremes of sacrificing and indulging. Some men do such a good job of burying these feelings that they don't even know they're there. But such men are more the exception than the rule. Most men are in close enough touch with these feelings to be aware of their presence or to need only the slightest nudge to reconnect with them.

But as I said earlier, becoming aware of these feelings is only the first step in the process that Bly calls the "descent into the ashes." The second step is to actually feel these feelings—to dispense with detached, dispassionate, defensive intellectualizing and let them come up and out as the real and painful emotions they are. Once a man has fully experienced and expressed these feelings, he's ready for the third step— which is to let them go. That's when real healing begins. Once a man lets go of his anger and pain, he begins to see his father for who he really is or was: no more and no less than a flawed, imperfect human being struggling to do his best by his family, just as dads are today. Only then can he genuinely forgive his dad for the pain his dad caused him and finally come to peace with his feelings toward him.

Once a man reaches this stage, he's often able to achieve a level of closeness with his dad that he wouldn't have thought possible before. One client, Larry, became aware during the course of counseling, for example, that he was more distressed than he'd realized by his lack of an adult relationship with his father—who invariably limited their long-distance telephone conversations to the same seven words: "Hi. How's it going? Here's your mom." A man of lesser emotional intelligence might simply have stewed in resentment at so uncommunica- tive a dad. Not Larry. After discussing how he could best at- tempt to foster more closeness with his father, we came up with a plan. That same week he began making weekly phone calls home—always placed when he knew his mother was out playing golf or bridge with her women's club—and engaging his father in friendly, undemanding, fifteen-minute conversa- tions during which he focused on showing interest in his dad: "What'd you do this week? Did you put in the new flower bed? How was Uncle Joe's retirement party? Have you decided what to do about the car?" When, during his second phone call, his dad asked laughingly, "What is it with all these questions?" Larry said simply, "You're my dad, remember? I love you. I want to know what's going on in your life." For three months that was the only question his father asked—but the fact that he asked it during each conversation told Larry he liked hear- ing the answer. During the fourth month the conversational tide began to turn, and his father began asking questions in return: "So, how's the job going? Are you still happy there? Are they treating you right? Are you still playing tennis? Have you done any fishing lately?'' The mention of fishing started father and son reminiscing about the fishing trips they'd taken together when Larry was a boy. Over the course of many months' conversations the reminiscing gradually gave way to loose talk about how great it'd be to go fishing together again someday—and, finally, to Larry's suggestion that they give that someday a firm date. His wife was taking the kids to visit her sister at the end of the summer. She'd already said he didn't have to come if he had something else to do. It had been thirty years since he'd last stuffed himself on his father's great camp-fire flapjacks. ''Whadya say, Dad?'' His father said yes.

I wish I could promise that every man can achieve a similar outcome. In reality, however, some fathers don't respond to their adult children's bids for more closeness. Some find close-ness too deeply threatening. Others desire it but don't know how to seek or accept it. Others are perfectly satisfied with their relationships just the way they are and see no reason to change things.

Another client, Ben, worked just as hard as Larry to estab-lish closer ties with his father—with no success. When his fa-ther mentioned during a telephone conversation, for example, that he'd been thinking of visiting his old hometown, where the family had lived until Ben was seven, Ben offered to make the trip with him. ''Let's go together, Dad,'' he said. ''It'll be fun. Just tell me when you'd like to go.'' His dad said he'd think about it. For an entire month, each time they talked, Ben asked again: ''Have you thought about when you'd like to go?'' His father hadn't decided. ''You'll let me know?'' Sure, said his dad. Two months later Ben learned through his step-mother that his father had made the trip three weeks earlier—with an aunt.

This latest in a long string of emotional rebuffs hurt Ben, of course. And, in some ways, his emotional intelligence made the pain worse—because instead of trying to numb the pain, he let himself feel it. But he also knew enough about his dad's traumatic early life experiences as the neglected youngest son of a tyrannical immigrant Italian father to have some insight into why his dad was so distant. And he had enough openness of heart to understand that, in his own closed-off, uncommunicative way, his father did love him. This didn't lessen his unfulfilled yearning for more closeness with his father. As Ben said, "I guess I just have to live with that." But emotional intelligence did enable him to accept and love his father for the imperfect father he is. It also helped him to see that he and his father would both be better served if he concentrated on appreciating the positive aspects of their relationship—their similar sense of humor, for example, and shared interest in world affairs—rather than torture himself or his dad by trying to get from him something he couldn't give.

Once a man has healed his relationship with his father, he's in a much better position to begin working through unresolved feelings toward his mother—which, because they're usually buried deeper, often don't become accessible to a man until the father issue is resolved. These unacknowledged feelings fall into two separate but related categories: the ones that date back to early infancy, when males are first forced to separate from their mothers; and the ones that characterize a man's adult relationship with his mother.

The first set of feelings are buried deepest and are hardest for a man to get in touch with on his own. Reconnecting with and working through these feelings is sometimes best attempted, therefore, with professional guidance. In Bruce's case, for example, they began surfacing only after our discussion of men's dependency needs prompted his dream about his mother disappearing under the water. With my help he was then able to finally mourn the trauma of this forced separation from his mother and set to work correcting the problems these long-buried feelings had been causing in his marriage.

One would think men would have readier access to their present-day feelings toward their mothers. Sometimes they do. But often they don't, because these present-day feelings are very often related to the feelings from earliest childhood. Nor are they very good at seeing how much these unacknowledged feelings also intrude on their relationships with their partners. I think of one man, for example, who had a habit of returning home after visiting his widowed mother and blowing up at his wife—a habit he didn't recognize until his wife pointed it out during counseling. He eventually came to see that it wasn't his wife who infuriated him. It was his mother—a robustly healthy, competent, self-centered woman who'd become insatiable in her demands on his time and attention ever since she'd been widowed six years before. Another man had a habit of shutting his wife down with an irritated "Not so loud" whenever she began talking about something with any hint of enthusiasm or excitement. Over the course of counseling he came to see that it wasn't loudness on the part of his wife that triggered this response. In fact, his wife seldom raised her voice. The real trigger was his unconscious fear that if he didn't cut her off she might "flip" and start screaming—as his now elderly mother had done literally every day of his life when he was growing up and still did all too frequently.

It takes emotional intelligence for a man to catch himself reacting inappropriately to his partner and recognize that these reactions may have more to do with his mother than his mate. Once he develops that intelligence, he's better able to identify and compartmentalize his feelings toward his mother in order to prevent them from spilling over into and doing damage to his relationship with his partner. Just as important, he can then begin the process of resolving these feelings in exactly the same way that a man works through unresolved feelings toward a father: by experiencing, expressing, and letting go of them; forgiving his mother for the hurts she has caused him; and accepting her for the person she really is— a flawed, imperfect human being who is doing the best she can. Men who do resolve these feelings often find they're then able to deal with their mothers more calmly, lovingly, and effectively than they would have thought possible before. The man who felt overwhelmed by his widowed mother's demands was able, for example, to start setting firm but loving limits on the amount of time and attention he allowed her to claim—

which not only made his visits with her more enjoyable but also motivated her to start rebuilding her social life. "She's gotten involved with a senior-singles' club at her church," he told me during one session. "She only joined two months ago, and she's already taken charge of planning all the social events. She says the other members have started calling her 'Spitfire.' " He chuckled appreciatively. " 'Spitfire.' Yep. That's my mom."

MEN AS FRIENDS

We talked earlier about the differences in the ways boys play together and girls play together. Boys generally prefer running around and whooping it up whereas girls generally prefer more intimate forms of play that allow for talking, giggling, and sharing secrets. The same gender differences tend to hold true in adult same-sex friendships. Female friendships tend to be built around intimate sharing, whereas male friendships tend to be built around doing things. As psychologist Drury Sherrod writes in Harry Brod's *Making of the Masculinities,* "Men prefer activities over conversation, and men's conversations are far less intimate than women's conversations. . . . According to the research, men seek not intimacy but companionship, not disclosure but commitment. Men's friendships involve unquestioned acceptance rather than unrestricted affirmation. . . . Men achieve closeness through shared activities, and on the basis of shared activities, men infer intimacy simply because they are friends."

Psychologist Dwight Moore has named this traditionally masculine style of relating "side-by-side intimacy." All men know what that is. Think of two guys spending a warm summer Saturday fixing up the engine in a '57 Chevy. Do they feel close to each other? Of course they do. Would either one say to the other, "You know, I really feel close to you as we work together replacing the valves on this old heap"? No way! Ditto for the various competitive sports and games that rank high among men's preferred shared activities. As psychologist Robert S. Pasick writes in *Men in Therapy*, "Men may not express 'intimacy' as we commonly think of it in such activities as a racquet ball or poker game, yet competitive activities play a vital part in their well-being. They offer men camaraderie, pleasure, a sense of accomplishment, and an affirmation of masculinity. While men may not share feelings during these endeavors, they do enjoy each other's company. The appeal of these activities should not be underestimated; many men report that their tennis or softball game is the one event they most look forward to each week." And it's not as though men don't talk at all while engaged in these shared activities. They joke and banter and tease. They poke and prod and give each other shit in a way men never feel free to do with women, knowing it's perfectly okay to lace their interactions with another man with playful verbal and physical aggression because the other man will give it right back—much the way a friend and I did when we were fourteen and our favorite greeting was to slug each other in the arm.

Easy and comfortable and enjoyable and gratifying as this traditionally masculine kind of "side-by-side intimacy" is, however, there are times, as Sherrod writes, "when a man becomes aware that something is lacking. Inferred intimacy seems to work well until a disturbing problem demands more from the relationship than unquestioned acceptance. At that point, many men find themselves without the kind of friend on whom they can rely."

Let's look at this point more closely. Sherrod isn't saying men can't rely on their friends in any way when they find themselves dealing with a serious problem. Nor is he dishonoring or undervaluing the unquestioned acceptance men do offer each other. As he writes, "Men have buddies, pals, lifelong ties—bonds of unspoken, unshakeable commitment—the kinds of friends for whom one would 'lay down one's life.'" All men know what that kind of friendship is about. I think, for example, of the way my friend Gary stood by me when I was going through a particularly tough time back in the sixties. My marriage had ended. I'd dropped out of medical school. I had no idea what I wanted to do with my life. In a word, I was a mess. As any true male friend would, Gary came through for me. Basically, he and his wife, Nancy, took me in—letting me live with them, no questions asked and no thanks necessary, until I got back on my feet.

That's one of many admirable traits of male friendships. Male friends are loyal to each other. They stand by each other. They come through for each other. When one needs the other, the other is there—no questions asked. So the point isn't that men don't extend themselves for each other during times of trouble. They most certainly do. The point is that they tend to do that extending in the traditionally masculine way, which is by swinging into action on a friend's behalf. What men tend to be less good at is extending themselves to a friend in the more traditionally feminine way, which is by "being there" on a purely emotional level—by making clear that they're available and ready to listen anytime the friend wants to talk over a problem or just unburden himself of painful feelings.

That's often the missing piece in male friendships. A small piece, some men would say. Perhaps. It all depends on the nature of the friend's problem. When the signs of trouble are obvious—as they were, for example, when my life fell apart— no words need be spoken to get a man swinging into action on a friend's behalf. But sometimes the signs aren't obvious. In an essay published in the February 13, 1994, edition of the *New York Times*, William J. Caunitz, a retired New York City police detective, recalled the suicide twenty-three years earlier of his partner, Frank Brown. The suicide came as a shock. Caunitz and Brown had been partners for more than four years. "We pulled long surveillances together, crashed through apartment doors together, one of us always covering the other's back," Caunitz writes. "Twenty months earlier Frank had taken a bullet in his left shoulder that had been meant for me. . . . I thought that I knew him so well. . . ." No one could explain why Brown had committed suicide. Caunitz finally uncovered the answer on his own. Brown had amassed large gambling debts, and the loan sharks had threatened him with bodily harm if he didn't pay them off, which he couldn't do. Desperate, ashamed, and unable to ask for help, he had resorted to what had seemed his only escape route.

This is obviously an extreme example of the kind of trouble that can go undetected when emotional sharing isn't part of a friendship. The kinds of trouble male friends more commonly fail to detect are often inconsequential in comparison. But even minor undetected trouble can pose a threat to men's friendships—especially when the trouble has to do with a problem in the friendship itself.

I know of one long-standing male friendship that came close to foundering, for example, when one man, Lou, failed to show up at a fund-raising dinner at which the other man, Harry, was being presented with an award. Instead of calling Lou the next day to find out why he hadn't shown up, Harry waited to see if Lou would call him. Meanwhile, Harry kept his phone-answering machine on so that if Lou did call—which he did a few days later—Harry wouldn't have to talk to him. He didn't want to admit to Lou that he was upset with him—because, after all, men aren't supposed to be emotionally vulnerable—and he was too upset to be able to talk to him without letting his feelings show. He didn't admit that. He wasn't upset, he insisted to me. Nor was he hurt. He simply needed time to think about whether he was getting enough out of the friendship to continue it—and the more he thought about it, the more it seemed to him he wasn't. Fortunately for the friendship, Lou was emotionally intelligent enough to realize that two weeks' worth of unreturned phone calls meant Harry was upset with him. He persisted in his overtures until, at the encouragement of his partner, Harry finally agreed to get together with Lou and talk things out. "I had to work," said Lou. "Yeah," said Harry. "That's always your excuse." "You're right," said Lou. "The truth is I'm not very good at social functions. I don't like them. I'm sorry. I should have told you I wasn't coming. But don't just cut me off like that. If you're angry at me, you have to let me know."

Another potential impediment to male friendships is men's deeply ingrained competitiveness. Competitiveness in and of itself isn't necessarily a bad thing. Healthy competition can in fact be the glue that holds close male friendships together. In her research on friendship styles, psychologist Cynthia Mitchell found, for example, that one predominantly male friendship style is "competitive/accepting" in which friends with complementary strengths use each other as a standard of excellence and compete with each other in a way both value in order to become the best each can be. This is another admirable trait of many male friendships, and many men take deep satisfaction in this kind of honorable male joust. It's the same kind of pleasure a man takes, say, in playing tennis with a partner who's just enough better than he is to keep him stretching his skills and improving his game. This same sense of competitiveness can damage a friendship, however, when men allow it to intrude where it doesn't belong.

Another client, Stan, told me, for example, about a conversation he'd had with his closest male friend during one of their weekly lunches. Both writers who'd recently started new books, they'd gotten to talking about how quickly the advance money publishers pay gets eaten up in research costs. "Take the book I'm working on now," said his friend, and then he named the dollar amount of the advance he'd received— which was substantially less than Stan's. "And you know what I felt when he told me that?" said Stan. "I felt relieved. And the truth is I also felt superior—like, 'Mine's bigger.' I think he wanted me to tell him how much I'd gotten, but I didn't want to do that. So instead I got on my high horse and told him that maybe he shouldn't have been so quick to accept the offer and that next time he should shop the book around more."

For the rest of the day Stan was aware of feeling vaguely bad about how the lunch had gone. It took him two days to figure out why. "If I'd really wanted to help him," he said, "I could have told him how much I'd been paid, and then maybe we could have compared notes on how we each went about selling our books to see if there was something I was doing that he wasn't. Or I could have just commiserated. I mean, he's right. It is hard to get a decent advance. The truth is that until this book, all my advances have been smaller than his. But instead of telling him that or offering any real help or moral support, I got on my high horse—because I felt competitive. That's the fact of the matter. Here he is my best friend, and I still had to compete with him. I still let that get in the way."

I give Stan credit for being in touch enough with his feelings to realize he felt bad about how the lunch had gone and for doing the hard work of tracking that feeling to its source. I was also impressed with the degree of emotional empathy he felt for the friend he realized he hadn't helped by turning competitive. A man has to overcome a number of facets of male gender-role training to achieve this kind of emotional connectedness with a friend. In *Men in Therapy*, Pasick lists some of the "barriers that prevent men from developing and maintaining closer relationships with other men." These include:

1. Adherence to a masculine code that emphasizes competition, autonomy, invulnerability, and power, none of which are "conducive to closer friendships."

2. A tendency to engage with male friends only in strictly masculine pursuits (attending sports events versus going out to dinner) for fear of otherwise being suspected of homosexuality.

3. Dependency on women for emotional support, which "diminishes [the] need for male friends."

4. Excessive devotion to work, which leaves little free time in which to pursue friendships, and an achievement-

oriented workplace atmosphere that encourages competition and mistrust among male colleagues.

5. Reluctance to face conflict or reveal emotional vulnerability for fear of appearing weak.

6. Unresolved relationships with fathers, which "may make men wary of other men. . . ."

In workshops and counseling sessions I often hear men express a yearning for the kind of emotional closeness with other men that the traditional male code discourages. No doubt this has partly to do with a certain self-protective desire on the part of men to diversify their emotional investments in this time of confusion and uncertainty in gender relations. It may also have to do with men's desire to compare notes with one another during this time of gender-relation confusion to find out whether other men are feeling as confused as they are. But I don't think this is all that's going on. I think the current crisis in masculinity that has started men rethinking their relationships with women has also started them rethinking their relationships with other men and stirred their desire to fill in the missing piece of more straightforward emotional connectedness that can make male friendships even more satisfying than they already are. The more men work to develop their emotional intelligence, the sooner they'll be able to fill in this missing piece, and the richer their friendships will become.

MEN AS MATES

It's been more than thirty years since the publication of Betty Friedan's *The Feminine Mystique* heralded the birth of the Women's Liberation Movement. As discussed earlier, mental-health surveys indicate that it's been a good thirty years for women, whose psychological health has benefited from the flexibility and balance they've achieved in their lives—not such a good thirty years for men, whose psychological health has declined. As divorce statistics indicate, it hasn't been such a good thirty years for marriage, either. Between 1965 and 1979, divorce rates more than doubled, and they've remained close to this peak ever since. Back in 1970, when divorce statistics first began to climb, demographers predicted that 50 percent of all first marriages and 60 percent of all second marriages would eventually end in divorce. More recently, that estimate has been revised upward. In a 1989 article, researchers T. C. Martin and L. Bumpass predicted that 67 percent of all marriages will eventually fail.

That's not to say the changes women have made in their lives are solely responsible for the rise in divorce rates. The advent of no-fault divorce and reliable birth control, which allows couples to delay childbearing, has also made marriages easier to dissolve. But women's increasing economic independence from men has made it easier for them to leave a marriage in which they're unhappy. And as marriage has become more fragile, so has men's psychological health. Men suffer when deprived of the nurturing, affection, and emotional sustenance they derive from a committed relationship with a woman. The simple truth is that men need women.

And women need men.

They just don't need men the way they used to. They don't need men to be the breadwinners anymore. They need men to be their partners—true partners in all aspects of marriage and family life. They don't want men to sacrifice themselves to work in order to be the good provider. They want men to throw off traditional gender-role training and join them in building a relationship that allows both partners to develop the full range of their potentials and experience the full range of life's satisfactions.

The key to achieving this kind of relationship is, of course, good communication. It'd be a lot easier for couples to resolve the misunderstandings and conflicts that inevitably arise in a marriage if both sexes received the same early life training in basic communication skills—and if males and females spoke the same language. But they don't. From birth onward, females are trained in the skills and traits required to foster relationship and intimacy, whereas males are drilled in the skills and traits required to protect and provide for their families. These gender differences in behavior reflect a deeper dichotomy in frames of reference—that is, in the ways males and females are trained to think, prioritize, interpret events and experiences, assign meaning and value, and envision their place and purpose in the world. The male frame of reference tends to be more instrumental. Men tend to see themselves as independent agents in the world and to view most life events from the perspective of, "What's the situation or problem here? And what can I do to improve the situation, advance my goals, or solve the problem?" The female frame of reference tends to be more expressive. Women tend to think in terms of relationship rather than autonomy and are more likely to approach most life situations from the point of view of, "How can this other person and I connect with each other in a genuine way? How can we reveal something meaningful about ourselves to each other so that we each feel more known, understood, and appreciated?"

And, of course, as males and females think, so also do they communicate—which can lead to communication problems of the sort Dave and Joyce ran into when she told him the legal case she and a female colleague had hoped to work on had been assigned to two junior male colleagues. He didn't know that what she was saying was, "Something awful happened to me today, and I'm really feeling down about it, and I could use some expression of emotional empathy from you." Interpreting her words in a typically masculine, instrumental way, what he heard was, "I've got a problem, and I could use help figuring it out."

In her 1990 book, *You Just Don't Understand: Women and Men in Conversation,* linguist Deborah Tannen names these gender-distinct styles of communicating "genderlects" and offers a variety of examples of the many ways in which these styles differ and the misunderstandings that can arise when a man and woman think they're communicating but aren't. That's one common communication problem between men and women. Another, more serious one arises, however, when a man is unable or unwilling to communicate enough to satisfy his partner's healthy desire for connectedness—when she keeps trying to get closer and he keeps backing off or pushing her away.

Known among mental health professionals as the "pursuer-distancer" cycle, this common marital pattern is often the root cause of the chronic frictions that eventually bring couples into therapy—usually at the wife's insistence. I can't count how often I've heard variations on the following exchange between wife and husband when I ask them why they've come for counseling:

"He never talks to me," she says. "He doesn't tell me what he's thinking. He doesn't tell me what he's feeling. He doesn't tell me anything. Like today. I asked him how his day went, and he said, 'Fine.' That's it—just 'Fine.' "

"Well, what do you want me to say?" he says. "That's how it went. It went fine. I didn't set a new sales record. I didn't get fired. The building didn't burn down. If there was something to tell you I'd tell you. But there isn't."

"You could tell me what you did today," she says. "You could tell me who you had lunch with. You could tell me how your new assistant is working out. I don't care—anything."

"You mean like you?" he says. "Look, if you want me to listen to you prattle about everything you thought, felt, and did during the day—okay. I'll do it. But don't expect to get the same out of me because you won't. It's too boring."

"That's what you think?" she says. "I try to tell you what's going on in my life, and you think it's *boring*?"

Yes, he does. Having been trained all their lives to be action-oriented, goal-achieving men of few words, many men fail to see the point of this kind of small talk. A man doesn't want to say so for fear of hurting his partner, but the truth is he often does consider this kind of talk boring. To him it serves no purpose, whereas to his partner it serves a very important purpose: to initiate a connection. When that purpose is made clear to a man, his desire to avoid this kind of talk may become even stronger—because, unlike his partner, he's uncomfortable with too much closeness and connectedness. So he fends her off by distancing—by clamming up or by telling her to clam up. The more he distances, the more unrecognized, unappreciated, and unconnected she feels and the more she hungers for and pursues closeness with him. The more she pursues, the more he distances—and so on in a vicious cycle that can ultimately lead to the breakdown of a marriage.

In a 1983 study, psychologists Frank Floyd and Howard Markman found, for example, that wives who are caught up with their husbands in this cycle—also known as the "demand/withdraw" cycle—often mistakenly attribute to their husbands the same hostility they feel toward them for being uncommunicative and withholding, and often vent their hostility by becoming increasingly angry in their demands for closeness and increasingly critical of their mates. Husbands respond, the researchers found, by not responding—that is, by ignoring or otherwise withdrawing from their wives' anger and negativity. End result: the exact marital pattern that Markman and his colleagues found, in a 1987 study, to be an extremely accurate predictor of marital breakdown—a pattern in which the wife angrily pursues the resolution of conflict and the husband withdraws from it.

In another 1983 paper, psychologist Neil Jacobson proposed that the reason for this pattern is that husbands tend to hold more power and authority in marriages and tend to use this advantage to control the nature, quantity, and quality of marital communication. In two recent studies psychologists Andrew Christensen, Christopher Heavy, and Christopher Layne found evidence to support this hypothesis. The researchers found that the overall pattern of wives pursuing and husbands withdrawing held true no matter which partner had initiated the discussion. Even when the conflict or issue was one the husband had decided he wanted to discuss, in other words, he was more likely than his wife to withdraw from the conversation at some point. This finding reflects the gender-based tendency for men to avoid emotional closeness. The researchers also found, however, that husbands were more likely to pursue a discussion they had initiated than they were to pursue one initiated by their wives. When a husband wants to talk, in other words, he's more likely to use his power and authority to see that an issue is discussed. When she wants to talk, on the other hand, he's more likely to indulge his impulse to distance.

Other researchers argue that men can no more control their impulse to withdraw from conflict than they can control their heart rate or galvanic skin response (a measure of skin-surface conductivity)—that, indeed, the three are connected. In a 1982 study by psychologists Clifford Notarius and Jennifer Johnson, and again in a 1988 study by psychologists John Gottman and Robert Levenson, researchers found that conflict or the anticipation of conflict triggers much more intense and prolonged physiological arousal in husbands than it does in wives. Because this arousal is unpleasant, it follows naturally that husbands would seek to avoid these unpleasant sensations—which is what they do. Gottman and Levenson found, for example, that in situations of low or mild conflict, husbands will attempt to smooth over the conflict or prevent it from escalating by being positive and conciliatory, or by being calm, logical, rational, and reasonable. In situations of high or hot conflict—which mild conflict often turns into when men try to manage emotional conflict with logic and reason—husbands withdraw, which Gottman calls "stonewalling." In a 1985 study in which Levenson and Gottman reevaluated levels of marital satisfaction among couples they'd assessed three years earlier, they also found that where they'd initially measured unpleasant arousal in a husband prior to simply talking to his wife about the events of his day, they were now likely to find that the couple's level of marital satisfaction had declined.

Hardly surprising, given that men who experience this kind of unpleasant arousal at the thought of talking to their wives are probably going to do their best to avoid actually talking to them—and are probably also going to be pretty quick to withdraw or stonewall when conflicts arise. The more interesting question is why husbands experience more extreme levels of physiological arousal than wives do when conflict looms. Gottman basically takes the position that this gender difference is innate—that males are simply more sensitive to stimuli than females are.

Possibly. But I don't think that's the only reason men become more aroused when confronted with the necessity of discussing and working through conflict. At most, I think it's one minor reason. I think the real reason men become so anxious and physiologically aroused when wives speak those five dreaded words, "Honey, we have to talk," is because the prospect of having to work through conflict brings them smack up against all the legacies of their early life experience and gender-role training that make this an extremely unpleasant and difficult thing for men to do. For a wife to say to a husband, "We have to talk," is for her to throw him hard up against:

1. His inability to experience, express, and interpret his emotions.

2. His inability to sense and respond to his partner's feelings.

3. The defensive autonomy, unconscious dependency, and sense of destructive entitlement that make him uncomfortable with intimate sharing and that give rise to the belief that he shouldn't have to engage in it— that it's his partner's job to sense and minister to his needs.

4. His loyalty to a masculine code that says men shouldn't have or express human feelings and needs and that any man who does will be shamed.

Women don't realize that their bids for emotionally self-revelatory communication throw men into this internal struggle. More to the point, neither do many men. The more perfect a product a man is of traditional male upbringing—that is, the more alexithymic he is—the more disconnected he is both from the physical symptoms of distress and from the emotions causing them. But, as we know, the fact that a man doesn't realize he's having an emotional reaction doesn't mean he's not having one. And the fact that his emotional reaction doesn't get expressed overtly doesn't mean it doesn't get expressed. It does. That's why he experiences unpleasant physiological arousal when conflicts arise: When emotions don't get expressed externally, they get expressed internally—through jumps in heart rate and galvanic skin response, or in the form of headache, or queasy stomach, or tightness in the chest, or any number of other often unfelt physical symptoms of emotional distress that I call "the buzz." And the fact that a man isn't aware of these unpleasant physical sensations doesn't mean he doesn't react to them. He does—by clamming up and stonewalling, or by turning cranky, nasty, insulting, or intimidating in an unconscious effort to escape his discomfort or drive the "threat" away.

And what is this threat he's trying to drive away? The very thing for which he hungers: true closeness and connectedness with his partner—the comfort, ease, and security of a truly intimate relationship with another human being.

This is the companion crisis to the current crisis in American masculinity. I call it the "crisis of connection." Men want closeness and connectedness with their partners. Like all human beings, they need closeness and connectedness. But they now find themselves being called upon to foster that closeness and connectedness in ways they never learned to do and were never required to do before. In this time of shifting gender relations, when even the most committed of mates must work as hard as they can to prevent their marriage from turning into another divorce statistic, men can no longer afford to leave the bulk of the relationship-nurturing work to women. They've got to pitch in and do more of their share. Men possess a host of admirable skills and traits that always have been and still are deserving of praise and that are invaluable when it comes to protecting and providing for the health and welfare of their loved ones. But the emotional skills required to foster closeness and connectedness tend not to be among them. That's what men need more than anything in this time of changing gender roles and shifting gender relations. For their own sake and for the sake of their loved ones, they need to become more emotionally intelligent men.

MEN AT THE THRESHOLD

So it's up to men. They can change. Or they can resist change. They can make the most of the opportunity being offered in the form of the current crisis in American masculinity to transform themselves, their relationships, and their lives for the better. Or they can go on leading their lives the way they're leading them now.

Perhaps you feel your life is plenty meaningful and satisfying just as it is. And maybe it is. But the fact that you've stayed with me to the end of this book indicates that some part of you senses that it could be more meaningful and satisfying. Perhaps you see yourself in one or more of the case histories I've shared but aren't yet sure what you want to do about the problem you recognize. Or perhaps you've gone a step further and tried one or more of the exercises included in this book and found them effective in helping you change some aspect of your behavior. Perhaps this taste of positive change has given you the nudge you needed to make a more serious commitment to re-examining and reconstructing your beliefs about manhood. Or perhaps you're already well enough into this work to know what a profoundly transformative effect it can have on a man's life.

I've done my best to give you a sense of the tremendous rewards awaiting men who do commit to doing the work I call reconstructing masculinity. This work basically consists of the following steps:

1. Re-examining their beliefs about manhood.

2. Separating out the still valuable traditionally masculine traits and skills that deserve to be honored.

3. Identifying those aspects of the traditional masculine code that have become obsolete or dysfunctional.

4. Applying their skills and strengths to the task of developing the emotional intelligence required to make the changes they want to make in their lives.

I've tried to communicate some sense of how rewarding this work can be. But a man can't really understand what a profound effect it can have on his life until he experiences these rewards for himself.

I recently received a letter from a former client who has experienced these rewards—one of a few clients who occasionally drop me a line to keep me posted on where they are and how they're doing in their lives. As this client, Tom, reminded me in his letter, he'd also felt pretty satisfied with his life when we first met in one of my workshops, which he'd attended only because a friend had wanted to attend and had prevailed upon Tom to come with him. A thirty-nine-year-old bachelor and successful documentary filmmaker who was half in, half out of a two-year relationship at the time, he sat through the workshop on "Men and Work" with his arms firmly crossed over his chest, speaking up only once, during a discussion of men's resistance to becoming more involved with their families, to say, "That's why I'm not married. The last thing I need is a wife trying to get me to spend more time at home. I didn't get where I am by sitting around on my ass. I got where I am by picking up and going wherever a job takes me. You have to be able to do that in my business. And I *like* doing it. I like the travel. And I like the freedom."

Not the kind of attitude that speaks of someone who's ready to re-examine his beliefs about manhood. And yet, six months later, that's what he was doing. The woman with whom he'd been involved but to whom he'd been unwilling to commit had ended their relationship two months after the workshop. "She said she was tired of waiting for me to grow up," he told me during our first session. "I said, 'If by "grow up" you mean get married, don't hold your breath.' " The breakup took him by surprise but didn't really faze him—he didn't think. Within a week he began dating someone else, and then someone else, and then someone else—until while having dinner one evening with his latest female companion he looked up from his meal to see her staring at him stone-faced.

"What's with you?" he asked.

"My name is Marge," she answered coldly. "Marge. Not Rita. You just called me Rita."

"Sorry," he said, smiling sheepishly. "I must've been thinking about the film I'm working on. That's my co-producer's name." Which was a lie. Rita was the name of the woman who'd broken up with him.

He'd have shrugged off the incident, he told me, if it hadn't been followed by a similar one two days later, when he picked up the phone to call his mother only to realize when he heard Rita answer that he'd dialed her number instead. Shaken, he hung up and called his friend Hank, who'd dragged him to my workshop and who'd already expressed concern about Tom's dating frenzy. Hank listened to Tom talk for a while and then, not for the first time, urged him to call me. He called, making it clear during our conversation that he wasn't interested in therapy—he just wanted to come in and talk. We ended up working together for six months. As he wrote in his letter, "I didn't make for what you'd call a cooperative patient, I know. I really resisted you there for a while, until you suggested I keep that emotional response log. It was almost like I knew that once we got into the emotional stuff, the jig would be up. I'm still not sure why the idea of keeping that log appealed to me so much. I guess I was just ready to face some stuff I hadn't wanted to face before. Thank God I did it, though. Because I can see now that that's what threw the switch." He was writing now, more than a year after our last session, "to fill you in on the latest. Remember I said when we were finishing up that I was thinking of giving it another shot with Rita if she'd let me? Well, check out the photo!" Enclosed was a snapshot of Tom, dressed in a hand-some suit, standing beside an attractive, dark-haired woman wearing a pink suit and hat and holding a bouquet of pink roses—the two of them with their arms around each other and beaming at the camera. "We did it!" he wrote. "We got hitched last May!"

And then comes my favorite part of the letter. "I remem-ber you said during the workshop that some of the men who work with you on this emotional intelligence stuff come back later and tell you how much their lives have changed," he wrote. "You said one guy said it was like his life went from black-and-white to color. I thought that was a load of bull at the time. Well, I don't anymore. I didn't understand what you were talking about then. And I see now why I didn't. It's like when I try to talk to some of my friends. I look at them, and I can see they're caught up in a lot of the same crap I was caught up in. You know—Who, me? Have feelings? Not me. I'm a man. I try to tell them, look, you don't have to do this to yourself. It's okay to be human. Really! You'll like it a lot better! But I guess you can't really tell that to anybody, just like you couldn't tell it to me. I guess you just have to hope that someday they'll find out for themselves."

Exactly my hope. If I've done right by the ideas I'm trying to share in this book and by the men whose case histories I share, you'll have at least been given some food for thought. Perhaps you'll put the book aside now and go on with life as you're living it—which, if you're already well into the work of re-examining and reconstructing your beliefs about manhood, is just what I hope you'll do. Or perhaps you'll decide to continue exploring the issues we've examined by discussing them with your partner and/or your male or female friends. Maybe you'll decide to educate yourself further by reading one or more of the many other good books now available to men who are wrestling with these issues. Or maybe you'll decide to do as Tom's friend Hank did and get a friend to accompany you to a men's lecture, seminar, or conference—just to see what it's about. Or maybe you'll decide that you and your partner would benefit from couples counseling—or that your problems with some of the issues we've examined are serious enough to make it worth your while to seek professional help for them.

Only you can decide where to go from here. I urge you, however, as you consider your options, to listen as closely as you can to what your heart tells you instead of doing what men usually do—which is to silence their hearts and listen only to their heads. Men can't afford to do that anymore. Because it's not what the world needs from them now. And it's not what their loved ones need from them. For their own sake and the sake of all they hold dear, men need to become emotionally intelligent.

I've done my best in this book to point out some of the most common obstacles that prevent men from accomplishing this goal and to demonstrate how other men have succeeded in overcoming these obstacles and making positive changes in themselves, their relationships, and their lives. I've done my best to inspire you to want for yourself a life as rich in pleasure, meaning, purpose, and satisfaction as these men have achieved, to suggest how you might also achieve it and to encourage you to do the work you need to do to accomplish this *fulfillable* goal. Only you know what that work is. And only you can do it.

The rest is up to you.

APPENDIX

Male Role Norms Inventory (MRNI)

A few years ago, I decided to investigate whether the shift in values I sensed occurring among the men with whom I come in contact professionally was indicative of something happening within the male population at large. To find out, my colleagues and I devised a test to measure how much and in what ways men's beliefs about "what a man's supposed to be" correspond with or contradict long-standing norms. To do this, we first had to determine which "male norms" comprise the traditional masculine "shoulds." After carefully reviewing the research literature, we isolated seven norms:

1. Avoidance of femininity

2. Restricted emotionality

3. Nonrelational attitudes toward sex (sex disconnected from intimacy)

4. Pursuit of achievement and status

5. Self-reliance

6. Strength and aggression

7. Homophobia

We then formulated 58 statements that either support or contradict these seven norms. (For example, the statement "A man should avoid holding his wife's purse at all times" supports the norm of "avoidance of femininity," while the statement "A man should be able to openly show affection to another man" contradicts the norm of "homophobia.") In the test we designed—which we call the "Male Role Norms Inventory," or "MRNI"—these statements are listed in random order down the left side of five pages and are each accompanied, on the right, by a number-scale that runs from one through seven. The person taking the test is instructed simply to read each statement and indicate the degree to which he (or she) disagrees or agrees with it by circling the number that corresponds with his view:

1. Strongly disagree

2. Disagree

3. Slightly disagree

4. No opinion

5. Slightly agree

6. Agree

7. Strongly agree

As my colleagues and I reported in the July 1992 issue of the *Journal of Mental Health Counseling,* our first sample included 117 predominantly white, predominantly middle- and upper-middle-class men, aged 18 through 68, who were studying or working in the fields of biology, educational research, engineering, and community health. In analyzing their responses to the test, we first averaged their individual scores on each statement to come up with a "mean" score for each of the 58 statements. (A score of 4 is neutral. A score below 4 indicates disagreement. A score above 4 indicates agreement. A score below 3 and descending indicates increasingly strong disagreement. A score above 5 and ascending indicates increasingly strong agreement.) We then grouped these mean scores according to the traditional norm each statement supports or contradicts (five to ten statements per norm) and averaged these mean scores to come up with an overall mean score for each norm. Following are our results:

1. Avoidance of Femininity
(Overall Mean Score—Disagree: 3.8)

1. Housework is women's work. (Disagree: 3.1)

2. Jobs like firefighter and electrician should be reserved for men. (Disagree: 3.1)

3. Boys should prefer to play with trucks rather than dolls. (Agree: 4.6)

4. A man should prefer football to needlecraft. (Disagree: 3.8)

5. Boys should not throw baseballs like girls. (Agree: 4.7)

6. A man should avoid holding his wife's purse at all times. (Disagree: 2.2)

7. Men should be allowed to wear bracelets. (Agree: 5.1)

8. It is too feminine for a man to use clear nail polish on his fingernails. (Agree: 5.0)

2. Restricted Emotionality
(Overall Mean Score—Disagree: 3.2)

1. Men should be detached in emotionally charged situations. (Disagree: 3.2)

2. Nobody likes a man who cries in public. (Disagree: 3.7)

3. It's not particularly important for a man to control his emotions. (Agree: 4.1)

4. If a man is in pain, it's better for him to let people know than to keep it to himself. (Agree: 4.9)

5. A man should never reveal worries to others. (Disagree: 2.6)

6. Fathers should teach their sons to mask fear. (Disagree: 3.0)

7. One should not be able to tell how a man is feeling by looking at his face. (Disagree: 3.1)

8. Men should not be too quick to tell others that they care about them. (Disagree: 3.5)

9. Men should be allowed to kiss their fathers. (Agree: 5.3)

10. Being a little down in the dumps is not a good reason for a man to act depressed. (Disagree: 3.5)

3. Nonrelational Attitudes Toward Sex
(Overall Mean Score—Disagree: 3.3)

1. A man should always be ready for sex. (Disagree: 3.8)

2. A man doesn't need to have an erection in order to enjoy sex. (Disagree: 3.3)

3. It is important for a man to be good in bed. (Agree: 4.9)

4. A man should love his sex partner. (Agree: 5.4)

5. Men should always take the initiative when it comes to sex. (Disagree: 2.7)

6. A man shouldn't have to worry about birth control. (Disagree: 2.2)

7. For a man, sex should be a spontaneous rather than pre-planned activity. (Disagree: 3.9)

8. For men, touching is simply the first step toward sex. (Disagree: 3.2)

9. Hugging and kissing should always lead to intercourse. (Disagree: 2.4)

10. A man shouldn't bother with sex unless he can achieve an orgasm. (Disagree: 3.0)

4. Pursuit of Achievement and Status (Overall Mean Score—Disagree: 3.9)

1. If necessary, a man should sacrifice personal relationships for career advancement. (Disagree: 3.4)

2. It's not important for men to strive to reach the top. (Disagree: 2.9)

3. In a group, it's up to the men to get things organized and moving ahead. (Disagree: 3.2)

4. A man should do whatever it takes to be admired and respected. (Disagree: 3.4)

5. It's o.k. for a man to buy a fast, shiny sports car if he wants, even if he may have to stretch beyond his budget. (Disagree: 3.5)

6. A man should always be the major provider in his family. (Disagree: 3.8)

7. A man should try to win at any sport he participates in. (Agree: 4.9)

8. Men should have goals and be determined to achieve them. (Agree: 5.9)

9. Men should make the final decision involving money. (Disagree: 3.3)

5. Self-Reliance (Overall Mean Score—Agree: 4.6)

1. A man should never count on someone else to get the job done. (Agree: 4.4)

2. A man should think things out logically and have good reasons for what he does. (Agree: 5.4)

3. Men should always be realistic. (Agree: 4.8)

4. A man should be level-headed. (Agree: 5.1)

5. A man should never doubt his own judgment. (Disagree: 3.3)

6. A man must be able to make his own way in the world. (Agree: 5.4)

7. A man who takes a long time and has difficulty making decisions will usually not be respected. (Disagree: 3.9)

8. It's o.k. for a man to ask for help changing a tire. (Agree: 5.0)

6. Strength and Aggression
(Overall Mean Score—Agree: 4.6)

1. A man should not force the issue if another man takes his parking space. (Agree: 4.4)

2. Boys should be encouraged to find a means of demonstrating physical prowess. (Agree: 4.1)

3. A man who has no taste for adventure is not very appealing. (Agree: 4.3)

4. Men should get up to investigate if there is a strange noise in the house at night. (Agree: 5.6)

5. A boy should be allowed to quit a game if he is losing. (Disagree: 2.7)

6. When physically provoked, men should not resort to violence. (Agree: 4.2)

7. It is important for a man to take risks, even if he might get hurt. (Agree: 4.9)

8. When the going gets tough, men should get tough. (Agree: 5.2)

7. Homophobia (Overall Mean Score—Disagree: 3.9)

1. Being called "faggot" is one of the worst insults to a man or boy. (Agree: 4.8)

2. A man should not continue a friendship with another man if he finds out that the other man is homosexual. (Disagree: 3.3)

3. A man should be able to openly show affection to another man. (Agree: 4.4)

4. There are some subjects which men should not talk about with other men. (Disagree: 3.6)

5. It is disappointing to learn that a famous athlete is gay. (Agree: 4.6)

Bibliography

Allen, J. G., and D. M. Haccoun. 1976. Sex differences in emotionality: A multidimensional approach. *Human Relations, 29*(8):71–722.

Averill, J. R. 1990. *Anger and aggression: An essay on emotion.* New York: Springer-Verlag.

Balswick, J., and C. P. Avertt. 1977. Differences in expressiveness: Gender, interpersonal orientation, and perceived parental expressiveness as contributing factors. *Journal of Marriage and the Family 39*:121–7.

Barnett, R. C., and N. Marshall. 1991. Physical symptoms and the interplay of work and family roles. *Health Psychology 10*:94–101.

Barnett, R. C., N. Marshall, and J. Pleck. 1991. Men's multiple roles and their relationship to men's psychological distress. *Journal of Marriage and the Family 54*:348–67.

Berardo, D. H., L. L. Shehan, and G. R. Leslie. 1987. A residue of tradition: Jobs, careers and spouse time in housework. *Journal of Marriage and the Family 49*:381–90.

Bergman, S. J., and J. Surrey. 1992. *The woman-man relationship: Impasses and possibilities.* Working Paper #55, Wellesley, MA: The Robert S. and Grace W. Stone Center for Developmental Services and Studies.

Betcher, W., and W. S. Pollack. 1993. *In a time of fallen heroes: The re-creation of masculinity.* New York: Atheneum.

Bly, R. 1990. *Iron John: A book about men.* Reading, MA: Addison-Wesley.

Boszormenyi-Nagy, I., and D. N. Ulrich. 1981. Contextual family therapy. In A. S. Gurman and D. P. Kniskern (Eds.), *Handbook of family therapy.* New York: Brunner/Mazel.

BIBLIOGRAPHY

Brod, H. 1987. *The making of the masculinities: The new men's studies.* Boston: Unwin Hyman.

Brody, L. 1985. Gender differences in emotional development: A review of theories and research. *Journal of Personality 53*(2):14–59.

Brody, L., and J. Hall. 1993. Gender and emotion. In M. Lewis & J. M. Haviland (Eds.), *Handbook of Emotions.* New York: Guilford.

Brooks, G. R. 1993. *Clinical implications of men's reactions to women's bodies.* Paper presented at Annual Meeting of the American Psychological Association, Toronto, Ontario, Canada.

Buck, R. 1977. Non-verbal communication of affect in preschool children: Relationships with personality and skin conductance. *Journal of Personality and Social Psychology 35*(4):225–36.

Buck, R., R. E. Miller, and W. F. Caul. 1974. Sex, personality, and physiological variables in the communication of affect via facial expression. *Journal of Personality and Social Psychology 30*:587–96.

Campbell, A. 1993. *Men, women and aggression.* New York: Basic Books.

Carnes, P. 1983. *The sexual addiction.* Minneapolis, MN: CompCare Publications.

Chodorow, N. 1978. *The reproduction of mothering: Psychoanalysis and the sociology of gender.* Berkeley, CA: University of California Press.

Christensen, A., and C. Heavey. 1990. Gender and social structure in the demand/withdraw pattern of marital conflict. *Journal of Personality and Social Psychology 59*:73–81.

David, D., and R. Brannon. 1976. (Eds.) *The forty-nine percent majority: The male sex role.* Reading, MA: Addison-Wesley.

Dinnerstein, D. 1976. *The mermaid and the minotaur: Sexual arrangements and human malaise.* New York: Harper and Row.

Douthitt, R. A. 1989. The division of labor within homes: Have gender roles changed? *Sex Roles 20*:693–704.

Dunn, J., I. Bretherton, and P. Munn. 1987. Conversations about feeling states between mothers and their children. *Developmental Psychology 23*: 132–9.

Eagly, A. H., and V. J. Steffen. 1986. Gender and aggressive behavior: A meta-analytic review of the social psychological literature. *Psychological Bulletin 100*(3):309–30.

Ehrenreich, B. 1983. *The hearts of men.* New York: Doubleday.

Eisenberg, N., and R. Lennon. 1983. Sex differences in empathy and related capacities. *Psychological Bulletin 94*(1):100–31.

Eisler, R. M., and J. R. Skidmore. 1987. Masculine gender role stress. *Behavior Modification 11*:123–36.

Faludi, S. 1991. *Backlash: The undeclared war against American women.* New York: Crown.

Fivush, R. 1989. Exploring sex differences in the emotional content of mother-child conversations about the past. *Sex Roles 20*:675–91.

Floyd, F., and H. Markman. 1983. Observational biases in spouse observation: Toward a cognitive/behavioral model of marriage. *Journal of Consulting and Clinical Psychology* 51:450–7.

Fogarty, T. F. 1979. The distancer and the pursuer. *The Family* 7(1):11–16.

Frodi, A., J. Macaulay, and P. R. Thome. 1977. Are women always less aggressive than men: A review of the experimental literature. *Psychological Bulletin* 84(4):634–60.

Fuchs, D., and M. Thelen. 1988. Children's expected interpersonal consequences of communicating their affective state and reported likelihood of expression. *Child Development* 59:1314–22.

Gilmore, D. 1990. *Manhood in the making: Cultural concepts of masculinity.* New Haven: Yale University Press.

Goodman, L. A., M. P. Koss, L. F. Fitzgerald, et al. 1993. Male violence against women. Current research and future directions. *American Psychologist* 48:1054–8.

Gottman, J. 1991. Predicting the longitudinal course of marriages. *Journal of Marital and Family Therapy* 17:3–7.

Gottman, J., and R. Levenson. 1988. The social psychophysiology of marriage. In P. Noller & M. A. Fitzpatrick (Eds.), *Perspectives on marital interaction*, 182–200. Clevedon, UK: Multilingual Matters.

Greif, E. B., M. Alvarez, and K. Ulman. 1981. *Recognizing emotions in other people: Sex differences in socialization.* Paper presented at meeting of the Society for Research in Child Development, Boston.

Grusznski, R., and G. Bankovics. 1990. Treating men who batter: A group approach. In D. Moore & F. Leafgren (Eds.), *Problem-solving strategies and interventions for men in conflict.* Alexandria, VA: American Association for Counseling and Development.

Hall, J. A. 1978. Gender effects in decoding nonverbal cues. *Psychological Bulletin* 85(40):845–57.

Harrison, J. 1978. Warning: The male role may be dangerous to your health. *The Journal of Social Issues* 34(1):65–86.

Haviland, J. J., and C. Z. Malatesta. 1981. The development of sex differences in nonverbal signals: Fallacies, facts, and fantasies. In C. Mayo & N. M. Henly (Eds.), *Gender and non-verbal behavior.* New York: Springer-Verlag.

Hochschild, A. 1989. *The second shift.* New York: Avon.

Hoffman, M. L., and L. E. Levine. 1976. Early sex differences in empathy. *Developmental Psychology* 12(16):557–8.

Hudson, L., and B. Jacot. 1991. *The way men think: Intellect, intimacy, and the erotic imagination.* New Haven: Yale University Press.

Hyde, J. S. 1984. How large are gender differences in aggression: A developmental meta-analysis. *Developmental Psychology* 20(4):722–36.

Jacobson, N. S. 1983. Beyond empiricism: The politics of marital therapy. *American Journal of Family Therapy* 11:11–24.

Juster, F. T., and F. P. Stafford. 1985. *Time, goods, and well-being.* Ann Arbor, MI: Institute for Social Research.

Karen, R. 1992. Shame. *Atlantic Monthly* 40–70.

Kessler, R., and J. McRae. 1981. Trends in the relationship between sex and psychological distress: 1957–1976. *American Sociological Review* 46:443–52.

Kessler, R., and J. McRae. 1983. Trends in the relationship between sex and attempted suicide. *Journal of Health and Social Behavior* 24:98–110.

Kimmel, M. S. 1987. *Changing men: New directions in research on men and masculinity.* Newbury Park, CA: Sage Publications.

Krugman, S. 1991. Male vulnerability and the transformation of shame. In W. S. Pollack, Chair, *On men: Redefining roles.* The Cambridge Series, The Cambridge Hospital, Harvard Medical School, Cambridge, MA.

Krystal, H. 1979. Alexithymia and psychotherapy. *American Journal of Psychotherapy* 33:17–30.

Krystal, H. 1982. Alexithymia and the effectiveness of psychoanalytic treatment. *International Journal of Psychoanalytic Psychotherapy* 9:353–78.

Kundtz, D. J. 1991. *Men and feelings: Understanding the male experience.* Deerfield Beach, FL: Health Communications.

Langlois, J. H., and A. C. Downs. 1980. Mothers, fathers, and peers as socialization agents of sex-typed play behaviors in young children. *Child Development* 51:1217–47.

Lamb, M. E. 1981. *The role of the father in child development.* New York: Wiley.

Lamb, M. E. 1977. The development of parental preferences in the first two years of life. *Sex Roles* 3:475–97.

Lamb, M. E., M. J. Owen, and L. Chase-Lansdale. 1979. The father daughter relationship: Past, present, and future. In C. B. Knopp & M. Kirkpatrick (Eds.), *Becoming female.* New York: Plenum.

Landers, S. 1989. In U.S., mental disorders affect 15 percent of adults. *APA Monitor* 16.

Levant, R. F. 1992. Toward the reconstruction of masculinity. *Journal of Family Psychology* 5(3/4):379–402.

Levant, R. F., L. Hirsch, E. Celentano, et al. 1992. The male role: An investigation of norms and stereotypes. *Journal of Mental Health Counseling* (in press).

Levant, R. F., and J. Kelly. 1989. *Between father and child.* New York: Viking.

Levant, R. F., and W. S. Pollack. 1995. *A New Psychology of Men.* New York: Basic Books.

Lever, J. 1976. Sex differences in the games children play. *Social Work* 23(4): 78–87.

Long, D. 1987. Working with men who batter. In M. Scher, et al. (Eds.), *Handbook of counseling and psychotherapy with men.* Newbury Park, CA: Sage.

Maccoby, E. E. 1990. Gender and relationships: A developmental account. *American Psychologist* 45:513–20.

Maccoby, E. E., and C. N. Jacklin. 1974. *The psychology of sex differences.* Stanford, CA: Stanford University Press.

Maccoby, E. E., and C. N. Jacklin. 1980. Sex differences in aggression: A rejoinder and reprise. *Child Development 51*:964–80.

Majors, R. G., and J. N. Billson. 1992. *Cool pose: The dilemmas of black manhood in America.* New York: Lexington Books.

Malatesta, C. Z., C. Culver, J. Tesman, et al. 1989. The development of emotion expression during the first two years of life. *Monographs of the Society for Research in Child Development 50*(1-2, Serial No. 219).

Markman, H. J., S. W. Duncan, R. D. Storaasli, et al. 1987. The prediction and prevention of marital distress: A longitudinal investigation. In K. Hahlweg & M. Goldstein (Eds.), *Understanding major mental disorder: The contribution of family interaction research.* New York: Family Process, Inc.

Marshall, C. 1992. *The expectant father.* Citrus Heights, CA: Conmar Publishing.

Moore, D. 1991. Men and emotions: Teaching men to be more emotionally expressive. In R. Levant, Chair, *Men, emotions, and intimacy.* Symposium conducted at Annual Meeting of the American Psychological Association, San Francisco.

Morgentaler, A. 1993. *The male body: A physician's guide to what every man should know.* New York: Simon & Schuster.

Nolen-Hoeksema, S. 1990. *Sex differences in depression.* Stanford, CA: Stanford University Press.

Notarius, C. I., and J. Johnson. 1982. Emotional expression in husbands and wives. *Journal of Marriage and the Family 44*:483–9.

Oliver, M. B., and J. S. Hyde. 1993. Gender differences in sexuality: A meta-analysis. *Psychological Bulletin 114*(1):29–51.

O'Neil, J. M. 1986. *Gender role conflict scale I.* Unpublished manuscript, University of Connecticut, Center for Social and Gender Role Change.

Ornish, D. 1990. *Dr. Dean Ornish's program for reversing heart disease.* New York: Random House.

Osborne, R. W. 1991. Men and intimacy: An empirical review. In R. Levant, Chair, *Men, emotions, and intimacy.* Symposium conducted at Annual Meeting of the American Psychological Association, San Francisco.

Osherson, S. 1986. *Finding our fathers: The unfinished business of manhood.* New York: Free Press.

Paley, V. G. 1984. *Boys and girls: Superheroes in the doll corner.* Chicago: University of Chicago Press.

Pasick, R. S. 1990. Raised to work. In R. L. Meth & R. S. Pasick (Eds.), *Men in therapy: The challenge of change.* New York: Guilford.

Pasick, R. 1992. *Awakening from the deep sleep: A powerful guide for courageous men.* San Francisco: HarperCollins.

Pennebaker, J. W. 1992. Putting stress into words: Health, linguistic, and therapeutic implications. *Behavior Research and Therapy* (in press).

Pleck, J. H. 1981. *The myth of masculinity.* Cambridge, MA: MIT Press.

Pleck, J. H. 1985. *Working wives/working husbands.* Newbury Park, CA: Sage Publications.

Pollack, W. S. 1990. Men's development and psychotherapy: A psychoanalytic perspective. *Psychotherapy* 27:316–21.

Pollack, W. S. 1991. Can men love? In R. Levant, Chair, *Men, emotions, and intimacy.* Symposium conducted at Annual Meeting of the American Psychological Association, San Francisco.

Pruett, K. D. 1987. *The nurturing father.* New York: Warner Books.

Rhodes, S., and M. S. Potash. 1988. *Cold feet: Why men don't commit.* New York: Signet.

Robinson, J. 1977. *How Americans use time: A social-psychological analysis.* New York: Praeger.

Rohner, R. P. 1976. Sex differences in aggression: Phylogenetic and enculturation perspectives. *Ethos* 4:55–72.

Rotundo, E. A. 1993. *American manhood: Transformations in masculinity from the revolution to the modern era.* New York: Basic Books.

Schell, A., and J. B. Gleason. 1989. *Gender differences in the acquisition of the vocabulary of emotion.* Paper presented at the annual meeting of the American Association of Applied Linguistics, Washington, D.C.

Shapiro, J. L. 1993. *The measure of a man: Becoming the father you wish your father had been.* New York: Delacorte.

Sherrod, D. 1987. The bonds of men: Problems and possibilities in close male relationships. In H. Brod (Ed.), *The Making of masculinities: The new men's studies.* Cambridge, MA: Unwin Hyman, Ltd.

Siegal, M. 1987. Are sons and daughters treated more differently by fathers than by mothers? *Developmental Review* 7:183–209.

Sifneos, P. E. 1967. Clinical observations on some patients suffering from a variety of psychosomatic diseases. *Proceedings of the Seventh European Conference on Psychosomatic Research.* Basel, Switzerland: Kargel.

Silverstein, L. B. 1993. Primate research, family politics, and social policy: Transforming "cads" into "dads." *Journal of Family Psychology* 7(3):267–82.

Silverstein, O., and B. Rashbaum. 1994. *The courage to raise good men.* New York: Viking.

Stapley, J. C., and J. M. Haviland. 1989. Beyond depression: Gender differences in normal adolescents' emotional experiences. *Sex Roles* 20(5/6): 295–308.

Stephenson, J. 1991. *Men are not cost-effective.* New York: Diemer-Smith.

Stoller, R. J. 1975. *Perversion.* New York: Pantheon.

Straus, M. A., and R. J. Gelles. 1990. *Physical violence in American families: Risk factors and adaptations to violence in 8145 families.* New Brunswick, NJ: Transaction.

Straus, M. A., R. J. Gelles, and S. Steinmetz. 1980. *Behind closed doors: Violence in the American family.* Garden City, NJ: Anchor Press.

Strickland, B. 1988. Sex-related differences in health and illness. *Psychology of Women Quarterly 12*:381–99.

Tannen, D. 1990. *You just don't understand: Men and women in conversation.* New York: Morrow.

Waldron, I., and S. Johnson. 1976. Why do women live longer than men? *Journal of Human Stress 2*:19–29.

Walker, L. E. 1979. *The battered woman.* New York: Harper & Row.

Walker, L. E. 1984. *The battered woman syndrome.* New York: Springer-Verlag.

Walker, K., and M. Woods. 1976. *Time use: A measure of household production of goods and services.* Washington, D.C.: American Home Economics Association.

Weinberg, M. K. 1992. Sex differences in 6-month-old infants' affect and behavior: Impact on maternal caregiving. Doctoral dissertation, University of Massachusetts.

Weingarten, K. 1994. *The mother's voice: Strengthening intimacy in families.* New York: Harcourt and Brace.

Weiss, R. S. 1990. *Staying the course: The emotional and social lives of men who do well at work.* New York: Fawcett Colombine.

Wong, M. R. 1992. *Shame and male gender identity.* Paper presented at the Annual Meeting of the American Psychological Association, Washington, D.C.

Wright, F. 1987. Male shame and antisocial behavior: A psychodynamic perspective. *Group 11*(4):238–46.

Yalom, I. 1985. *Theory and practice of group psychotherapy.* New York: Basic Books.

Zilbergeld, B. 1992. *The new male sexuality.* New York: Bantam.

Index